The Corners Are Glowing

The Ottawa International Animation Festival (OIAF) began in 1976 and stands today as one of the oldest and largest animation events in the world. One of the unique features of the OIAF is the inclusion of commissioned writings that provide attendees with a more in-depth background into the festival's special screenings. These writings have not only contextualized the festival presentations but have also contributed significantly to animation education and scholarship.

The Corners are Glowing is a selection of the best writings (many unseen for decades) culled from past OIAF catalogues. These wide-ranging texts cover the spectrum of animation from the familiar (Daffy Duck, Pee Wee Herman, Bob Clampett, Joanna Quinn, Hiyao Miyazaki, Frank Tashlin) to the more esoteric (Robert Breer, Emily Pelstring, Taku Furukawa, Michael Sporn, and even the use of furniture in animation!).

The Corners are Glowing is a valuable time capsule that celebrates animation's past and present, and the styles of writing are as diverse, enlightening, and fun as the animation subjects being written about.

The Corners Are Glowing

Selected Writings from the Ottawa International Animation Festival

Edited by
Chris Robinson
Tom McSorley

CRC Press
Taylor & Francis Group
Boca Raton London New York

CRC Press is an imprint of the
Taylor & Francis Group, an **Informa** business

Ottawa
International
Animation
Festival

First Edition published 2023
by CRC Press
6000 Broken Sound Parkway NW, Suite 300, Boca Raton, FL 33487-2742

and by CRC Press
4 Park Square, Milton Park, Abingdon, Oxon, OX14 4RN

CRC Press is an imprint of Taylor & Francis Group, LLC

ISBN: 978-1-032-26379-3 (hbk)
ISBN: 978-1-032-26377-9 (pbk)
ISBN: 978-1-003-28802-2 (ebk)

DOI: 10.1201/9781003288022

Typeset in Minion
by Deanta Global Publishing Services, Chennai, India

Contents

Author Bio, ix

INTRODUCTION, 1

CHAPTER 1 ▪ In Search of Raoul Barré (1976)   3
BY ANDRE MARTIN

CHAPTER 2 ▪ The Importance of Being Fischinger (1976)   21
BY WILLIAM MORITZ

CHAPTER 3 ▪ Segundo de Chomon: Spanish Magician (1978)   33
BY CARLOS FERNANDEZ CUENCA

CHAPTER 4 ▪ German Animation Pioneers (1988)   41
BY LOUISE BEAUDET

CHAPTER 5 ▪ The Evolution of Daffy Duck (1988)   47
BY MARK LANGER

CHAPTER 6 ▪ Frame by Frame: Animated Commercials
1920–1990 (1990)   53
BY LOUISE BEAUDET

CHAPTER 7 ▪ The Personal Side of Ernest Pintoff, Filmmaker   59
BY MAUREEN FURNISS, PH.D.

CHAPTER 8 ▪ Drawing on Both Sides of Their Brains (1996):
The Art and Careers of Derek Lamb and Kaj
Pindal   67
BY MARC GLASSMAN

vi ■ Contents

CHAPTER 9 ■ A Taste of Tashlin (1998)   79
BY MARK LANGER

CHAPTER 10 ■ The Animation of MTV (1999)   85
BY KELLY NEALL

CHAPTER 11 ■ Phil Mulloy: An Appreciation (2001)   89
BY RICHARD MELTZER

CHAPTER 12 ■ Rex, Epicurus and Me: The Search for
Pleasure (2001)   93
BY CHRIS ROBINSON

CHAPTER 13 ■ Narrow Roads: The Wor (ks) (lds) (ds) of Taku
Furukawa   97
BY TINA PAAS

CHAPTER 14 ■ Piotr Dumala: Notes from Underground
(2002)   103
BY TOM MCSORLEY

CHAPTER 15 ■ Janie Geiser's Uncanny Silence (2002)   109
BY BARRY DOYLE

CHAPTER 16 ■ The Fecal and the Feral: John Kricfalusi,
Theme & Variation (2002)   113
BY RICHARD MELTZER

CHAPTER 17 ■ Ominous Beauty: The Animation of
Jean-Francois Laguionie (2003)   119
BY TOM MCSORLEY

CHAPTER 18 ■ The Wage Of Mersh, The Fart Of Art: Oscar
Grillo In The 21st Century (2003)   123
BY RICHARD MELTZER

CHAPTER 19 ■ Miyazaki Magic (2004)   129
BY MARK LANGER

CHAPTER 20 ■ Robert Breer: Dadanimator (2004)   137
    BY GEORGE GRIFFIN

CHAPTER 21 ■ Transforming Realities: The Work of Co
    Hoedeman (2004)   141
    BY BARRY DOYLE

CHAPTER 22 ■ Animating Pee-wee's Playhouse (2005)   145
    BY CHRIS ROBINSON

CHAPTER 23 ■ Bob Clampett at Warner Bros. (2006)   151
    BY MARK LANGER

CHAPTER 24 ■ Showing Scher (2006)   159
    BY RICHARD O'CONNOR

CHAPTER 25 ■ Bawdy Politics: The Animation of
    Joanna Quinn (2007)   163
    BY TOM MCSORLEY

CHAPTER 26 ■ Dušan Vukotić – A Canonical Modernist of
    Animated Film (2007)   167
    BY HRVOJE TURKOVIĆ

CHAPTER 27 ■ Saul Steinberg and Animation (2007)   173
    BY GEORGE GRIFFIN

CHAPTER 28 ■ Don't Throw Out Your Television: The
    Works of Christopher Mills (2008)   181
    BY JERRETT ZAROSKI

CHAPTER 29 ■ There's a Party in My Tummy: The Yo
    Gabba Gabba Revolution (2008)   187
    BY CHRIS ROBINSON

CHAPTER 30 ■ Jonas Odell: Revolver Bang! Bang! (2008)   191
    BY TOM MCSORLEY

CHAPTER 31 ■ Michael Sporn (2008)   195
    BY RICHARD O' CONNOR

CHAPTER 32 ■ Jim Blashfield: "And Things Were Looking Like a Movie" (2009)   199

BY RICHARD O'CONNOR

CHAPTER 33 ■ Stan Vanderbeek (2009)   203

BY AMID AMIDI

CHAPTER 34 ■ Furniture of My Mind (2010)   209

BY GEORGE GRIFFIN

CHAPTER 35 ■ The Genius of Osamu Tezuka (2010)   215

BY TOM MCSORLEY

CHAPTER 36 ■ Decoding Narrative: The Animated World of Gil Alkabetz (2011)   219

BY MADI PILLER AND PATRICK JENKINS

CHAPTER 37 ■ Don't Stop: Animating Hip Hop (2011)   223

BY MARLEY ROSEN

CHAPTER 38 ■ Remembering Karen Aqua (2012)   227

BY KELTIE DUNCAN WITH KEN FIELD

CHAPTER 39 ■ Unseen Forces: A Spotlight on Emily Pelstring (2020)   231

BY KELTIE DUNCAN

CHAPTER 40 ■ Flannel Fever Dream: The Films of Mike Maryniuk (2021)   237

BY DEVIN HARTLEY

INDEX, 243

Author Bio

Chris Robinson is a Canadian writer and author. He is also the Artistic Director of the Ottawa International Animation Festival (OIAF) and is a well-known figure in the animated film world and was recently given the 2020 award for Outstanding Contribution to Animation Studies by the World Festival of Animation Film - Animafest Zagreb.

Robinson has been called "one of the stylistically most original and most provocative experts in the history of animation. He made a name for himself with a unique and eclectic magazine column *Animation Pimp*, which became a book of the same name (the column was later renamed into *Cheer and Loathing in Animation*).

Mastering different methods and styles in critical and scholarly approaches, Robinson covers a broad range of Canadian and global subject matters in his books *Estonian Animation: Between Genius and Utter Illiteracy, Unsung Heroes of Animation, Canadian Animation: Looking for a Place to Happen, Ballad of a Thin Man: In Search of Ryan Larkin, Animators Unearthed, Japanese Animation: Time out of Mind* and *Mad Eyed Misfits: Writings on Indie Animation*.

In addition to his writing on animation, Robinson also wrote the award-winning animated short, *Lipsett Diaries* (2010) directed by Theodore Ushev.

Currently, Robinson is writing two books on animation and is working with German artist, Andreas Hykade, on *My Balls Are Killing Me*, a graphic novel about his experience with cancer. He is also collaborating with Theodore Ushev on a live action feature film, *Drivin'*.

Tom McSorley is Executive Director of the Canadian Film Institute. He is also an Adjunct Research Professor of Film Studies at Carleton University, and the film critic for CBC Radio One's "Ottawa Morning."

McSorley is the editor of *Rivers of Time: The Films of Philip Hoffman* (2008), *Elective Identities: The Moving Images of Garine Torossian* (2010) and *Entre Nous: The Cinema of Denis Cote* (2011); *Intimacies: The Cinema of Ingrid Veninger* (2012); *Forms of Light: The Films of Malcolm Sutherland* (2012); *Time Being: The Moving Images of Daniel Cockburn* (2013); *Dark Mirror: The Films of Theodore Ushev* (2014); and co-editor, with Andre Loiselle, of *Self Portraits: The Cinemas of Canada Since Telefilm* (2006); with Mike Hoolboom, *Life Without Death: The Cinema of Frank Cole* (2009); and, with Scott Birdwise, *The Transformable Moment: The Films of Stephen Broomer* (2014). He has published numerous articles and book chapters on Canadian and international cinema for various international film journals and magazines, and is the author of *Atom Egoyan's The Adjuster* (University of Toronto Press, 2009) a book-length critical study of Egoyan's 1991 feature film.

Introduction

S INCE ITS DEBUT IN 1976, the Ottawa International Animation Festival (OIAF) has grown into one of the oldest, largest, and most respected animation events in the world. A major part of the success has been the festival's fearless championing of animation's underdogs: the more esoteric, experimental, and personal voices not seen on TV screens, cinemas, or whatever streaming route you might travel down. The OIAF has never been one to pick a single lane. One of the unique and enduring features of the OIAF is the blending of the commercially friendly and the decidedly daring and uncommercial. Since its inception, the OIAF has seen itself as a bridge between different worlds of animation art and has acted accordingly.

Over the years, the OIAF catalogue has served as deep background for the films and filmmakers, offering in-depth texts written by assorted animation aficionados, historians, enthusiasts, curators, and scholars. These writings take OIAF attendees beyond the screens and more substantively into the works, providing valuable insight as well as supplying ample historical and cultural context. Whether the topic was Daffy Duck, Hip Hop, Pee Wee Herman, Ren and Stimpy, Furniture (yes, furniture), or more eclectic figures like Robert Breer, Janie Geiser, Stan Vandenbeek, and Phil Mulloy, the OIAF treated them all with respect but not without a bit of cheekiness (check out Meltzer's maybe not so flattering take on Oscar Grillo). Respectful *and* irreverent, OIAF writings are nothing if not honest!

The OIAF has been fortunate to have received generous contributions from many fine writers, scholars, and misfits: notably, Mark Langer, George Griffin, Richard O'Connor, Amid Amidi, Madi Piller, Patrick Jenkins, Maureen Furniss, Marc Glassman, Hrvoje Turković, Richard Meltzer

DOI: 10.1201/9781003288022-1

(mostly known to folks as a rather notorious music writer). In addition to these voices, we've also heard from current and former OIAF staff (most of whom came from film theory backgrounds): Keltie Duncan, Devin Hartley, Tina Paas, Kelly Neall (the OIAF's current Managing Director who has been with the festival since 1994), Jerrett Zaroski, Marley Rosen. We'd also like to give a great raucous scream of thanks to a few of those who have left us: William Moritz, André Martin, Louise Beaudet, Barry Doyle.

We are so thankful to all the contributors included here for allowing us to reprint their material. One of our motivations was a worry that many of these pieces might be swallowed by the dustbins of history. *The Corners are Glowing* is our attempt to keep those voices alive and moving forwards so that a new generation of animation fans, critics, historians, and passers-by can discover these rarely seen writings, as we regard them as essential contributions to both the history of and critical discourse about one of cinema's most important and perhaps least understood forms.

Finally, we'd like to thank Ben Compton and Angie Mosher for their invaluable assistance scanning, proofing, and editing the articles included here. And a tip of the hat to the very fine musician and painter, Tobin Sprout, for allowing us to pinch his song title for this publication.

Chris Robinson/Tom McSorley
Ottawa, December 2021

CHAPTER 1

In Search of
Raoul Barré (1976)

by Andre Martin

T HE HISTORY OF THE visual arts in Québec is characterized by as many areas of obscurity and inaccuracy as is the history of the American animated film. Among the chapters yet to be written, one will have to be devoted to Raoul Barré (1874–1932), the Québec painter, illustrator, commercial artist, and pioneer animator who was a co-developer of the American animated film. Barré is one of the most fascinating yet least known figures of the early years of animation in the last century.

In many ways, Barré's lifestyle explains the silence of film historians on the subject of his life and work. He was at home anywhere in the Atlantic area. Moving between Montreal, Paris and New York, he was never where one expected him to be; a puzzle to those who tried to like him and always one step ahead of those who tried to imitate him. Since he devoted most of his time to the development of comic strips and film animation, he neglected to exhibit his paintings, and consequently was never considered a major Canadian painter. Up to the present time, he has also been ignored as one of the originators of the newspaper comic strips in Québec, the history of which is just beginning to be considered noteworthy by chroniclers of popular culture. Paradoxically, he is best known outside Québec for his contribution to the invention and development of animated film in America.

DOI: 10.1201/9781003288022-2

In 1913, when his colleagues in New York were bogged down by the basic problems of controlling animated movement, it was Barré who developed the primary technical procedures for controlling the picture-by-picture drawing and frame-by-frame shooting of the animated cartoon. It was he who initiated the first generation of animators in New York to the craft that he had just invented.

"Everybody respected him. He was our idol. He not only showed us how to draw the image of a step but also how to make it move and to provoke laughter. He was a great help, a pleasure to work with at the Sullivan Studios." We can believe this testimony since it came from Otto Messmer, the creator of the best animated and comic strip adventures of *Felix the Cat*. But unfortunately, for many years, virtually no one has seen the films of Raoul Barré.

In order to have a better understanding of his life, we shouldn't consider him simply as a gifted amateur or a dilettante who dispersed his energies in too many directions. He was truly innovative, a trail-blazer who explored new ideas and techniques where others lost their way.

Vital-Achille-Raoul Barré was born in Montreal on January 29, 1874. In his family of twelve children, he was considered the "artist." After completing his studies at the Institut du Mont Saint-Louis, he planned to become a painter and was encouraged in this direction by his father (a wine importer, particularly church wine – not a small detail, given the religious enthusiasm of turn-of-the-century Québec).

In July 1891, Raoul Barré left for Europe to study at the Ecole des Beaux-Arts and the Academie Julian in Paris. The trip to Europe, especially Paris, was considered a necessary ritual for young Canadian painters. Barré was there at about the same time as Ernest Lawson, Suzor Cote, Clarence Gagnon and other artists of that generation. Many of the Canadian artists who had gone to Paris in order to master the traditional European academic figures unexpectedly acquired a whole range of pertinent techniques for representing the sky, the rivers and the snows of their homeland. On their return to Canada, they became the nucleus of an impressionist school in Montreal and Toronto.

Some of Barré's works, including *La Baigneuse* (1913), *Les mines de l'ensoleillee* (1929), and several series of sketches, reveal a highly sophisticated use of impressionistic techniques in the tradition of Daubigny and Sisley. *Au bord de la mer* (1911) suggests the vigour of Cezanne in the treatment of the mass of rocks and vegetation dominating the canvas, revealing what Barré could have done had he pursued a less diversified career.

Barré also painted in the pictorial tradition of Krieghoff and Henri Julien, best exemplified by his *L'homme ii la meule* (now in the Musee du Québec) and *Le voyage de bois*. His interest in this type of picturesque representation of habitants and explorers is further emphasized in the many pen drawings which he did to illustrate the novels of Honore Beaugrand, Pamphile LeMay and Rodolphe Brunet. But the form which he preferred was the large portrait done in oils, given the ease with which he could capture a likeness (*Portrait de Madame Roy*, 1929).

In the early 1900s, illustrations for books, magazines and newspapers were still done entirely by hand, providing young artists with a good opportunity to test their talents as illustrators or caricaturists. Whether in "La Revue Nationale" (August 1895 to January 1896), in "La Revue des Deux France" (April to August 1898) or in "Le Monde Illustre" (1902), Barré's prolific contributions were worth notice. While other artists usually supplied two or three illustrations for a publication, he used to provide the frontispiece, illustrated titles, initial letters, vignettes and all the remaining illustrations. He also illustrated many of Pamphile LeMay's books, notably, *Mariette* (1902) and the second 10th edition of the *Contes Vrais* (1905). While these drawings were typical "fin de siecle" illustrations, often hastily composed, they demonstrated his ability to present expressive characters and lively activities capturing people and places with intensity and intelligence.

While in Paris, Barré worked for several satirical magazines. During the general battle for the appeal of the famous Dreyfus case, he produced a series of caricatures for the magazine "Le Soufflet" which openly supported the accused. In this way, Barré received recognition equal to that of the great caricaturists of the time, such as Caran d' Ache and Florian. Clemenceau, too, commented favourably on Barré's courageous drawings in the paper he edited.

Barré returned to Québec in 1898, intending to divide his time between painting, caricaturing and illustrating. In 1901, he produced a satiric album entitled "En roulant ma boule." Done in the precise style of Caran d' Ache, it satirized the traditional preparations for the St-Jean-Baptiste Day festivities.

That same year, he married Marie-Blanche Antoinette Skelly in Montreal and left immediately to live in Paris for a year. Their daughter Marguerite was born there in July 1902. In November of the same year, the family returned to Québec.

Montreal, at this time, had a population of 326,000 and though it was the largest city in Canada, it could not sustain the hopes and curiosity of the young painter nor allow him to earn a living. Thus in 1903, Barré left Québec and moved to New York, where he lived for the next twenty-five years. At first, he worked as a portraitist and illustrator, participating, despite the distance, in Canadian exhibitions.

At this time, the photographic image had not yet come to dominate magazines, newspapers and advertisements. Barré worked for George Batten and Co., a firm that specialized in commercial art. With his solid background, he soon began to direct and run the production of ads, posters and illustrations. Since the founder of the company was getting old and his son showed little interest in running it, Barré was in a position to take over the direction of the firm.

Barré, however, had not completely forgotten Québec. He continued to send drawings and illustrations to newspapers and magazines. In 1902, when he was still living in Montreal, the daily newspapers were just beginning to include caricatures and cartoons in their copy. But in Chicago and New York, a new wave of cartoon characters in comic strip form was emerging and along with it a new enthusiastic audience. The December 20, 1902, issue of "La Presse" took an innovative and radical step, in Montreal, by publishing a block of eight images by Barré entitled "Pour un diner de Noel." The successive images depict a farmer, his wife and their sons chasing a reluctant turkey. While the precision of the drawing and the detailed background relate to the comic style of the last century, the intensity of the action, the exaggeration of form and movement typify Barré's graphic vitality and drive. This series, the first done by a Québecois, represented the birth of the comic strip in Québec. In 1904, with strips by Bourgeois, Busnel and Beliveau in "La Patrie" and by Bourgeois and Charlebois in "La Presse," the comic strip came into its own as an art form with broad popular appeal. Unfortunately, this early "blossoming" only lasted for six years.

In June 1906, a full page of Barré's cartoons, "Les Contes du Pere Rhault," were published in "La Patrie." These alternated weekly with Busnel's "Les aventures de Timothee." This continued until 1909 by which time a total of 57 episodes had been published.

In the tradition of the mischievous children of Dirk's "Katzenjammer Kids" and Outcaut's "Buster Brown," Barré produced between eight and ten images at a time to describe the pranks played by Fanfan and P'tit Pit on their father, Aunt Frizine and finally almost everyone else, each episode usually culminated in a vigorous spanking of the two brats, a compulsory ritual in an era richer in rectitude than our own.

On January 11, 1913, after nearly four years' absence, Barré appeared again in "La Patrie" with a strip entitled "À l'hôtel du Père Noé" and signed V ARB (a pseudonym formed with the initials of his name). It was first produced in 1912 for a New York newspaper and distributed by the McLure Newspaper Syndicate. It appeared weekly twenty-one times until June 1913. The strip detailed animal life, and it was a combination comedy–parody metaphor of human life: animals living together, enduring each others' presences, quirks, etc. At the very bottom of the strip, lilliputian animals living their own set of adventures comment on the main action taking place above them. Four years later, Barré again used this device introducing the "Joys" and "Glooms" in the animated series *The Phables*.

Precisely at this point, new systems of images suddenly appeared which impelled the young painter and illustrator along a new course.

One night at the cinema, Barré saw his first animated film. (Was it by Winsor McCay, Emile Cohl or Stuart Blackton?) He was both intrigued and amazed by the enormous possibilities that seemed to lie open to graphic artists. The growth and multiplication in the number of nickelodeon and film production companies at this time can only confirm his impression.

It is likely that Barré had made contact with the Edison workshops about 1912. Soon after, he began to work with William C. Nolan making advertising films either in actual shooting or in animation. These films were made for cinemas as well as for projection in Times Square. He also directed some films which served as prototypes for his future series.

In 1914, Raoul Barré, in the Bronx, opened one of the first animation studios designed and organized to produce animated films regularly and continuously. It was in this studio that he and Bill Nolan initiated such famous animators as Gregory La Cava, Frank Moser, Pat Sullivan and Dick Huemer into the art of making animated films. Things seemed to be going well for Barré on all fronts.

From a distance, what these men achieved may not seem impressive, but in fact, they created a graphic and dynamic system of representation without precedent. We are only just beginning to realize that the artists of the New York school of animation, in the anonymity of their studios, had to construct from nothing a precise craft and resolve a whole series of fundamental problems in the areas of structure and form: notably inking the outline, careful superimposition of the different animated phases during the drawing and shooting, insertion of backgrounds and halftones. Indeed, they refined their baroque art to a classical level which should find its place between the monsters of Bomarzo and the Nanas of Niki de St-Phalle.

The problem of strict positioning and superimposition of the successive images, whether during drawing or shooting, constituted a major hurdle. Projection onto a large screen revealed the quality of superimposition and of the succession of animated images which give the illusion of movement. Sometimes the characters, along with the background, would jiggle uncontrollably only to freeze completely as soon as there was a scene without animated action. They tried a number of solutions, with no great success. For example, Winsor McCay and Paul Terry used a paper cutter to give perfectly straight edges to the sheets of paper and right-angle forms to keep them exactly superimposed, one on top of another. Bray made use of a system of crosses in the four corners of the drawing, a form of registration borrowed from colour printing techniques.

In 1914, Barré resolved the problem of registration and superimposition by creating the "peg system." Each drawing could now be mechanically perforated. These holes in the sheets of drawings allowed them to be perfectly aligned on a pegboard. In this way, the successive phases of the animation process were assured of exact correspondence. Holes perforated in tracing paper, celluloid or backgrounds found in every animator's studio are paying homage, as discreet as it is enduring, to Raoul Barré. The drawing technique used by Barré was that of drawing on paper. It was a demanding discipline. The characters, outlined only in pencil or pen, totally lacked the coloured opacity that painting on celluloid would later provide. They could not move too freely without the background becoming visible through their silhouettes. A method had to be found whereby characters could be animated without overlapping or becoming entangled with the background elements. This is why, in all the animated films of this time, backgrounds were reduced to a minimum, a few simplified forms lost in an immense white field. The pieces of background were simply paper cut-outs, which were placed around the edges of the image frame at a respectful distance from the characters, and which freed for them a kind of shining arena. Sometimes, an element of the background, the line of the horizon or of the floor, or of a door opening, had to be redrawn around the character at every phase of animation. For these reasons, some elements of the background were often reduced to a single line.

From 1915 onwards, Bray and Hurd, along with Paul Terry, were to be responsible for the spread of the technique of cell animation which was to dominate the field in the 1920s. However, Barré, and later on Sullivan, deliberately continued to draw on paper. They wanted to preserve the qualities of contrast and graphic simplification required by this approach, which was further accentuated by filming on positive stock. Thus, there appeared a style of black and white animation, typical of the New York School, which started with the works of Winsor McCay and continued with Barré's *Animated Grouch Chaser*, Fleischer's *Out of the Inkwell*, and Sullivan and Messmer's *Felix the Cat*. It always remained close to the graphic and typographic tradition which inspired it, and in which pen and ink and the hand of the artisan played the major roles.

Barré was always searching for ways to perfect the disassociation of the three dynamic elements – characters, background and special effects – and in his *Grouch Chaser* series, he made use of transparent material. At first, he used plates of glass on which he drew such special effects as cigar smoke, smells and splashes of liquid. Glass also allowed him to insert an element of foreground and make a character walk behind a tree without having to draw the process step by step.

Eventually, Barré made use of cell animation techniques for these foreground effects. In his studio, beginning in 1915, Bill Nolan put the background itself on long strips of paper in such a way that it could be moved horizontally (or vertically) behind a moving animated character who, although stationary, would appear to be going forwards, backwards, up or down. Similarly, by using translucent or transparent foreground (glass or celluloid), they could put specific foreground elements in front of moving animated characters and eventually could even animate the whole background.

Finally, in order to reduce the incredible amount of work involved in the preparation of successive phases in the animation process, Barré introduced the "slash system," whereby the moving parts of a character (the arms, legs or head) were separately superimposed on the stationary parts (for example, the torso). The latter, of course, need not move for a number of seconds.

The spread of the cell animation technique (patented by John Randolph Bray in 1915) was a decisive trigger in the industrial organization of American animated film. Bray Studios Inc. which in its first year (1914) seems to have produced only five short films (the series *Colonel Heeza Liar* and *Bobby Bump*), the next year turned out no less than thirty (notably, the *Out of The Inkwell* films of Max Fleischer), and in 1916, it produced forty films, including Paul Terry's *Farmer Alfalfa*. However, this increase in production was not without production mistakes, such as reflections off the celluloid and uncontrolled background movements. Meanwhile, Barré stuck with his technique of animation on paper, and in 1915 still successfully produced 15 Animated *Grouch Chaser* films. He managed to resolve many of the problems of producing animated shorts, both in quantity and quality, by combining the advantages of a still primitive but powerful style with a technical setting and mode of operation superior to those of his colleagues. All the conditions necessary for systematically organizing the production of animated films were now fulfilled, and the stage was set for the emergence of the large studios of the 1930s.

The main characteristic of Barré the entrepreneur, as well as of Barré the producer, was his great confidence in the development of animated film. As early as 1910, he was exploring the possibilities of sound and colour. He tried sticking pieces of transparent coloured paper onto his figures to give them colour. He realized that one day this would be done, and it was not too early to think about it.

Otto Messmer remembers certain predictions Barré made in 1914 (fifteen years before the arrival of sound and eighteen years before that of colour) which could only at the time be considered futuristic dreams:

> I remember one gathering – some dinner. It was the only time all the animators of New York got together. Previous to that each studio kept by themselves, but they had one big gathering, and Barré made a speech. This was in the very early days. He predicted that someday the cartoons would speak, you know, and have sound effects. Everybody roared, they thought he was crazy. He said not only that, but they will all be in colour and they laughed at that as if it was a wild dream. But as you see it all came true – everything he said. If he had gone into it and could have experimented on sound and colour as well as effects, he would have been an expert.

And so it was in May 1915, that Barré undertook, for the Edison Studios, the production of one of the very first series of American animated films, the *Animated Grouch Chaser*: *The Animated Grouch Chaser*, *Cartoons in the Kitchen*, *Cartoons in the Barber Shop*, *Cartoons in the Parlour*, *Cartoons in the Hotel*, *Cartoons in the Laundry*, *Cartoons on Tour*, *Cartoons on the Beach*, *Cartoons in a Seminary*, *Cartoons in the Country*, *Cartoons on a Yacht*, *Cartoons in the Sanitarium*, *The Black's Mysterious Box* and *Hicks in Nightmareland*, *The Adventure of Tom the Tamer and Kid Kelly*, *The Story of Cook vs Chef* (the first PHABLE cartoon) and *Hicks in Nightmareland*, *The Story of Hicks in Nightmareland* and *Love's Labour Lost*.

In this series, the unfolding story was told in sequences of live-action, which alternated with episodes of animated cartoons more or less related to it. Encouraged by the graphic simplification of the paper animation, Raoul Barré developed, in these episodes, a caricatural tone, inventive burlesque and carefree animation in strong contrast to his colleague's work, which remained too close to their typographical sources. At that time, the drawings done by animators were filmed directly without first being traced, recopied or complemented by assistants. Also, animated film was produced on the basis of 16 frames per second, which were often functioning in blocks of 4 to 12 frames. Thus, it was possible for gifted animators to capture directly the projected movement in personally expressive and daring phases. Barré, with his spontaneous and highly developed techniques of animation, gave to certain characters like Jip, Kid Kelly's little dog, not only movement, but their own personalities, paving the way for such divergent and soon-to-be-firmly established figures as Koko the Clown and Felix.

While most animators around 1910 were content to pattern their work on the elegant and descriptive style popularized by 19th-century magazine illustrations, Barré introduced an entirely different approach. His drawing was simple, cursory and firm, and he pioneered a style of comedy and graphic humour pretelling new theatrical and musical modes which would flourish with the coming of sound to animated film. The lecherous and ugly character of Silas Bunkum, the insects of *Cartoons in the Country*, the eccentric germs of *Cartoons on the Beach*, and *Cartoons in the Laundry*, the imaginative adventures of the little Kid Kelly, his dog Jip, and the nightmarish visits to the hell of Hercules Hicks set the stage for all the scenes of burlesque and controlled excess which would be the hallmark of American animated film for the next fifty years. His films were innovative and expressive, establishing a figurative visual language that animators in New York, as well as Hollywood, would later pick up and develop.

Animation is a graphic art of total creation, which offers all the freedom of a blank sheet of paper. Inherent in it are at least as many fantastic possibilities as the magical effects gained through the use of trick pictures and the "stop-action" technique in live shooting as practised by Melies, Smith, Blackton and Dickson. We know that in the early days, filmmakers starting with Melies and Smith demonstrated the absolute realism and unrealism which could be attained in film. They gave new credibility to magical and archaic visions of the world by populating their films with ghosts, dwarfs, giants, severed heads and multiple beings. They could also create the effects of disappearance, apparition and metamorphosis, using the "stop-action" method. All it takes is for this method to become a technique in itself, and for entire films to be constructed around it, and animated film is born. "One turn, one picture!"

From 1906, animated filmmakers applied this frame-by-frame animation technique to real living people and inanimate objects in such films as *L'Hotel Electrique* by Secundo the Chomon and *The Haunted Hotel* by Blackton (1907). Clothes would leave their wearers, pens would write by themselves, pieces of furniture would leap into the air and fly around, enhancing the already classical level of fantasy and the inexplicable, which characterized some of these early films.

On the other hand, a second mode of expression occurs, when this frame-by-frame procedure is applied to animate drawings rather than live characters and real objects. The pandemonium is replaced by a quieter atmosphere. For example in Cohl or Blackton, it produces dreamy associations of images and ideas, comic metamorphoses, and strange autonomous growths in drawings. We have to remember these random successions of ideas and metamorphoses, invented by these early filmmakers to better understand the third trend of comic action and impossible happenings, began in 1911 with the work of McCay, Bray and Raoul Barré.

Of course, if Barré lacked inspiration, he could always fall back on old formulas like random transformations, which had worked before, as is illustrated by the somewhat hasty carefree succession of caricatures in *Cartoons on a Yacht*. But in the *Grouch Chaser* series, he uses new forms of anthropomorphism. Not only do animals assume human characteristics as in fables (insects in love, a juggling grasshopper or an acrobatic dog) but also inanimate objects are endowed with lives of their own. In *Cartoons on a Yacht*, a chair painfully stretches out its legs when a fat lady gets up from her seat, while in *Cartoons in the Country* a chair leaves the screen after having been juggled by the grasshopper.

The *Grouch Chaser* series developed examples of logically structured metamorphosis and nonsense that defined the standard of caricature in American animated drawing for the next thirty years. In *Cartoons on the Beach*, Mr. Hicks gets lost in the sky and casually takes a bite out of a cloud, as a result of which he suddenly sprouts wings. In *Cartoons in the Hotel*, a cow eats Silas Bunkum's beard, immediately grows a beard of its own and heads for the barbershop; a chicken eats ostrich feed, grows to gigantic proportions, and lays an enormous egg from which hatches a small car. It is obvious that Barré consciously introduced surreal elements into his animation. A young girl's chaperone is literally transformed into a dragon in an episode of *Cartoons in the Parlour*. In Black's *Mysterious Box*, two hairy arms emerge from a fantastic box, drag the hero inside and end up grabbing anything within reach.

Barré's early experiments prepared the way not only for the fables of Paul Terry, the Van Beuren Corporation, and the great Disney fantasy world, but also the paroxysms of Bob Clampett and Tex Avery. He spared nothing in his exploration of the world of imagination: Hercules Hicks visits, in turn, Heaven and Hell and discovers the fountain of youth; in Barré's *Phables*, the abstract concepts of happiness and sadness are personified by the "Joys" and the "Glooms," tiny gnomes who trot around at the bottom of the frame. The evocation of the supernatural or fantastic was even used to produce changes in shape and dimension in sequences of Felix in *Germ-mania*. The same fundamental anxieties which, in the works of Lewis Carroll and Kafka, or in classical fairy tales, are the basis of scenes of metamorphosis and the perpetual search for food, are also present in animated film. The morbid hunger which devours the cadaverous ogre in *Cartoons on the Beach* is later found in such industrious and ever-hungry characters as Sullivan's Felix the Cat and Lantz's Woody Woodpecker.

By 1915, it was obvious to media tycoons that the public preferred images to words. "Syndicated" comic strips appeared in the newspapers of the smallest cities and towns. Even Hearst's King Features Syndicate decided to finance animated films based on popular comic strip characters in order to broaden their popularity. Gregory La Cava and Frank Moser left Barré to animate *Jerry on The Job*, *Krazy Kat* and *Bringing Up Father*.

Like Barré, Frank Moser and George Stalling worked on Tom E. Power's *Phables* (Joy and Gloom*)*. But the seven *Phables* that Barré directed in 1916 – *The Phable of a Busted Romance, Feet is Feet, A Newlywed Phable, The Phable of a Phat Wooman, Cooks versus Chefs, T'was But a Dream* and *Never Again* – were indisputably the best of the series. In these *Phables*, Barré succeeds in animating the relatively elementary drawings of Tom Powers even better than his colleagues, and these films have a vivacious tone and intense level of caricature which outstrips and contrasts with the more moderate humour of most of the films being made at that time. Ridicule reached a peak in *Feet is Feet* with the trials of the fat lady whose shoes are too small for her. In *The Phable of a Busted Romance*, he voluntarily saturates the unfolding story with seemingly unending successions of intertitles supporting the situation. Similarly, throughout the series, the little Joys and Glooms follow every incident, be it fortunate or ill-fated, and alternately chase each other off the screen, sometimes quite brutally.

After the *Phables*, Barré produced and animated a new film series based on the comic strip characters Mutt and Jeff, created by Harry Conway, Bud Fisher (1884–1954). The opportunity to work on one of the most important 12 and popular comic strips of the era was quite a coup for Barré and his workshop. The strip was so sought after that newspapers struggled for the rights to print it.

In 1916 after many attempts, Charles Bowers (1889–1946) and Raoul Barré founded the Barré-Bowers Studio. The studio brought together Dick Friel, Burton Gillette, Ben Sharpstein, newcomers like Dick Huemer, William Tytla, and later, Nat Collier, Ted Sears, Mannie Davis, Isadore Klein, John Foster and Harry Bailey. In three years, Mutt and Jeff, the heroic stars of the world of comic strips, appeared in such films as *The Interpreter, Promoters, The Chamber of Horrors* (1916), *Harps and Halos* (1917), *Cramps, The Dog Pound, The Hospital* and *The Inventors and Wall Street* (1918). These films reveal marked progress in the capacity to introduce drawn characters in continuous and well-developed action: the true Hitchcockian scenario of *The Interpreters*; the burlesque duo in *Dog Pound*, with Jeff playing a fool and Mutt his guardian, in an attempt to fool the police; the economic but effective scene in *The Promoters* where administrators who are "straw men" are literally made of straw and manipulated by strings.

By 1919, the animated film industry in New York was quite clearly established. Four major animators, considered the most competent and reputable, dominated the production: Raoul Barré, John Randolph Bray, Early

Hurd and later, Paul Terry. However, relations between Barré and Bowers were becoming strained. Perhaps Barré feared that Charlie Bowers was seeking to take over more and more control of the studio. Very depressed by this situation, Barré suddenly abandoned not just his studio, but the whole field of animation. Happily enough, he was not well suited to neurosis, and his depression did not last long. Without really leaving New York, he withdrew to Glenn Cove. In this quiet spot on Long Island, which at that time was right out in the country, Barré was able to devote himself completely to painting and illustration.

He did a series of portraits of actresses and high society women, entitled "The Blond of the Month," which was used in magazines to advertise Marchand Hair Treatments. He also worked on some stained glass windows for a church in New York.

Soon Barré was again working in New York. He did some animated cartoons for Rube Golberg and for the *Tad's Indoor Sports* series of Thomas A. Dorgan. During 1926 and 1927, he spent some time in Pat Sullivan's workshop, participating in the production of about ten *Felix the Cat* films. Along with such people as Otto Messmer, Al Eugster, Rudy Zamora, Geo Cannata, Dana Parker and Sullivan himself, who was delighted to have the help of such an eminent animator and director.

Barré mastered completely particular characteristics of visual irony which made Felix the first superstar of animated cinema. His preoccupied walk, cannibalistic smile, endless ingenuity and all-purpose tail made *Felix the Cat* popular throughout the world. Barré also introduced some of his favourite themes to the films he worked on: a comic zoo in *Hunts the Hunter*, evil and gluttonous germs in *Felix in Germ-mania*, funny fat women in *Felix Trumps the Ace*; Noah's Ark in *Pedigreedy*. He directed the best sequences of *Two Lip Time* (watering the tulips with gin) and of *Felix Busts a Bubble* (the sabotage of the screen tests by putting a distorting lens on the camera).

Then, for once in his life, Barré encountered an obstacle he could not immediately overcome. He was ill and had to leave the competitive world of New York for Montreal and the care of family and friends (Elzear Roy and Ozias Leduc). He began to paint again in his studio on Sherbrooke Street West and exhibited some of his works at the Royal Canadian Academy and at the Art Association of Montreal in 1929 and 1930.

During this same period, Dr. Gaspard Fauteux, the young dental surgeon whom his daughter had married in 1923, became involved in politics. In the 1931 provincial elections, he ran against the everlasting mayor of Montreal, Camilien Houde. In order to counter the influence of the journal "Le Goglu," which supported Houde, the young candidate started one of his own, no less satirical, with very few resources. It was called "Le Taureau." In March 1930 the first issue appeared, produced almost single-handedly by Barré and Fauteux. The journal was filled with political manifestos and editorials, elaborate puns, humourous insults, false chronicles, cartoons and parodies. Naturally taking no payment, Barré, under the pseudonym E. Paulette, provided a whole comedy of illustrations and caricatures. The main figures were the well-known silhouette of the elegant mayor (a little like the Penguin character in Batman), the enormous Executive Committee president, and a somewhat clumsy and foolish maiden representing the city of Montreal.

Once again, Barré put his energy to good use. In 1931 Fauteux defeated Houde, and again at the federal level in 1945. Unfortunately, Barré didn't live to see him appointed Speaker of the House of Commons from 1945 to 1949, or become Lieutenant-Governor of Québec in 1950, the youngest in the history of Canada to hold this position. Barré's short foray into partisan journalism did not halt his interest in film and animation. He prepared the scenarios for two films for the provincial Department of Roads, called "Tourism in Québec."

In an interview for "Le Devoir" he revealed a truly philosophic faith in the value of movement:

> Nothing is immobile in nature, everything is movement; that which stops begins to move backwards, and all that moves backwards dies. The most beautiful painting, whether it be a landscape, a portrayal of daily life, or a person's portrait, must first of all capture life, which is movement. One can only understand a living being, a tree, or a machine when one sees how life animates the first, how the wind rustles the leaves of the second, and how the third works.
>
> Beyond that, there are only engineers' blueprints, intelligible only to specialists. Even a monument gains its value only when people visit it. The architect's design is of interest to no one but himself.

DR. FRÉDÉRIC PELLETIER, "THE EDUCATIONAL FILM:
A CONVERSATION WITH A CINEMA TECHNICIAN" IN
LE DEVOIR, DECEMBER 6, 1930, P. 2.

In New York, Barré had worked on a program of films for fine art students. It was designed to use drawing to develop the student's powers of observation and synthesis, to encourage them to consciously reflect on a projected movement and to teach them to master the necessary graphic techniques and gestures. Some reels were completed or ready for production on how to translate ideas into lines, how to create forms that suggest movement, and how to draw animals (using "stop-action" to study a movement or a pose).

Through advertisements and articles, Barré announced the creation of the "Educational Art and Film Company of Montreal." He cited the names of famous artists that he had trained such as La Cava, Milton Gross and Charles Bowers as proof of his capacity to recognize young promising talent. He confirmed his prophetic ability by foreseeing the possibilities which recreational and educational films would offer in the future. He foretold commercial television when he explained how radio would soon call upon visual means to show the products which they could only describe orally on the radio. The students in this co-operative school were paid to work on actual productions. In 1930, they participated in a project called "Le Roi Microbus 1er," from which some of the work schedules, the scenario, some sketches and animated drawings have been preserved.

In this project, as earlier with his *Grouch Chasers*, Barré starts with a live-action sequence to tell the story of a too eager "bon vivant" who is examined by his doctor and told to drink water constantly in order to recover his health. Parallel to these live sequences are animated images of happy germs in the rich man's stomach, who build an ark in anticipation of the flood, and take refuge in it until everything gets back to normal. In a triumphant finale, the man exits from a street urinal to the sound of an invisible brass band playing the Marseillaise. There are whole pages of sketches of a complete menagerie of small animals, zany birds, strange rabbits, pigeons with crankshafts for bills, sad-looking germs wearing funerary top hats and a couple of remarkable monstrous multipedes named Samson and Delilah. All this material was more a preview of the riotous burlesques produced by the Warner Studios under Leon Schlesinger than of the harmonious products of the golden age of Disney. Barré envisioned a possible co-production with France. In October 1931, his brother Hercule, who was Canadian Trade Commissioner in Paris, wrote to him that he had received the sample reels of "*Roi Microbus 1er*" and that he would try to find people in France who might be interested in it. A young

French animated filmmaker, Jean Regnier, offered to collaborate on the project and was especially interested in working on the soundtrack.

Some careers are cumulative, everything leads to final triumph. Others are more evanescent, and in Raoul Barré's life, when he received the warm and devoted letter from his brother, it seemed that the past weighed as little as the future. Hercule Barré said: "I am living in a small apartment and I can put you up when you arrive. So, you see everything looks promising." But Raoul Barré was coming to the end of his career which was in some sense, inverted. He began as a successful painter and illustrator, he became an indisputable pioneer of American animated films, and at the end of his life, he had reached the stage where he had to prove himself. As for the future, he would succumb within six painful months to cancer.

Raoul Barré died at the age of 58, on May 21, 1932, at the home of his brother Georges in Outremont. He was buried in the Cote-des-Neiges cemetery in Montreal. Although some details of this full life were printed in the newspapers at the time, they were empty tributes and could not shield him from obscurity for the next forty years.

Thus the life of one of Québec's boldest and most enterprising creators came to an end. Ever advancing, yet never established, he tried to do too many things at once. Like Charles Cross, Lewis Carroll or Nadar, he was at the very source of 20th-century consciousness, caught between traditional forms of expression and new means of reproduction, between Victor Hugo and the linotype, between Monet and Kodak, Sarah Bernhardt and Melies, and finally between the Art of the single hand and the imperative suggestions of the emerging technical facilities. He too was a good painter, a good animator and, incidentally, a good cook, not to make his own way, whether he was living in Montreal, New York or Paris. He practised daily the maxim summarized by the melancholy Amie! in his personal diary: "Wherever you bring joy, you are almost certain to find it."

It is clear that the time has come to rediscover and collect the widely dispersed works of Raoul Barré, to hunt for the unknown owners of his paintings, to rephotograph the original plates of his satirical drawings, his illustrations and his comic strips and to search out whatever copies of his films are left; in short, to celebrate the centenary of his birth, which passed unnoticed in 1974. It is indeed our loss that we have so long neglected such a stimulating example as the life and work of Raoul Barré. Finally, as a salute to our era, where "survival of the fittest" could make such things as "Grouch Chasers" as rare as the buffalo on the prairies or the turtle dove of

Québec "tourtieres," I would like to close this dossier with a small advertisement that could never be printed elsewhere:

HELP

WANTED

People like Raoul Barré to help make life bearable. Good opportunities for the future but marginal benefits. Diplomas and cars unnecessary.

For more information, RE-READ THIS BROCHURE.

CHAPTER 2

The Importance of Being Fischinger (1976)

by William Moritz

THE ABSOLUTE, EXTERNAL FACTS of Oskar Fischinger's life are simple enough.

Oskar Fischinger was born June 22, 1900, in the small town of Gelnhausen, Germany, the son of a prominent local family who owned a drugstore and a brewery restaurant. He was educated with scientific-technical training, but his love of music led him to apprentice to an organ builder. When World War I closed down that business, he became an architectural draftsman, then a machinist draftsman and engineer for a turbine factory. Around 1920, in Frankfurt, Fischinger met Dr. Bernhard Diebold at a literary club; seeing Fischinger's abstract scroll sketches of the emotional dynamics of dramas, Diebold urged Fischinger to take up abstract filmmaking. At the world premiere of Walther Ruttmann's Opus I (April 1921), Diebold introduced Fischinger to Ruttmann. Although Ruttmann had now moved his film production company to Munich, Fischinger kept in contact with him and sold him the wax-slicing machine, an animation tool (of Fischinger's invention) which could translate a spatial cross-section into a time-lapse duration/movement. In August 1922, Fischinger resigned from his engineer's job and moved to Munich to become a full-time filmmaker. In addition to his abstract films prepared with the wax machine and other animation techniques, Fischinger also joined in partnership with Louis Seel to produce

DOI: 10.1201/9781003288022-3

half-a-dozen rotoscoped, representational cartoons for a theatrical run. He also collaborated with composer Alexander Laszlo on Farblichtmusik, a multiple-projection light show which toured theatres and exhibitions throughout Germany. By June 1927, financial difficulties related to the failure of the Seel Co. and general inflationary troubles forced Fischinger to leave Munich, so he walked to Berlin, where he re-established himself with difficulty. In July 1928, he went to work for UFA doing rockets and other special effects for Fritz Lang's science fiction feature, Frau im Mond. A year later, he accidentally broke his ankle at the UFA studios and, while hospitalized, decided that this must be a sign for him to devote himself full-time to abstract filmmaking, which he then did, producing over the next three years a remarkable series of black-and-white studies tightly synchronized to music. These STUDIES, screened widely in Europe, Japan, and America, came to be in such demand that by 1932 Fischinger had engaged his brother Hans, his wife Elfriede, and three other girls to work at Fischinger Studio. This also freed him to pursue experiments with drawn synthetic sound and to collaborate with Bela Gaspar on the development of a three-colour subtractive tripack film and camera process, Gasparcolor, which allowed him, in December 1933, to complete his first colour film, Kreise. Fischinger's subsequent colour films, Muratti Marches On and Composition in Blue, gained so much critical and popular acclaim that Paramount offered him a contract; in February 1936, he set sail for Hollywood, never to return to Germany. Fischinger's independent temperament and language difficulties made it extremely hard for him to work in studio situations, although he endured episodes at Paramount (1936), MGM (1937), and Disney (1938-9), and later (1941-2) sat out a stint with Orson Welles for an unrealized project. His frustration at not being able to produce independent film as he had in Berlin, led him to take up oil painting. Through the success of his canvases, he came under the patronage of Hilla Rebay, curator of the Solomon Guggenheim Foundation, who extended several grants to him during the difficult war years. Unfortunately, Fischinger and Rebay quarrelled over the artistic merits of his film Motion Painting I (1947) and he never again received adequate financial support – from Rebay or other sources – to complete another film. For the last twenty years of his life, Fischinger had to content himself with endless unfulfilled projects, with his paintings (which involved him in dozens of gallery shows), and with a home light-show instrument, the Lumigraph, which he invented in the early 50s but for

*which he never found commercial distribution. After some years of relative
ill-health, he died on January 31, 1967.*

The internal facts of Fischinger's life, on the other hand, are perhaps
among the most difficult things to establish and comprehend.

He left few formal writings, and those are mostly hampered by linguistic limitations, as he tried to match his new American citizenship with
a command of the English language that he never quite mastered to a
degree commensurate with the obvious subtlety and variety of his visual
thoughts. His private writings – notes and letters – not only are elliptical and fragmentary but also usually deal with his artistic thoughts on
the most superficial level. He was an avid reader – both in German and
English – but his habitual poverty kept him from owning many books
or subscribing to many journals; he haunted libraries, public and private,
but what exactly did he read? In cases where we know he did read some
certain thing, like *Scientific American*, how can we know what he thought
about it?

He was relatively shy and reserved in personal relationships, but he
could also be a brilliant and witty conversationalist among friends. All
indications are that he regarded most social situations, even "private"
ones, as performances, since he seems to have behaved radically differ-
ently to various people and the same people at different times. He loved
chess, and he loved argumentation as another form of mental sports: he
would heatedly debate almost any subject from almost any point of view
(and alternately from opposite viewpoints) just for the enjoyment of the
challenge. Few people, perhaps none, enjoyed anything like his comprehensive confidence. With one friend he might discuss music but not painting, with another astrology but not tantra.

His regimen betrays profound mysticism. He lived constantly by some
sort of astrological principles – working and abstaining according to
moon cycles and other portents. For certain periods, he stayed awake only
at night, sitting on hilltops in meditation contemplating the moon. He
locked himself away (which was probably necessary with five children) for
hours to practice yoga. He moved his bed around periodically to compen-
sate for magnetic currents in the earth, and to realign his energy flow in
various relationships with it. He may have been somewhat psychic, as he
reports several premonitory dreams; in any case, he believed intensely in
the validity of his visions and at one point, for example, ate nothing but

millet for several months because he sensed that he had been or would be a bird in a separate incarnation, and felt that he could tap that spiritual energy of his bird-ness by feeding it properly. He constructed an electric Tibetan prayer wheel that whirled aloft his mantras even after his death. I certainly do not mean to describe any of these things in a supercilious or negative light; in fact, they all seem quite reasonable and vanguard to me. I only wish I knew exactly how and why he did some of them.

Lack of time and money and fierce individualism, among other reasons, prevented him from ever becoming a regular or active member of any group over any period of time. This makes it very hard to judge the extent and nature of his involvement with formalized ideas. We know he studied Ms. Blavatsky's theosophy and Rudolph Steiner's anthroposophy and Yogananda's Vedanta, but we may never know how deeply or inclusively or lastingly he was impressed by their concepts. It would seem from correspondence that Rebay more or less forced Fischinger to attend Ding le Mei's Institute of Mental Physics as part of the terms of one of his grants; did he enjoy it or respect it anyway?

The last person to have known such details, unfortunately, would have been another artist – precisely the persons most likely to understand. Because of several tragic experiences with friendly rivals and collaborators in his mid-twenties, Fischinger developed an almost paranoid suspicion of other artists. Though he could be a polite social friend of someone like Mohely-Nagy, he would never speak to him about any important spiritual or technical matter related to his art. He seems to have harboured a silent resentment against filmmakers like Alexeieff and Bute, who duplicated his cigarette tricks for later ads. He rarely went to other artists' shows (partly because he wished to preserve the integrity of his own creativity), and he seems to have been relatively blind to the possible merits of work different from his own. He dismissed the Whitney brothers' *Exercises* as "gadgetry," and, though he recognized Jordan Belson's genius after seeing his first film (and recommended him to Rebay for a Guggenheim grant), Fischinger never attempted to speak seriously with him on spiritual or aesthetic matters and died without seeing those ripe masterworks of Belson's middle period which are, in so many ways, the fulfillment of all Fischinger's strivings.

I firmly believe, however, that some of Fischinger's spiritual qualities rubbed off on the young Whitneys and Belson, even though at the time they may have regarded much of his work as trivialized by the seeming dominance of the banal music tracks over the visuals. Ah, but those visuals contain formulas and gestures that communicate with us subconsciously, directly, without being appreciated or evaluated.

And what of Harry Smith?

Bashe telephoned
today long distance – Is it
snowing over there?

We know from Calvin Tomkins' *Bride and the Bachelors*[1] that John Cage sees Fischinger as something of a seminal figure in his own development. Cage's work with Fischinger is somewhat more colourful than Tomkins relates.

Galka Scheyer had introduced Cage (and Edgar Varese) to Fischinger shortly after his arrival in America (1936) in the hope that Cage might provide Fischinger with some original and modernist music more suited to the extraordinary, radical potential of his animations. Fischinger, round and jolly as a Chinese Buddha, explained to Cage that he had tried writing sound himself a few years earlier by drawing ornaments and photographing them into the soundtrack area of film so that their inherent spirit, that gave them visual shape, might also be released to give them equivalent auditory values. This notion that each object contained its intrinsic sound spirit – undoubtedly articulated with bilingual aleatory whimsy – intrigued Cage immensely and led him to embark on his percussion pieces. When Cage proposed doing a soundtrack of percussion music for one of Fischinger's films, Fischinger suggested that Cage should actually work on animating a film to better understand the process and potential of the medium – that incredible freezing of time, and that tedious thawing. Cage dutifully came to observe and help Fischinger on his current work-in-progress, Optical Poem, for which dozens of paper objects were suspended on strings throughout the deep space of a stage area. Cage's lesson involved taking over from Fischinger the long pole topped by a chicken feather with which each circle would have to be moved to a small, even increment, then steadied to motionlessness in preparation for the next exposure. Fischinger merrily sat beside the camera, puffing his smoke, supervising, waiting for the next take. But in the hands of a novice, the set-up took such a long time! Gradually Fischinger dozed, and his cigar, falling to the floor, ignited some rags and papers lying nearby. Cage seized a bucket of water and splashed it over the fire, coincidentally inundating the camera. That was the end of John Cage's apprenticeship in film (though Fischinger wrote him a few years later asking if he had ever done a suitable music track).

What does this all mean in a practical sense? Well, I suppose it means that Fischinger's primary statements are, as he wrote in the *Art in Cinema* catalogue, in his works themselves. Which raises two more problems: what are Fischinger's works? and how should we interpret them?

I confess that, as I review my biofilmography in *Film Culture* 58-59-60,[2] 1974, and this program "The Working Process" that Mrs. Fischinger and I prepared for Ottawa, I see with some trepidation that I have created a bit of a "Frankenstein."

During his lifetime, Fischinger remained fanatically scrupulous about which films were shown and how they were shown, as a reflection on his name and the purpose of his work.

- Fischinger was opposed in theory to representational imagery. In the spirit of nonobjective art, he maintained, correctly, that his (major) films were absolute experiences in and of themselves, not representations of some other objects or experiences. Because of this, he would never have shown (or even discussed) things like *Pierrette* or the advertising films on any program of his "works"; nor, I believe, would he have shown *Spiritual Constructions, Munich to Berlin*, or *Swiss Rivers and Landscapes*, regardless of how good these pieces might now seem in the context of Independent Cinema.

- Fischinger did commercial work only as a means of gaining much-needed money to support himself and his heartfelt abstract film work. Whenever possible (e.g., *Study IIA, Kreise, Muntz*) he used abstract imagery as the basis of the ad films and after the contractual rights of the original sponsor had expired, he prepared purely abstract versions which would then be suitable for screening as part of his oeuvres. He seems to have purposefully destroyed prints of films like the Euthymol toothpaste ad, Meluka and Borg cigarette ads, and the Rota titles which knowledgeable filmmakers who remember seeing them have told me were masterworks of their genre. Even the celebrated colour Muratti film, which (as a single exception) he did keep 35mm and 16mm prints of and occasionally show "for fun," was never included in a serious or official show of his works (e.g., Art in Cinema, Pasadena and San Francisco museums, or Museum of Modern Art distribution). Thus he would undoubtedly grit his teeth at the rape of seeing the Tolirag ending restored to *Kreise*, etc. Even the majestic rolling moonscapes and rockets of *Frau Im Mond*, relevant as they are to an understanding of the origins of some of the figures and movements in the contemporaneous black-and-white studies, would be rejected.

- How did Fischinger feel about his early films? We may never know. During his first 25 years in America (his major, mature period), he had no access to these films since he was officially not allowed to take film out of Nazi Germany in 1936 and only snuck away with single prints of the major sound films. We know he respected *Studies 2, 3 and 4* because he once attempted to get grant money to recover them. We know that, despite his ill-health, he began to build an optical printer in the '60s to transfer some of the silent nitrates to safety film. I fear, however, that his idea may have been only to reconstruct an "experiment reel" like the one he used to keep in Berlin (which Mohely-Nagy used to screen at the Bauhaus), containing merely brief excerpts from several early films chosen to represent various techniques he had employed. There may have been other reasons for this, of course. Some items like WAX and SPIRALS are definitely not complete, structured films as we now see them; we can not even be sure of the provenance of the elements or fragments that make up the compilation we see today. Now, Fischinger was fastidious about the structures of his films, composing them carefully (even when music dictated to some extent a general flow or climax) to represent visual statements and dialogues with some sort of meaningful conclusion. When he speaks in the Pasadena Museum notes (1956, reprinted in *Film Culture*, p. 188) of creating "sentence after sentence of moving, developing visual images," we can see an important aspect of his artistic credo and an important reason why he may not have wanted to preserve or exhibit fragments of early films in which the basic intentions or conclusions of the conceptual dynamics behind the imagery may not be comprehensible. Or indeed, like Jordan Belson, he may not have felt that the early pieces expressed sufficiently mature ideation.

But there is another group of films which Fischinger also did not show. *Radio Dynamics*, the most lucid, diverse and successful of his visual communications, may never have been shown publicly. We know from the Rebay correspondence that he worked on a film for Ding le Mei's Institute in the mid-'40s; *Radio Dynamics* was that film, and did Fischinger feel its message too particular or specialized to be screened outside the Institute? Did he withhold it merely because it had no soundtrack, and he considered silent films theatrically risky? (How sad that seems in the context of Independent Cinema!)

Study 11A was not brought to America along with the other sound films in 1936, but even after two good prints did arrive in the early '60s, Fischinger never screened it or had other prints of it made. He probably considered it an artistic failure since he mentions several times in his writings that the power of the simple purity of his black-and-white studies can hardly be equalled by a colour film, in which just the rainbow multiplicity is bound to absorb or dissipate or distract a certain amount of energy from the main flow of the argument.

- Fischinger would never have discussed his working process. He felt, first of all, that production techniques should be invisible and truly unimportant – that since they were merely the instrument of "writing" the new non-verbal language, then they should never be obtrusive or consequential in their own right. Thus, he took great pride in having hand-crafted each of his films without recourse to secondary machinery or artificial colouring methods (again this refers to his "serious works" from which *Wax* and *Study 11a* are "exempt"), and thus (naturally, if unfairly) he would reject out of hand the Whitney brothers' pendulum sound and optically printed imagery. On the other hand, Fischinger also imbibed the film business' competitive spirit, which led him to a justified pride in the ingenious tricks that he used to make the cigarettes walk or his abstract figures flow and metamorphose so fluidly. For both these reasons, he would never have submitted to a "working process" show.

Of course, whether Fischinger would approve or not, his "unpublished" film works provide valuable insights and aids to the appreciation of his major creations, so I'm not sorry I've done this. A peek at the rejected motions and gestures lets us appreciate the tantric restraint of the perfected

Composition in Blue. When I first saw *Swiss Rivers and Landscapes*, though I knew *Motion Painting I* well and could say hundreds of things about it, I was staggered by the range of new information it invoked, such as the basic rapport between rivers and landscapes; the basic analogy between representational landscape and mental (abstracted) landscape with the corollary suggestion of ideational, psychic and psychobiological "rivers"; the rapport between the "documentary" gesture of the handheld diagonal tracking shots along river banks and the formalized layering of *Motion Painting I*'s spiral "projections"; the time lapse (or perhaps not?) of the clouds snuggling against the sides of distant triangular mountains vs. the sense of rhythm and timing inherent in the dash-outlining middle-section of *Motion Painting I*. And all this, though I know Fischinger would have considered *Rivers and Landscapes* an insufficiently balanced work and not shown it. Or maybe I, as a practitioner of our contemporary Independent Cinema, am unduly attracted to the tension between the informal imagery and the heavily structured sound...?

One thing is certain: Birds know how to talk through some articulation lost to music.

Now that we have decided what the corpus of work fairly constitutes, how do we deal with it? I suspect the only answer to that is: "In as many ways as possible!" One of the inherent characteristics of the non-objective image allows (or rather requires) us to digest the information in terms of one or more external systems, frames of reference, programs, whatever you wish to call them. This doesn't mean just saying, "Oh, that reminds me of a comet!" or "The handling of spirals is certainly radically different between the *Spiral* film and *Motion Painting I*" (although those are both valid approaches). Rather you have to set up whole attitudes towards the material, saying, "I'm going to treat the colour-shape continuum in purely formalist terms" or "I'm going to handle the configuration-movement symbiosis as an analogy to naturalistic gesture" or even "I'm going to get stoned and pretend it's a light show." Some art critics claim one or more of these approaches are simply *de trop* or *pas engage*, but after all, each of us is left victim (or beneficiary?) to the shortcomings (or advantages?) of his approaches, or the limitations (?) of his linguistic structures, if you would. But it in no way damages or limits the richness of the original films, for like pieces of exquisite music, they can be experienced again and again, and each time we bring with us our new selves to have a new relationship with the event. The a-concentric circles of *Composition in Blue* – are they a virtuosic epitome of Art Deco design principles? Or an invocation of the "expansor" sigil of the great Renaissance Magus Giordano Bruno? Or tantric orgasmic rhythms? Odour...?

I remember as one of the most moving passages in all Literature, the description by Kandinsky in his memoirs[3] of his returning home late one night to find a canvas he had been working on accidentally left upside-down on the easel illuminated by a shaft of moonlight (I have not reviewed this text for some years – perhaps it was a little less romantic). What a thrill that discovery was to him, and in his range from dismay to elation, what a tale we can read of academic repression and rebellious revelation, of the prison behind every breakthrough. On an emotional level, that's really quite incomprehensible to me. Abstract art has always been such a natural part of my environment that I could never consider it secondary, artificial, trivial, or taboo. And perhaps more importantly, I could never consider anyone blind to its obvious cogency as being more than an unfortunate Ignorant.

Fischinger straddles a bridge between Kandinsky and me. Though Kandinsky must have known in his heart (that same heart which first remembered colours from his nursery) that he had perfect right to paint his patterned canvases, still he felt it necessary to rationalize and defend himself against charges ranging from insanity to unprofessionalism to wall-papermaking. Fischinger was just enough younger than Kandinsky that I think he shared my utter confidence in non-objective consciousness, and though he was frequently subjected to the same inane accusations and pedantic challenges that Kandinsky was (and, indeed, I still am), Fischinger never felt obliged to reply with more than polite condescension.

Fischinger was not a pioneer in Kandinsky's sense of forging a new format in the face of respected opposition, truly experimenting with new possibilities to find out how far you could go and what would happen if you did. Fischinger didn't experiment; he knew exactly what he had to say and exactly how to say it, and exactly what the reaction would be, then and now. He was a pioneer in that absolute (perhaps American?) sense of a settler in a new land. The non-objective world had always existed. Fischinger was not surprised to find himself living there, nor was he unsure about how to handle the flora and fauna, nor was he afraid to venture beyond its mountains and rivers for fear of falling off or coming across some impassive desert. For surely, Plato and Buddha and the Hopi shaman had lived there before.

NOTES

1. Ref: Viking Press, New York, 1968 (pp. 86-87)
2. "The Films of Oskar Fischinger" by William Moritz in Film Culture, Nos 58-59-60, New York, 1974
3. Wassily Kandinsky, "Text, Artist, Autobiography" in In Memory of Wassily Kandinsky (Solomon R. Guggenheim Foundation, New York, 1945). p. 60.

CHAPTER 3

Segundo de Chomon

Spanish Magician (1978)

by Carlos Fernandez Cuenca

THE BEGINNINGS

Segundo de Chomon was "a man of great knowledge and exceptionally gifted".[1] Son of Isaac Chomon and Luisa Ruiz, he was born in Teruel on the 18 October, 1871. He died in Paris on May 2, 1929. He was a descendant of Henri de Chaumont, third son of Hugo de France, who died in the Crusade of 1130; around 1550, the De Chaumonts (or De Chomons) settled themselves in Spain and obtained recognition of their nobility.[2]

The young man from Teruel, who was then working in an office, decided to enlist in the army to fight in the Spanish-American War in Cuba. Discharged, he returned to Barcelona in 1897 and his encounter with the film producer Lumiere completely changed his life; from then on, his intelligence and will were constantly devoted to the service of the newborn art.

The first thing he was interested in was the colouring of films, and after thoroughly studying the system currently used and

DOI: 10.1201/9781003288022-4

experimenting with several mixtures of anilines, he obtained a perfect transparency of an everlasting quality. In his home at 61 Poniente Street in Barcelona, he installed the first Spanish workshop and one of the world's first for hand-coloured films. This happened in the middle of 1902 and, in October of the same year, Pathé became one of his best clients, sending him films from Paris to be hand-coloured in Barcelona.[3] The first one was *Samson et Dalila*, a 140-metre film. Following a letter of 14 October 1902, in which the French technicians describe "how well produced it was," he received seven more films: another print of *Samson et Dalila*, one of *Bolero Espagnol* (20 metres) one of *Danse Cosmopolite* (30 metres) and four of *Quadrille En Robe* (20 metres). Chomon charged two francs per metre for the hand-colouring of these films.

THE FIRST TECHNICAL DISCOVERY

At the same time, he was performing the difficult and tiresome task of hand-colouring the films, Chomon set up a small laboratory to print cinematographic titles; it was there, in 1902, that he made his first discovery which opened great possibilities of fantasy for the movies.

At that time, there was no special apparatus to print subtitles which were photographed with an ordinary camera and on positive film, so as to obtain a better contrast. However, the positive film was less sensitive than the negative, and it needed a relatively long exposure to the light while the handle was turned as slowly as possible. One day, in the middle of his work, Chomon did not notice a fly walking on his subtitle. When he saw it on the screen, he was surprised to discover the fly moving in a very strange way, sometimes very fast, sometimes with abrupt and incredible jumps. The novelty of such a show made Chomon think about its possible origin. He immediately reached the conclusion that filming only one object frame-by-frame and changing it slightly each time from its original place could convey the impression that the object moved by itself.

This was the birth of the so-called "one turn, one picture" technique which enabled Chomon to make many of his magic films and which constitutes one of the infallible means of creating laughter. For the man from Aragon, the cinematographic apparatus began to be a source of wonder; "he wanted to do with it what had never yet been achieved."[4]

THE SPIRIT OF IMITATION

The first films undertaken by Segundo de Chomon were documentaries or, as they were called in those days, "natural scenes" as, for example, some views of the mountains in Montserrat, taken in Barcelona in 1902 and which Zecca hurried to offer to Pathé[5].

Chomon's beginnings in the field of cinema are closely related to the spirit of imitation existing at that time. The man from Teruel had been appointed head of the technical section in the organization founded in Barcelona by Luis Macaya and Alberto Marro who were able to obtain the commercial representation of Pathé Freres in Spain. Macaya and Marro wanted to take advantage of the success of a film by Fructuoso Gelabert, and, in 1905, they entrusted Chomon to produce another film with a similar title.

Gelabert's film, which became the first great success of the new Spanish film industry, was entitled *Los Cuapos De La Vaqueria Del Parque* (The Dandys of the Vaqueria Del Parque). It was based on a real event which at that time had very much amused the population of Barcelona: it concerned a Vaqueria del Parque licence-holder's clever advertising to attract customers to his rather deserted snackbar.

The trick consisted of putting an ad in a newspaper reading as follows: "Beautiful young lady with a one million dowry, wishes to marry a handsome and elegant young man. Rendez-vous at the Vaqueria del Parque, between 11 a.m. and 12. He shall wear a gardenia in the buttonhole of his jacket – I will have a white fan."[6] Several hundred young men, responding to this ad, gathered in this place with a gardenia in their buttonholes hoping to be the "sesame" able to open the heart of the fabulous rich lady. Gelabert made a sparkling film, 250 metres long, which was shown in Barcelona with enormous success.

The actors were Carmen Vital, the director Juan Morales, Juan Alarma (brother of another prestigious director), Jose Vico (son of the famous actor of the same name); the tenor Jose Pineda, Antonio Riba, Juan Solsona, Jose Parera, and numerous extras. The outdoor scenes were shot in the Ciudadela Park, and the author Vicente Raspail was the set decorator. The imitation produced by Chomon (as author as well as director and cameraman) under the direction of Macaya and Marro, was far from being the servile copy which we find in the work of Melies or Zecca in France. Even if the title *The Dandys of The Park* is almost identical, the action was quite different. In this 100 metre film, the protagonist is a rich Catalan farmer whom many girls wanted to marry.

It is certain that Chomon was not satisfied with *The Dandys of The Park*, nor with *We Serve Meals*, another of his successful 150-metre comedies produced around 1905. The Aragonian believed that cinema should not be limited to reproducing nature nor to repeating scenes played on the stage, but rather that its main purpose was to use this medium precisely to create what could not be done before the invention of this new wonder called "cinema."

And it is said that he built, for his own personal use, a camera with a wooden box generally used in Malaga to export raisins.[7] Such a camera really existed and was known at the Pathé Studio under the name of "apparatus No. 12."[8] Its particularity was that the film could run forwards and backwards, which was a great advantage in producing his trick-filled films.

His first important film *El Hotel Electrico* (150 metres) plainly dealt with the different aspects of the everyday life in a hotel. The owner had substituted all kinds of electrical systems in place of the staff. Chomon showed an extraordinary world of inanimate objects which seemed to act almost like humans, thanks to the development of his "one turn, one picture" technique – that is, shooting the film frame by frame. In this way, napkins were cleaning dishes alone, knives were cutting food by themselves, docile shoes hurried to fit their owner's feet. One of the most surprising and perfect moments of the film was a brush lathering the face of a client, leading up to the razor which shaved him without a barber, in a fast and proper way.

In 1905, Chomon took a high quality shot of an eclipse of the sun from the Observatory of the Jesuits in Tortosa and made one of the first films on astronomy. The next year, he did an excellent documentary on the wedding of Alfonso XIII which made Pathé decide to call him to Paris to work directly for him. It was not the documentary film, however, but the films with tricks which were to give the Spaniard his prestige as one of the most important collaborators of Pathé.

IN THE REALM OF FANTASY

Chomon stayed four years in the Pathé Studio in charge of the production of films with special effects. During this period, he directed some 150 films of 100 to 200 metres, besides contributing his initiative and technical advice to other productions and sometimes working as cameraman for various directors, mainly Zecca and Nonguet.

Upon his arrival in Paris, he won Charles Pathé's first prize, rewarding imaginative and technical achievement with his film *La Legende Du Fantome*. His success established his great reputation in the French film industry and gave him a great deal of confidence.

The technique of "one turn, one picture" served him to produce *Liquefaction Des Corps Ours*, a 105 metre film, which constituted one of his first triumphs, provoking the envy of all specialists due to its amazing technical skill. At one point in the action, Chomon substituted the live actors for perfect wire puppet reproductions, which he photographed frame by frame until they became a liquefied formless pile.

In *Le Roi Des Aulnes*, he achieved a prodigious effect of superimposition: taken in close-up, he made the clear image of two cavaliers appear in the eye of a live toad whose eyelid was constantly moving.

In the film *Les Ombres Chinoises* in January 1901, he used – for the first time – transparent backgrounds which gave him the means to accomplish countless displays of fantasy. With excellent photographic quality in *La Maison Hantee* (1907), he showed a man lying down and seeing his own shadow attacked by two devils.

That same year, he produced *Le Chevalier Mystere*, a heroic and spectacular fantasy featuring the young comedian Andre Deed, with whom he also made the special-effects comedy *Le Roi Des Tetes A Claques*. Chomon also produced films in the fantastic trips genre, so highly appreciated in those days. To name a few: *Voyage Dans La Planete Jupiter*, *Voyage Au Centre De La Terre* and the Chinese fantasy *Voyage Dans La Lune* (1908) which bears no relation to the Melies film of the same title.

The main idea of *El Hotel Electrico* reappeared in *Cuisine Magnetique* and *La Table Magique; Cauchemar Et Doux Reve* is a delightful description full of fine poetical values; *Les Jouets Vivants, Fabrique D'argent* and *Sculpteur Moderne*, with new technical resources, widely developed the system of "one turn, one picture." Of course, in Chomon's work, the fairy tale, intended for children but also enjoyed by adults, could not be absent. *La Poule Aux Oeufs D'or, Peau D'ane* and *La Belle Au Bois Dormant* are to be put in this category.

WONDERFUL CONQUESTS

With these films, Segundo de Chomon gave a new stimulus to already-known techniques and was responsible for many inventions. For instance, double exposure combined with slot masks to duplicate the characters; an original assortment

of little curtains to open and close the scenes; optical surprises obtained through stop motion animation to achieve a metamorphosis of characters and objects, etc. But his personal contributions went much further. Besides the tricks over which he attained incredible mastery – the frame-by-frame technique and the use of a transparent screen to animate shadows – we owe to him the first attempts to produce cartoons, early in 1907, in the Vincennes Studio. For this purpose, he had built a special wooden scaffolding that vertically held the camera over a table where the drawings were placed.

He did not dare to produce a complete cartoon but limited himself to include short animated sequences in some of his films, like *La Maison Hantee*. On the other hand, the task was very difficult since the drawings were made on heavy paper and the repetition to give the illusion of movement took a very long time.

As far as the future of the artistic possibilities of the cinema were concerned, perhaps the most impressive of all the technical innovations which Segundo de Chomon brought to the Pathé films was the invention of a support to move the camera about freely. The primitive model, used for the first time in *Life and Death of Our Lord Jesus Christ*, consisted of a platform mounted on two brake-blocks guided by a long wooden pointer.

The contribution of de Chomon to the development of the cinema is truly important.

Originally appeared in Carlos Fernandez Cuenca, Historia def Cinema, Vol. 1, Ch. IV, pp. 345-354 (Madrid: Ed. Afrodisio Aguado, 1948). Trans: Santiago Gubern.

NOTES

1. In the already quoted article "The Precursors of the production of Spanish Film" by Joaquin Freixes Sauri, in the magazine Arte y Cinematografia, Barcelona, 1926.

2. These and other very important data of Chomon's biography were passed on to me by the son of the great film expert, Mr. Robert de Chomon Ruiz, the excellent photographer and cameraman in Turin. The present study devoted to the amazing personality of Segundo de Chomon, supported by first-hand documentation, will serve, I do trust, besides putting this Spanish pioneer in the place he historically deserves, to clear certain vagueness and to dispel current errors with regard to his work, so little known.

3. Several texts about the first years of the French film industry (Bardeche et Barsillach: Histoire du Cinema, p. 22; Mesguich: Tours de Manivelle, p. 31, etc.) explain the hand-colouring film workshop of Chomon. It is believed that they refer to Chomon's workshop, because his family name had been often spelled in the French way, as also did Jean Mitry in his already mentioned work on Ferdinand Zecca et son ecofe.

4. "The Contribution of Two Spaniards to the Fast Development of the Cinema," article by J. Soler Moreu in the special issue of Arte y Cinematografia, Barcelona, July 1936, to celebrate its silver anniversary. The author mistakenly calls him Facundo instead of Segundo de Chomon.

5. This is clear from a letter of Chomon to Pathé, dated January 19, 1903.

6. Transcribed by Gelabert in his "Contribution to the History of the Cinematography in Spain" in the magazine Primer Plano, Madrid, November 3, 1940.

7. Mendez-Leite: Forty-Five Years of Spanish Cinema, already quoted, p. 14.

8. Sadoul: Les Pionniers du Cinema, p. 313.

CHAPTER 4

German Animation Pioneers (1988)

by Louise Beaudet

D ESPITE THE SIGNIFICANT CONTRIBUTIONS of German animation pioneers, it is in vain that we look for a comprehensive history of German animation. And yet the experimental work of a small group of German avant-garde artists searching for a universal language of abstract symbols was seminal for the development of film, a medium to which all soon turned. Painters like Viking Eggeling, Hans Richter, Walter Ruttmann, collaboration with Fernand Léger and Man Ray revolutionized graphic arts, paving the way for the modern "non-figurative" animators. Eggeling's *Diagonal Symphony* became the movement's cornerstone: Tristan Tzara unhesitatingly called Eggeling a precursor, while Standish Lawder described the film as "a duo of comb-like objects, one angular, the other curved, abandoned to some sort of mechanical dance, one dominating, the other pulling back, each in perfect rhythm with the other's movements."

Eggeling was born in 1880 in Lund, Sweden, and moved to Berlin in 1919, where he began a brief collaboration with Hanz Richter. It was on his own, however, that he made *Horizontal–Vertical Orchestra* (1921), a film (no longer available) which displayed his innovative experimentation. He later produced, under considerable strain, the famous *Diagonal Symphony* (1924), which confirmed his reputation as a master animator. His success,

DOI: 10.1201/9781003288022-5

however, was short-lived: he died in Berlin in 1925, shortly after the film's release.

Hans Richter, a student of art and architecture, was born in Berlin in 1888. By 1919, his insights led to new perspectives. He thought the rhythm of a painting could be prolonged almost endlessly if, instead of limiting the work to the canvas' rectangular borders, scrolls, such as the Chinese used to depict their countryside and illustrate their fables, were used. By transferring the art to celluloid and projecting it on a screen, the laborious manual unravelling could be avoided.[1] In 1921, he produced *Rhythmus 21*, the first of his abstract films, notable for its substitution of the conventional form of painting for a frame-by-frame breakdown of the standard canvas, which had the effect of highlighting the temporal elements (rhythm, artificial unravelling of time and movement).[2] Thus was the effect of film on painting and, conversely, of painting on film.

Though Richter and Eggeling shared the same goals, their methods differed. What Richter attempted to do by changing from black to white and from negative to positive, Eggeling achieved by moving the diagonal axes and organizing figures temporally. In trying to fuse music with painting, however, Eggeling was the more successful of the two. For film definition, Richter's work better captured the creative tension of the filmmaker faced with the materials of his art.[3]

As with other avant-garde artists, Richter abandoned abstraction once dadaism caught hold. The transition was evident in *Filmstudie* (1926), a polyphony of associations and analogies achieved by alternating abstract and figurative shapes. The changeover went a step further in *Ghost Before Breakfast* (1927–28), a deliciously absurd, iconoclastic comedy. It was originally produced for the Baden-Baden International Festival of New Music, with a Paul Hindemith musical score that was unfortunately destroyed by the Nazis. Hindemith and Richter appeared in the film sporting beards and, in one scene, moved toward the camera with Darius Milhaud at their sides.

For Richter, theory and practice were never far apart. In 1929, he published *Film Enemies Today – Film Friends Tomorrow*, in which he described his experience as an avant-garde artist and explained his "film-as-poetry" theory. On his film *Ghosts Before Breakfast*, he wrote: "We are permanently surrounded by objects we consider to be inanimate. But these objects are beings in their own right. They have natures and a life of their own; if we let them 'live,' they reveal, both to themselves and to us, unsuspected originality."

Between 1930 and 1939 Richter travelled extensively, dividing his time between Russia, France, The Netherlands and Switzerland, before finally emigrating to the United States in 1940. From 1942 onwards he devoted his time to teaching, writing and filmmaking. He died in Locarno in 1976.

Walter Ruttmann, a fellow abstract film experimentalist, was born in Frankfurt-on-the-Main in 1887. A musician and painter, he began his filmmaking career in 1919, producing a four-film series entitled *Lichspiel*, numbered *Opus I, II, III and IV*. The London *Times*, after their premiere at the London Film Society in 1925, described them as "'Absolute films' – a succession of motifs in movement... enthusiastically greeted by the audience." These films revealed perceptive analogies between film and painting, while the music added significantly to the visual process. Using light and colour to highlight the film's music was also central to Ruttmann's art: sequences were orchestrated with themes and variations.

The critical success of *Opus* brought offers of collaboration from Julius Pinschewer, Piscator, Lotte Reiniger and Fritz Lang, for whose film, *Niebelungen I*, Ruttmann contributed the hawk's dream sequence. He turned to live-action filmmaking in 1927–28, however, directing the internationally acclaimed *Berlin, Symphony of a Great City*. After brief stays in Paris and Italy, he returned to Germany to film documentaries on urban life. In 1936 he made *Olympia* with Leni Riefenstahl. He died in Berlin in 1941.

There is yet another filmmaker whose non-figurative, pure cinema stands next to Ruttman's, Richter's and Eggeling's for its contribution to German avant-garde cinema in the 1920s: Oskar Fischinger. Born in Gelnhausen in 1900, he was initially a graphic artist and, later, an engineer. But it was while living in Frankfurt, where he met Ruttmann at the premiere of *Opus* (which greatly impressed him), that he started experimenting with film. This new interest eventually led him to Munich where, in 1922, he began making short films with Louis Seel. When Seel's studio failed, Fischinger continued to experiment until he produced, in 1927, a film called *Spiritual Constructions*. Made with thin cutouts of a wax and clay mixture and set on glass lighted from beneath, it is a meditation on violence in the form of a psychedelic fable: "...The abundance of signals in certain scenes hints at a quest for polyphony and counterpoint that is not picked up at first sight."[4] Even in his figurative films, Fischinger, we see, tended toward abstraction.

After a troubled stay in Munich, Fischinger moved to Berlin. Hired by UFA studios, he applied his talents to the special effects of Fritz Lang's *Woman on The Moon*. Around 1929, before the end of his UFA contract, he began his charcoal drawing studies. Of these black and white studies, according to animation specialist and Fischinger biographer William Moritz, No.8 was the most complex, the most striking, the most important and the one Fischinger preferred best. In 1936, lured by Paramount Studios, Fischinger emigrated to the United States. His adjustment was difficult, but he stayed, working until his death in 1967 in Hollywood. His oeuvre will be remembered for its continuity and polytechnical diversity.

Guido Seeber was born in 1879 in Chemnitz. A photographer by training, he became interested in cinematography in 1896. As early as 1903 he utilized follow shots, and by 1909 he had perfected a method of sound recording, dubbed the Seeberophon, while heading Deutsch Bioskop Gesellschaft, a studio whose organization provided the model for future German studios. In 1919, Seeber founded with a partner, the Deutsch Kinotechnik company and became publisher of the magazine *Kinotechnik* as well as co-publisher of *Filmtechnik*. He spent a good part of his time exploring and popularizing cinema. His efforts to systematize research, improvements and inventions contributed to the advancement of film techniques on many levels. At one point, with so many innovations to his name, he decided to forego patenting and simply published his results in magazines, thus giving unrestricted access to his innovations. As hoped for, his writing nurtured scientific interest and eventually helped popularize the medium.

Seeber's predilection for tricks was apparent in *Kipho-Film*, the publicity film he had made for the Film-and-Photo Show in Berlin in 1925. It contained almost all his tricks with elements specific to photography and cinematography, presented in a way that highlighted the whole filmmaking process. Fluid images overlapped and melted into each other, creating a mosaic of elements in perpetual motion, unified by a common theme.[5]

It was Julius Pinschewer (born in Hohensalza/Poznan in 1883) who produced *Kipho-Film*. In order to distribute theatrical commercials, which he invented and first introduced into theatres in 1912, he started his own studio. His preference lay with the experimental works of the more important film animators of the 1910s and 1920s, namely Walter

Ruttmann, Lotte Reiniger, Oskar Fischinger and Hans Richter, animators who, in some instances, also collaborated with him. In 1933, to escape Nazism, he emigrated to Switzerland. He died in Berne in 1961.[6]

Hans Fischinger, Oskar's brother, was born in 1909. Around 1931, the two brothers collaborated on various films and experiments. Two years later, eager to be on his own, Hans left his brother's studio and created the astonishing *Dance of the Colours*. Drafted into the army at the outbreak of the war, he was killed in 1944 in Romania.[7]

Hans Fischer was born in 1900 in Kösen (Thuringia) and began his career in the early 1900s – under the name of Fischerkösen. He went on to become a brilliant film animator. Pinschewer was greatly impressed by his films and provided encouragement from the beginning. Becoming his own producer, Fischerkösen won many awards in the 30s and 40s. Among his greatest films were *The Ravaged Melody* and *The Snowman*, made during the war. He also worked on theatrical commercials, displaying his immense talent and imagination in *Blue Wonder*. His work was interrupted when he was sent with the German army into the Soviet Union, and again when he fled the German Democratic Republic. He eventually set up a studio in Mehlem-on-the-Rhine. He died in 1973. After Pinschewer, he was, without a doubt, the most successful filmmaker in the history of German animation.[8]

So, we see that from early in the 20th century, effervescence and dynamism infused all sectors of German animation. Provocative avant-garde art interacted with the most disparate forms of animation, from publicity shorts to Chinese shadows. Of the latter, Lotte Reiniger was certainly the most famous practitioner. Born in 1899 in Berlin, she began cutting out figures at a very early age. At 15 she became captivated with animation after meeting Paul Wegener, the director of *The Golem*. Having studied acting, she was given minor roles by Wegener and, at the same time, was also allowed to try her hand at decorative titles. She made her first of animated silhouettes, *Ornament of The Loving Heart*, in 1919, under Wegener's guidance.

Reiniger met her new collaborator and future husband, Carl Koch, in Berlin's Kulturforschun. She worked on various screen adaptations of popular fairy tales, among them *Cinderella* (1922), before embarking, with the help of Walter Ruttmann and Berthold Bartosch, on her first feature-length film, *The Adventures of Prince Achmed* (1923–26), considered one of the most outstanding examples of German expressionism. Jean Renoir, a friend at the time, asked her to contribute a sequence of Chinese shadows for his film *La Marseillaise*. Working with the newly created soundtrack, she then made films inspired by music. In 1936, at the invitation of John Grierson, Alberto Cavalcanti and Basil Wright, Reiniger and her husband moved to London, joining the staff of the General Post Office Film Unit. At the end of the war, she produced 13 films for British television. She came to Canada on several occasions, giving seminars and making films: in 1975 she made *Aucassin and Nicolette* for the National Film Board, and in 1979 *The Rose and Ring* for Canadian television. This pioneer of German animation continued working until only a few months before her death in Dettenhausen, June 19, 1981.

This history of German animation reveals, if only briefly, the vitality and creativity of its ground-breaking pioneers.

NOTES

1. Herbert Read in Catalogue of Hans Richter exposition "Painting and Cinema."
2. Hans Richter
3. P. Adams Sitney in *Une Histoire du cinéma.*
4. André Martin in *"Pourquoi il faut voir, revoir et revoir encore les film d'Oskar Fischinger."*
5. Biographical notes were taken from the Kalëidoscpoe of German FIlm Animation, edited by the Deutscher Trickfilmverband and the Deutsche Kinemathek (Berlin, 1979).
6. ibid
7. ibid
8. ibid

CHAPTER 5

The Evolution of Daffy Duck (1988)

by Mark Langer

T HE RETURN OF DAFFY Duck in *The Duxorcist* (1987), after an absence of almost 20 years, is a major film event. Since his creation, this animated character has become as well known as his live-action contemporaries. "Writing for Daffy Duck is like working with Groucho Marx or Cary Grant," says *Duxorcist* writer/director Greg Ford. "A true legend of the screen comedy." All legends have a beginning. Daffy's beginning was in the Warner Bros. animation studio, although the genesis of the duck lies not with a single film or creator, but in the very history of American animation and the organization of the film industry.

Animated cartoons made by American studios were traditionally disseminated in much the same way as live-action pictures, which were distributed to theatres through a system known as block-booking. Under block-booking, theatres could not rent films individually; they had to book entire packages of movies, sight unseen, from film distribution companies. Without the ability to pre-screen the films to be exhibited, the only guarantee a theatre owner had of a film's potential box-office success was the commercial reputation for the production company and the popularity of the film's stars. Through this system of distribution, the persona of the star took on a name-brand quality: the star became a commodity with great commercial value.

DOI: 10.1201/9781003288022-6

Large-scale production of American animation began at the same time that the block-booking system was being instituted. Since the entire yearly output of a studio's cartoons had to be block-booked, series cartoons tended to be designed around continuing star protagonists such as John Bray's *Colonel Heeza Liar* (1913), Mutt and Jeff (1916) of Charles Bowers and Canadian Raoul Barré. So important was this system, that cartoon experiments in forms of narrative without continuing characters, such as Disney's *Silly Symphonies*, or Max and Dave Fleischer's *Song Car-Tunes*, were only made possible because of the presence of star personalities featured in separate cartoon series, like Disney's Mickey Mouse or the Fleischers' Betty Boop. The pervasiveness of block-booking made it crucial to the marketing of cartoons that they feature established, identifiable and popular characters.

The *Looney Tunes* series, produced by Leon Schlesinger for Warner Bros. began with a continuing character – Bosko. The Bosko of these early cartoons, directed by Hugh Harman, was a simple black humanoid variant on Mickey Mouse. Although not as popular as Disney's character, Bosko afforded enough continuity to the *Looney Tunes* series to make it marketable. (Harman's partner, Ruby Ising, directed a parallel animated series without continuing characters. These *Merrie Melodies* films promoted Warner Bros. songs in a manner somewhat similar to today's rock videos.)

Schlesinger lost Bosko when Harman and Ising left Warners in 1933, taking their character with them. Without a star, the studio hastily improvised a replacement named Buddy. Unfortunately, this bland white retread of Bosko never appealed to the public. Even the addition of colour to the *Merrie Melodies* series in 1934 failed to reverse the declining fortunes of Schlesinger's little production company. The studio began to desperately cast about for stars. In 1935, director Friz Freleng introduced a number of characters such as Porky, Beans, Ham and Ex in the film *I Haven't Got a Hat*. Although the latter three had limited popularity with the public, Porky caught on. By mid-1936, Porky had become the lynchpin of the effort to merchandise the *Looney Tunes* series.

While Porky was popular with the public and did succeed in turning around the fortunes of Schlesinger's studio, there were several limitations to what Porky could do. Porky was a reactive character – essentially a well-meaning innocent coping with remarkable circumstances. As a result, Porky was not usually funny himself but the victim of humorous situations or characters. An Everyman figure, Porky represented a kind of populist small-town or rural virtue and, as such, was hampered by the same kind of limits experienced by Disney with Mickey Mouse. Disney once complained that he was "trapped with the mouse... Mickey couldn't do certain things – they would be out of character. And Mickey was on a pedestal – I would get letters if he did something wrong. I got worried about relying on a character like the mouse. You wear it out, you run dry."

The answer at Warners was to be the same as at the Disney Studio. Disney's reactive star had been paired with other characters, such as Goofy or Donald Duck, who were funny because of their inherent peculiarities, like stupidity or bad temper. In *Porky's Duck Hunt* (1937), Warner's director Tex Avery and writer Ben "Bugs" Hardaway, sent the pig in pursuit of his dinner – a dinner named Daffy Duck. Daffy was designed as the yin to Porky's yang: Porky was passive, Daffy was active; Porky spoke with inarticulate stuttering, Daffy was uninhibitedly verbose, peppering his conversation with a "hoo-hoo-hoo" laugh in imitation of comedian Hugh Herbert; Porky was staid, Daffy was insane. Not a completely realized personality, the early Daffy Duck was simply a bundle of comic attributes in the same spirit as a later character written by Hardaway – Woody Woodpecker. Daffy was designed to reinvigorate the *Looney Tunes* series through his wild and unpredictable behaviour. So successful was this new character that a rabbit clone of Daffy was introduced in *Porky's Hare Hunt* (1938).

Through such films as Freleng's *You Ought to Be in Pictures* (1940), Frank Tashlin's *Porky Pig's Feat* (1943), and Chuck Jones' *Duck Dodgers in the 24 1/2th Century* (1953), Daffy often was paired with Porky in a relationship where Porky continued to play the straight man to Daffy's comedian. But with the passing of time, the character of Daffy Duck changed. Simple lunacy was not enough to sustain a marketable persona. The continuity provided through the use of a series star allowed the development of richly articulated personalities in American animation. Each succeeding Daffy cartoon embellished Daffy's characteristic, drawing on the audience's previous familiarity with the duck in order to create an increasingly more detailed personality. Beginning as comic relief in Porky Pig films, Daffy soon became more and more central to the action. Opposed to Porky's bourgeois placidity, Daffy evolved from an unmotivated zany disruptor into the quintessential parvenu. Aggressive and urban, Daffy soon became representative of the dark side of the upwardly mobile Horatio Alger myth in American society, the mirror image of the conventionalized social model to which we aspire. Striving and scheming to better himself in the world, he continually failed to conform to the demands of any given situation. Daffy's attempt to pass as a doctor in *The Daffy Doc* (1938), to replace Porky as the studio's star in *You Ought to Be in Pictures*, to emulate Errol Flynn in *Robin Hood Daffy* (1958) or the Man of Steel in *Stupor Duck* (1956) all met with a similar lack of success. Daffy's aspirations continually exceed his capabilities. The later Daffy was often a team player, but his backslapping aggressiveness, seen at its best in Tashlin's *Nasty Quacks* (1945), coupled with an over-competitive nature, assured that Daffy remained the outsider striving to be the insider. Rarely successful, Daffy responded to every defeat with redoubled effort, irrepressibly a game bird. Comparing Daffy to Bugs Bunny, director Chuck Jones observed that "... nobody could be Bugs Bunny. Bugs Bunny is an aspiration. It's what you'd like to be like. But what you're sorely afraid of is that you're probably much more like Daffy. He expresses all the things we're afraid to express."

Within these general parameters of Daffy's character, a number of individual variations were developed by each major Warners director. Following Avery's prototype lunatic came Bob Clampett's variation on the duck. Clampett's films portray a world of illogical metamorphosis and emotional extremes. His malleable mallard is a character in constant plastic variation, from the inflatable iron lung victim of *The Daffy Doc* to the startled zoot-suited scat singer who turns briefly into a giant eye in *Book Revue* (1946). Clampett's films often took recognizable cultural icons and myths, and restated them in hallucinatory form, as exemplified by Daffy's frenetic imitation of Danny Kaye, careening among caricatures of big band personalities while playing out a jitterbug variation of *Little Red Riding Hood* (*Book Revue*), or Daffy as Duck Twacy, fending off wildly exaggerated Chester Gould-ish villains with names like Pickle Puss and Neon Noodle in *The Great Piggy Bank Robbery* (1946). Clampett's Daffy is less a psychological figure than a rubberized absurdist participant and commentator on the clichés of contemporary culture.

Frank Tashlin's Daffy is an aggressive vulgarian – the loud-mouthed avatar of patriotic platitude and bonhomie. Utterly oblivious of his lack of social graces, Daffy soldiers on in films like *Nasty Quacks* and *Plane Daffy* (1944), confident of his charms that drive others to the point of murder. The obnoxious boosterism of Tashlin's Daffy makes him a caricature of the go-go-get-it ethos of middle-class striving. While the physical environment of Tashlin's cartoons lacks the rubberized quality of Clampett's work, Tashlin's extreme angles, quick cutting, his contrasts between static and kinetic action, and his fondness for emphasized key poses produce a unique sense of comic timing.

Daffy Duck as interpreted by Chuck Jones is at the opposite extreme from that of Clampett and Tashlin. There are touches of psychological pathos in Jones' characterization of the little black duck. Jones' Daffy is basically a supporting actor in a starring role – somehow never quite up to the demands of the part, but unstinting in his efforts. Daffy's grasp always exceeds his reach, but he perceives his shortcomings in terms of social injustice – the ultimate self rationalizer pitted against a harsh world in which other characters, such as Bugs Bunny, effortlessly prevail. Richard Corliss has pointed out a scene from Jones's *Rabbit Seasoning* (1952), where Daffy, hiding with Bugs in a burrow, is asked to stick his head up to see if Elmer is near. When Daffy does, he is shot in the face and drops back down into the burrow croaking "Still lurking about!" States Corliss, "The voice is broken, but maniacally chipper, defeated but indomitable." Only Jones was capable of such shadings of character. Even in a film like *Duck Amuck* (1953), where Daffy suffers every possible physical transmutation, his psychology remains detailed and complete. In contradistinction to this is Jones's increasing tendency toward modernist stylization and formalism, seen at its most extreme in the settings of *Duck Dodgers in the 24 1/2th Century* and the reflexive filmic environment of *Duck Amuck*. This tension between naturalism and formalism is one of the chief characteristics of Jones' expression.

One constant through all of these variations on the theme of Daffy Duck has been the voice of actor Mel Blanc. Blanc was hired the year of Daffy's birth to provide a new voice for Porky Pig. He later went on to provide the voice for many of the Warners characters, such as Bugs Bunny, Sylvester and Pepe Le Pew. Blanc's original voice for Daffy Duck was a speeded-up imitation of producer Leon Schlesinger. His intonation and sense of comic timing have contributed greatly to the richness of Daffy's personality.

Animation is a collaborative art. The hundreds of people involved in the production of Warner Bros. cartoons over the past 51 years cannot be named here. The effort of the people mentioned above, and that of many other directors, voice artists, animators and writers form the true source of the entity we know as Daffy Duck. A tribute to Daffy Duck is a tribute to the talent and vitality of this host of artists who have developed one of the most enduring of cartoon performers.

CHAPTER 6

Frame by Frame

Animated Commercials
1920–1990 (1990)

by Louise Beaudet

ADVERTISING GOES AS FAR back as 1638, when Theophraste Renaudot first produced a flyer entitled "Business Office." Ads – as they began to be called – appeared in 1835, in a variety of printed matter. Poster artists such as Daumier, Bonnard, Toulouse-Lautrec, as well as decorative artists were soon to follow suit. Actually, cinematography took up advertising from the very first. As early as 1897, Edwin S. Porter projected an ad for Dewar's Scotch Whisky on an outdoor billboard in New York's Herald Square. In 1899, in England, Arthur Melbourne-Cooper produced *Matches Appeal* for the match manufacturer Bryant and May. This film is considered to be the first animated ad in the history of animation. Later, between 1920 and 1940, British businesses used animation widely to promote their products, taking advantage of the fact that animators could not compete with the American entertainment films which were being massively imported at that time by distributors. To ensure their own survival, they were forced to turn to industry and trade and to accept the conditions which prevailed there. This was the situation in most European countries. British animation really took off with John Halas and Joy Batchelor in 1940. This prolific studio was, and still is, a leader in the fields of advertising and scientific and educational filmmaking.

DOI: 10.1201/9781003288022-7

In Germany, in 1911, Julius Pinschewer founded a studio that specialized in advertising and set up an organization that systematically distributed his productions through a wide network of cinemas. In 1933, he owned a thousand of them. As producer and filmmaker, he associated himself with artists of great talent such as Lotte Reiniger, Walter Ruttman, Oskar Fischinger and Hans Richter. In 1928, the famous production and distribution studio, UFA, which produced the films of Fritz Lang, followed suit and opened an advertising department. By the end of the silent movie era, 86 advertising production companies competed in the German market.[1]

Meanwhile, in France in 1919, Lortac (Robert Collard), with the part-time collaboration of Emile Cohl, opened an animation production department while he was head of Publi-Ciné. Long before this, in 1904, the Lumière brothers themselves produced, in the form of a brief two-minute documentary, a very discreet ad for Moët et Chandon Champagne. In the period between the two wars, artists became involved in advertising in a big way. Cassandre was probably the most accomplished in poster-artistry, and Alexander Alexeïeff, in animation. At that time, the French-Swiss poet Blaise Cendrars wrote: "... Yes, advertising is truly the most beautiful expression of our era, the greatest novelty, a veritable art." Blaise Cendrars, *Aujourd'hui*, Paris, 26 février 1927

Until the liberation in 1945, animation in Hungary was almost completely devoted to advertising, except for the odd individual project. This form of production carried on even after the nationalization of the Hungarian film industry, a unique event in Eastern Europe at the time, unless one considers Yugoslavia. Indeed, from 1948 to 1950, a team specializing in advertising films worked under the direction of film pioneer Gyula Macskassy, under the auspices of the government studio. This team was to become the key group of the future Pannonia studio. Macskassy, along with his team, directed nearly 300 advertising films in the course of his career, apart from his own films.

As for Czechoslovakia, Hermina Tyrlova, as well as Irena and Karel Dodal, had begun to engage in animation in the mid-'20s, but their work was strictly limited to advertising. Ten years later, Dodal was to found his own studio, IRE Films; and in 1935, he created, along with his wife, *A Game of Bubbles*, for the Saponia soap company. The film is remarkable for its time, even though Fischinger's influence is evident throughout. In 1922, the Pole Sergije Tagatz set up shop in Zagreb. To alleviate his difficult financial situation, he became involved in the production of animated advertising films. In 1931, the three Mondschen-Maar brothers, escaped from the Nazi threat, sold their studio in Berlin and also settled down in Zagreb. They created the Maar sound-film advertising studio and carried on their activities in the field of animated advertising. For over five years, this enterprise, which produced nearly two hundred ads a year, was a great business success. Due to their skill, talent and workmanship, the Maar brothers were able to take Yugoslavian animation beyond an amateur level and onto the road of professionalism.

The history of Italian animation is so intimately associated with advertising that the two are said to be inseparable. As had been the case in Hungary, Czechoslovakia and Yugoslavia, the first small animation advertising teams were responsible for the further growth of animation in that country. The production of ads in Italy in the '20s was a good way of gaining experience. Later on, this country was to develop a particular style of animation. During most of the '50s, Italian animators invented what were called "commercial extravaganzas," aimed at cinemas, where the quality of the product itself was overwhelmed by a taste for the spectacular. When television first made its appearance, Italian advertising was subjected by the IAR, between 1957 and 1977, to a strange regulation called "carosello." This policy stipulated that an advertising film should not exceed two minutes fifteen seconds in length. Of this total running time, it was formally forbidden to mention, to show or even to hint at the product for one minute fifteen seconds. As for the actual message itself, it could be presented only in the final thirty seconds. This strict regulation gave rise to a host of ads featuring the "greats" of the Italian star system. When it finally began running out of breath, the "Carosellian star system" discovered animation, and for a time, in Italy, a new star was born.[2]

We can safely conclude, as a result of this brief retrospective, that it was advertising which led to the introduction of animation into a large number of European countries. In our time, the "iconosphere" in which we live began to manifest itself in an explosive fashion at the beginning of the 50s. In this era of "hypersignalisation," even "the written word has become aware of its image." This graphic civilization matured at an early age and animation easily emerged within this context. This ideographic writing is expressed "in sharp symbols, in forms that are clearly readable and powerful, like those found in the commercial and industrial arts."[3]

When television first came on the scene around 1930 in New York and London, it made little or no impression. Only after the war did it truly impose itself. As was the case with its role model, the film industry, television was quickly invested with the stuff which "dreams are made of" and at once constituted a fabulous opportunity for the industry, which rapidly sought to take advantage of this new marvel.

Most of the broadcasting bodies of the Western hemisphere, realizing the value of animated graphic pieces, warmly welcomed this form of advertising film. The small screen with all its idiosyncrasies, required the invention of ultra-synthetic imagery to convey a message that was sensory, rigorously concise, minutely rhythmic and unmistakably striking. One might describe it as a sort of conditioned reading. Has it not been said that, because of its broad scope and its immediacy, one televised half minute is worth three theatrical minutes? Thus the televised ad must at once provide instant reference and be eye-catching without being repetitious for fear of overtaxing the viewer and, all the while, respect the viewer's own visual literacy. The design must be based on a concept and, therefore, reveal a clue, something easily recognizable, as well as set a style and create a visual and auditory mood. The script must never overshadow the image. At the same time, because of the lack of perspective, tight time slots, tough budgets and constrained techniques, artists are narrowly confined in their efforts. The messages, through their graphic symbolism, must bring about an almost imperceptible persuasion, always in line with broadcasting the vertical orientation of television, as opposed to the horizontal orientation of the big screen. Indeed, "graphic creation for TV demands a greater inventiveness and daring than film-making does, and the challenge is therefore more difficult to meet."[4] Everyday, animators must put their imagination to the test in order to face the hazards of an uneven terrain. "In filmmaking, one could say advertising is a long-term operation... In the television industry, production is short-term, tense, dynamic, often short-tempered and generally very unnerving."[5]

This "frame by frame" retrospective features productions made for both the small and the large screen. It does not pretend to provide a complete chronology, but instead it is an attempt to simply build some bridges, establish some landmarks, comparisons and affinities. It seeks to show the eclecticism and evolution of techniques, and at the same time, illustrate the influence of certain artists, studios and feature films. The most important of these influences came from United Productions of America (UPA). Breaking radically with American classic cartoon esthetics, UPA, with its avant-garde style, changed the look of advertising in the '50s. Creator of the famous Muratti cigarette ads, Oskar Fischinger inspired Alexander Alexeïeff and Etienne Raïk, amongst others. The latter, in turn, left an ever-lasting impression on filmed advertising. Stanley Kubrick's *2001: A Space Odyssey* (1968), sparked an infatuation for special effects. The impact of George Dunning's *Yellow Submarine* (1968) was immediate. This feature's design left its mark on an incalculable number of commercials, and there were still traces of its influence well into the '70s.

We shall also point out the social tendencies which blended with the style and sensitivity of a given era, coupled with its national character-istics. "Advertising is not only an important cultural factor, it is also the faithful reflection of the civilization of peoples, of the spirit of an era."[6]

Thus, a group of films will reflect the traditional image of woman and man (rather, the male species), as it prevailed and unfortunately, more often than not, still does. Whole families of products will be grouped so as to appreciate the variety of approaches used to sell a given commod-ity. For example, at a time when life's pleasures were not under the sharp scrutiny they are today, alcohol and cigarettes were widely celebrated in a number of fashions. Alcohol and cigarette lovers were continuously called upon to buy. And the proverb which holds that it is the effect that counts, not the bottle, does not ring true in advertising. The image, the labels, the presentation, all are given careful consideration, often more so than the content itself. On the other hand, another more virtuous category is aimed at children, using the drawing power of famous Hollywood cartoon characters. Daffy Duck and Bugs Bunny help to increase Tang and Kool-Aid sales; Olive Oyl, Popeye and Bluto sing the value of Famous Fried Chicken. Betty Boop, as the perfect housewife, praises the efficiency of a particular brand of detergent.

Whether innovative, imaginative or sophisticated, at times adopting a slice-of-life approach or drifting off into the sphere of surrealist humour, all these films are magnificent examples of graphic art. Through their cre-ative daring and their new style, these artists have stayed clear of the rut of coded, conventional, predictable styles, leaving the Coricidin and Colgate platitudes for the less gifted. "The image itself is not an idea, though the image can become a sign or more precisely cohabit with an idea within a sign," according to Claude Levi Strauss. These creators grasped this prin-ciple superbly and rendered it graphically. They refused to tread the beaten path of history and completely upset the notion of advertising itself.

Surprising at times (we shall see some "curiosities" of historic interest), at other times awesome, this march through time unveils gems that can be compared positively with some of the best "conventional" works.

In 1965, Gerard Blanchard wrote: "All contemporary images have to face the advertising image." This is truer now than it ever was.

NOTES

1. Westbrock, Ingrid, Der Werbe Film, citee par Roland Cosandey in «Julius Pinschewer – 50 ans de cinéma d'animation», 1989.
2. Cf. Spotcartoon de Chiara Magri, Zagreb 90
3. MARTIN, André in Cinéma 65, #98, juillet-aout.
4. Dorfsman, Louis in Film & TV Graphics 2, 1976.
5. Halas, John in Film & TV Graphics, 1967.
6. Pinschewer, Julius in Reklamefilme, 1924.

CHAPTER 7

The Personal Side of Ernest Pintoff, Filmmaker

by Maureen Furniss, Ph.D.

*E*RNEST *P*INTOFF HAS HAD *a long and varied career in the arts and media, having written, produced, directed and often scored live-action theatrical features, short films, television pilots and series' episodes, as well as animated shorts and commercials. Aside from these accomplishments, he has also worked as a fine art painter, a musician and a writer of books. The truth is, the films being showcased at this festival represent only a small portion of Pintoff's total accomplishments – yet they quite accurately reflect what is at the core of many of Pintoff's artistic expressions: the search for self-understanding.*

Ernest Pintoff was born in New York City but grew up in Watertown, Connecticut, where he and his one brother attended Baldwin School and Watertown High School. His father, who was Polish, and his mother, who was Russian, both immigrated to the United States at the turn of the century. As a teenager, Pintoff had aspired to a career as a professional athlete, playing basketball or baseball, but says his brother talked him out of it: "I'd say my brother convinced me that the competition gets rougher as one gets older and that, living in Watertown, I was just a big fish in a small

DOI: 10.1201/9781003288022-8

pond. And that I perhaps had an inflated sense of my athletic prowess." Instead of sports, Pintoff earned a BFA in Painting and Design at Syracuse University. Later, he received a graduate assistantship at Michigan State University, which allowed him to acquire an MA in art history; and just this year, he was awarded an honorary doctorate from St. Michael's College in Vermont.

Although Pintoff has had a lifelong love of professional sports, his interest in the arts also developed early in life. He began playing the trumpet in grammar school, when he was nine years old and, shortly thereafter, took up piano and the cello as well. In high school, he acquired an interest in improvisational jazz, which developed rapidly in college. Greatly influenced by such musicians as Miles Davis, Dizzy Gillespie, Charlie Parker, Thelonius Monk and Bud Powell, Pintoff later played in jazz clubs and even did a brief stint with another of his mentors, Flip Phillips.

On the other hand, Pintoff's "serious" interest in painting did not develop until he was in college. Inspired by such "illustrative" artists as Thomas Hart Benton, John Riggs and Grant Wood, as well as the cartoon drawings of James Thurber and Saul Steinberg, Pintoff began college hoping that he could one day become an illustrator for publications like the *Saturday Evening Post* or *Colliers*. During the early 1950s, while he was in college, he managed to have a few line-drawing illustrations published in *Metronome* and *Downbeat*, both jazz magazines.

As the character of the American art world changed, Pintoff's aesthetic sensibilities evolved from representational to abstract expression. He says his paintings "matured" as he first studied the abstract tradition of the Cubists, Georges Braque and Juan Gris, and subsequently came to admire the work of Paul Klee, Henri Matisse, Piel Mondrian and the hard-edged painters.

After receiving his graduate degree from Michigan State University, Pintoff married and moved to Los Angeles. Having seen some United Productions of America (UPA) films, he decided that he would like to enter the animation industry, which he thought would encompass all of his interests. Though he had no formal training in this field, he felt qualified because of his education and general abilities in music and graphic art. Initially, he was hired to do inbetweening at the Disney Studios, but he worked there for "just a couple of days." Pintoff says that he really was not very interested in Disney material, which he associated primarily with animal characters and stories for children.

Pintoff left Disney and applied at UPA, which was expanding its work-force in order to produce animated segments for its half-hour television series, *The Gerald McBoing Boing Show* (aired on CBS from December 1956 to October 1958). Herb Klynn and Steve Bosustow reviewed Pintoff's portfolio and hired him to be an apprentice inbetweener, pairing him to work with John Whitney, who also had been recently hired. Whitney had become renowned for his pioneering work in abstract animation, and Pintoff feels he benefited greatly from the opportunity to work with him, saying, "Whitney was very open and receptive to my ideas and he intro-duced me to a lot of non-objective animation possibilities. John was free with his knowledge and very encouraging." Working together for about a year, the team produced such animated shorts as *Aquarium*, *The Lion Hunt*, *Fight on For Old*, *Performing Painting* and *Blues Pattern*, the two latter being relatively abstract in their design. When *The Gerald McBoing Boing Show* was cancelled, UPA no longer needed an extended production crew and the studio's focus moved to other, less innovative work; Pintoff and others were soon on the move.

Next, Pintoff moved to New York and went to work for Terrytoons, where he stayed for only a short time. He was hired by Gene Deitch, whom he had met at UPA, and brought with him a concept that he had developed at the West Coast studio: the animated short, *Flebus* (1957). In his book, *Of Mice and Magic*, Leonard Maltin says of *Flebus*, "it was certainly the most cerebral cartoon the studio ever released. Like many others to follow it, it resembled a UPA cartoon in visual style, point of view and format." Together with veteran animator Jim Tyer, Pintoff brought his idea to life; reflecting the 1950s vogue for experimentation with wide-screen formats, *Flebus* was created in CinemaScope, the only one of Pintoff's animated shorts to have been designed and filmed in this way. Though Terrytoons' Studio Head Bill Weiss was not very supportive of the project, Deitch was encouraging, to the extent that he allowed Pintoff to compose the film's musical score – against contractual regulations. As a result, the score is attributed to studio composer Philip Scheib, who conducted the piece for recording.

After he completed *Flebus*, Pintoff went into business with Robert Lawrence in New York City, forming Pintoff-Lawrence Productions; however, this venture was short-lived. Pintoff soon opened his own com-pany, Pintoff Productions, which specialized in the production of televi-sion commercials for advertising agencies – a booming market during the 1950s. With a staff of artists that included Jim Murakami, Jim Hiltz, Jack Schnerk, and Howard Beckerman, Pintoff Productions created advertisements for such companies as Tip Top Bread, Lucky Strike Cigarettes, Norelco, and Renault, as well as numerous regional firms.

Pintoff enjoyed the economic freedom that resulted from his work for advertising agencies, investing the profits made from commercials into a series of independent films that were also produced by his company: the animated shorts, *The Violinist* (1958), *The Interview* (1959), *The Old Man and the Flower* (1960), and *The Critic* (1962), as well as the live-action short, *The Shoes* (1962).

Pintoff approached several studios regarding the distribution of the films but found little interest. When he showed *The Violinist* to Columbia executives, they turned it down, saying it was "too simple." Taking matters into his own hands, Pintoff successfully promoted the film through screenings in a series of small New York City theatres, such as the Paris and the Sutton, all of which were owned by Donald Rugoff. *The Violinist* garnered favourable reviews by Bosley Crowther of *The New York Times* and others and especially drew attention when it won a British Academy Award and was nominated for an Oscar. Not surprisingly, Columbia changed its mind about *The Violinist* and eventually became the sole distributor of all Pintoff's short films.

For *The Violinist*, as with all of Pintoff's animated shorts, elements of the soundtrack including voice, sound effects and music were premixed, so that the animation could be created to follow along exactly; this method also allowed for fast and economical production. In the case of *The Violinist's* soundtrack, Carl Reiner – who had gained renown for his work on *The Sid Caesar Show* – read directly from the storyboard (rather than from a script) and improvised freely.

Reiner was also an important figure in regard to another of Pintoff's short films, *The Critic*. Reiner knew Mel Brooks, who was writing for *The Sid Caesar Show* and introduced him to Pintoff. Pintoff explains that Brooks conceived *The Critic's* story line: "I think Mel got the idea while sitting in an 'art film' theatre. He overheard someone mumbling something like 'What the hell am I paying two dollars for this piece of junk on the screen?' Mel was amused by the idea and told me about it, and I liked it. I could identify with the reactions." Apparently, Pintoff related to the concept because of his own experiences as an abstract painter. He further explains, "I loved the idea... I was dealing with my own non-objective paintings and wanted to poke fun at myself and many of the reactions that people – from my mother to general viewers – had over my own work, saying things like 'What the hell is that?'"

As a basis for the film, cameraman Bob Heath was asked to create visuals composed of what Pintoff considered to be "pretentious" abstract forms. Pintoff says that Heath "improvised, by doing things like dripping paint and using Q-Tips. I told him to create anything he wanted. Heath was an amateur artist, and it turned out quite campy, which I liked." From Heath's footage, Pintoff edited down 30 minutes of film. This material was screened for Brooks, who freely improvised wisecracks to the footage, using the voice of an elderly Jewish man. Finally, Pintoff edited the voice track and visuals down to the film's running time of approximately three and a half minutes, a process that took nearly a year to complete. *The Critic* was not the first of Pintoff's films to satirize an art form close to the director's own heart. Such was also the case with *The Interview*, which takes on the subject of jazz music. The film is based on an interview with an inarticulate musician, made from a recording by Henry Jacobs and Woodrow Leafer. A jazz trumpeter for many years, Pintoff explains that he particularly enjoyed poking fun of what he considers to be a reflection of himself as a musician.

Though the subjects of Pintoff's short films vary, in each there can be found a link to the director's own life. Indeed, it seems that the opportunity to explore personal themes was in large measure what motivated the films' production. While Pintoff felt it was important to exhibit his works to as wide an audience as possible, it is also apparent that the animated shorts were not made primarily as a commercial venture. Pintoff says he wanted these films to "be personal reflections of my own work. I did want to try to sell them, obviously, but that was not my motive for making them."

Perhaps the most personal element of these works comes in the form of the "poor soul" character, which is a motif of the animated films *Flebus, The Violinist* and *The Old Man and the Flower*. Pintoff explains that "this lonely, grubby kind of character, who is always struggling to communicate and find love," was reflective of his own inner questioning at that time. He provides an example in discussing *The Violinist*, which he says was inspired by "my own personal struggles as an artist. I was in psychoanalysis at that time, and I was dealing with the whole question of whether psychoanalysis would affect my art or alter my spontaneity. Ultimately, the violinist remains happy and grubby, so I guess the answer to that question is to remain as you are." Animation historian Donald Crafton and others have said that animated films tend to be very self-reflexive in nature, that independent animators, especially, often depict themselves in their work or create story ideas out of personal experiences. In the case of Pintoff's series of short films, Crafton's thesis certainly seems to hold true.

Pintoff's first live-action short, *The Shoes*, in many respects continues in the style of the director's animated films. Pintoff points out that in this film, too, there is a "poor soul" character: the starring role, which was originally to be played by Jackie Gleason, but was eventually performed by Buddy Hackett. Pintoff also notes that the live-action character played by Hackett is in some respects "like an animated character – kind of a fat and lonely, but funny, guy." Another similarity is that a second starring role in the film is played by a dog, which is somewhat typical of Pintoff's work since he liked to include little dogs and cats in his animated shorts as well.

Despite its similarities to earlier works, *The Shoes* also marked a turning point in Pintoff's career. He explains, "at that time, I was losing interest in animation and was captivated by the prospects of communicating to a broader audience of people through live-action. Also, I think I became more true to myself in that I was losing interest in material primarily for children. First it was animals at Disney, then it was the relationship of children to animation. I was getting more interested in adult subjects and broader audiences, and covering more variety of subjects. Cartooning and animation was mostly humour, and I had become more interested in drama and serious subjects dealing with adults."

It is likely that Pintoff's experience with *The Shoes* and his newly-earned Oscar for *The Critic* were key factors in Columbia's decision to encourage him to direct live-action films, the first of which was *Harvey Middleman, Fireman* (1965). Pintoff wrote, composed, directed and produced the feature, which stars Gene Troobnick, Hermione Gingold and Charles Durning. After this turn of events, Pintoff stayed away from animation production for many years. Instead, he involved himself with other aspects of the entertainment industry. He wrote, directed, and produced a number of live-action features, including *Bullitt* (1968), which stars Steve McQueen, and *Dynamite Chicken* (1971), which features Richard Pryor, Paul Krasner, and Peter Max, among others. Pintoff entered television directing in the early 1970s after he produced a 16mm feature, *Blade* (1973), starring John Marley, Karen Machon and Morgan Freeman, which he used as a sample to break into the television industry. He directed many television pilots and series' episodes, having a special interest in programs from what he calls the "tough cop" genre, such as *Hawaii Five-O, Kojak,* and *Policewoman.*

Pintoff had little personal investment in his television work, saying, "it was very difficult to establish my own story mark. Directors function mostly as production people..." Other aspects of his career, however, continued to be more personal in nature. For example, in the mid-1960s, he began the first in a series of teaching positions, by lecturing on writing at the New York School of Visual Arts. He also had positions at Michigan State University, the American Film Institute, the University of California at Los Angeles, and the University of Southern California.

Other projects that reflected Pintoff's more personal interests included his record company, for which he wrote, produced and distributed under Dateline Records. Pintoff recorded Moms Mahley, Pigmeat Markham and others, sometimes coordinating the soundtrack with animated visual images. For example, Markham's recording of "Healthy Baboon" was accompanied by animated line drawings, which were aired on television – the visuals were projected over dancers on Dick Clark's television program, *American Bandstand.*

But of all Pintoff's work, his books are perhaps the most autobiographical in nature. Interestingly enough, Pintoff suggests that the written word is, for him, probably the most difficult form of creative expression. He explains, "graphics and music come rather easily to me, and naturally... [but] I'm not very well-read, and it is a particular challenge for me to 'write.' The very act of using the language is not natural to me, which I think has a lot to do with my family and background. My parents were not highly educated, so as a youth, I wasn't surrounded by literature or the subtleties of the English language."

Pintoff describes his first book, *Zachary* (Paul S. Eriksson, publisher, 1991) as "a young adult novel and very autobiographical, which is usually the case with first novels. It is about my growing up in Watertown, Connecticut, involved in a fictional adventure mystery. It's about a Jewish boy who has grown up in a Gentile town, about to be bar mitzvahed. It includes a lot of my interests in Judaism, coming of age and the Second World War." The book received critical acclaim, being nominated for an Edgar Award for "Best Young Adult Mystery." The story is also currently under consideration for production as a feature film.

Pintoff's other books also draw upon personal experience, especially his *Bolt from The Blue* (Northwest Publishing, 1992), which is a chronological account of his rehabilitation from a massive stroke in 1984. In the epilogue of the book, Pintoff discusses his role as a teacher, stressing that students should not specialize too soon, but instead would be wiser to prepare themselves for the future with a broad liberal arts background. This same philosophy informs Pintoff's other books, *The Complete Guide to American Film Schools* (Viking, 1994) and *The Select Guide to Studies in Animation and Computer Graphics* (currently in production).

Without a doubt, Pintoff has followed his own advice throughout his life, having involved himself in a broad spectrum of work in the fine arts and entertainment media. After his stroke, he was reinspired to work in animation, since it did not necessitate the mobility and strenuous activities required for directing other forms of motion pictures. He is currently working on a new animated film and teaching a course called "Concepts and Writing for Animation" at the University of Southern California. Pintoff is also writing another novel; like *Zachary*, his current book is quite autobiographical, in this case spanning the entire period from childhood to the present.

Pintoff now resides in Los Angeles with his wife, Caroline, whom he met in London 25 years ago; like her husband, Caroline is an artist (specializing in batik and printing) and a teacher (at a pre-school). Pintoff has two children from his previous marriage: a son, Jonathon, who is a professional musician in Los Angeles, and a daughter, Gabrielle, who has a family in San Francisco, where she is employed as a business professional.

Note: This article draws, in part, on an interview conducted with Ernest Pintoff on 24 July 1994 at his home in Los Angeles.

CHAPTER 8

Drawing on Both Sides of Their Brains (1996)

The Art and Careers of Derek Lamb and Kaj Pindal

by Marc Glassman

KAJ PINDAL AND DEREK Lamb have been making wonderful animated pieces for so many years that one is tempted to use words like "pioneering" and "distinguished" to describe their works and assume that they are ready to rest on their laurels. During their careers, singly or collaboratively, as creators of Peep, the Old Lady, Nesbitt Spoon and the Karate Kid, they have won awards from Ottawa to Salerno to Melbourne to, of course, Hollywood. Yet both men continue to push the envelope into such necessary and new fields as CD-ROMs and Third World Animation. Their work remains as relevant in the wired world of today as it was to animators in their cels thirty years ago.

The two have kept to the highest principles of animated art during a period when hack commercial work often seemed like the only option available to them and their colleagues. Instead, they have contributed together, or in partnership with others, to some of the finest animated moments created in the past four decades. Pindal and Lamb exemplify the best elements of the National Film Board: their films have not only been

DOI: 10.1201/9781003288022-9

of consistently high quality but they have also said relevant things about social situations that exist in the world today. Never afraid to shy away from hard topics, they have dealt with death, AIDS, substance abuse, car culture and the mistreatment of children. Yet most of their films are funny and human, not grim and didactic. As animators, producers and educators, Lamb and Pindal have always made sure that their messages were apt, interesting and fun to comprehend.

They met in the late 1950s in Montreal, then, and now, the site of the main animation studio at the National Film Board. The son of a wealthy Englishman who loved to perform as a magician on the weekends, Derek Lamb had rebelled from a future as a "manager of a Malaysian rubber plantation" to become a cartoonist. Pindal, an extremely gifted animator, had been recruited from Copenhagen to come to the Board to work on a technical film depicting the engineering of jet engines. A number of other remarkable young talents arrived at the Board during that period. Among them were Gerry Potterton, a charming and voluble Brit who went on to work with Buster Keaton, Harold Pinter and Ivan Reitman; the tragic and supremely talented Arthur Lipsett, who turned down an opportunity to work with Stanley Kubrick on *2001: a Space Odyssey* and Jeff Hale, latterly a key contributor to Sesame Street.

These young artists were trained by Norman McLaren, whose credo "animation is movement," seems to have influenced them all. Lamb (who went on to teach at Harvard and discover Caroline Leaf) and Pindal (latterly an inspirational force at Sheridan College) remember the brilliant Scotsman's use of loops and coloured gels in his informal seminars at the Board. McLaren's role as a mentor was a key element in their growth as artists – and signposts for their methodologies as teachers to the next generation of animators.

It was Potterton who persuaded Colin Low, then head of the animation studio, to allow his young artists the chance to create one-minute spots for government agencies and the CBC. Lamb and Pindal joined eagerly in these commissioned pieces, the best of which are on the compilation films *Hors d'oeuvre* and *Pot-pourri*. Earlier experiences doing commercial work in Sweden and at Denmark's Nordisk Film had prepared Pindal for this work; he has continued to make "short stuff" throughout his career. Lamb recalls that the pieces "were excellent training. You can't go far wrong in one minute and even if you do, there are ways to rescue the work." Two decades later, as executive producer for the English Animation

Department, Lamb often used the popular Canada Vignettes series to test out young colleagues. (An example of the vignettes, though hardly a test, is John Weldon's *Log Driver's Waltz*, a superb folk video.)

By the early sixties, the animation unit was ready for more challenging work. Lipsett received an Academy Award nomination for his first signed piece *Very Nice, Very Nice* (1961); Potterton directed a skillful adaptation of Stephe Leacock's *My Financial Career* (1962), and Pindal made a charming rustic short, *The Peep Show* (1962). Derek Lamb began to write two films, *I Know an Old Lady Who Swallowed a Fly* with Pindal and *The Great Toy Robbery* with Jeff Hale. Both proved to be memorable.

Pindal achieved his mature style in *Old Lady*. Against a white backdrop, a series of vignettes authored by Lamb play out. An admitted "victim of Walt Disney," Pindal creates a memorable assembly of brilliantly drawn characters to play out the darkly comic fable of greed that is the basis of the classic folk song performed by Burl Ives. There's the spider, looking like a cross between Anansi and a magician; a cat with a terrorist's gleam in its eyes; a bird that could be Peep; a dog wearing a derby hat and bearing an uncomfortable resemblance to a member of Mackie's gang in *The Three Penny Opera* and Old Lady – grey-haired, wearing a black dress, orange petticoats and red shoes dancing about, delighting in a bowl of grapes that contains a fly within it. Although Lamb does not like Ives' rendition of the song, and one can hear a chorus of Derek's livelier interpretation of the tune in *Laugh Lines* – the dynamic interplay between Pindal's characters marks this film as a true animated classic.

Lamb collaborated closely with Jeff Hale on his other 1964 short *The Great Toy Robbery*. A fast-paced pastiche of the Western genre, the film is populated by a pure, square-jawed and utterly fatuous hero who anticipates Canada's own Brian Mulroney in his looks and attitude; three villains led by a slim mustachioed type right out of 1920 penny-dreadfuls; an ineffectual sheriff and the requisite barman, a dancing girl and a piano player needed for a melodrama to take place. A delicious exercise in camp aesthetics, *Robbery* has the three wise men from the Nativity stealing Santa Claus's gifts so they can play with hula hoops, balls and horns instead of the kids that "deserve" them.

An offbeat Christmas entry, *The Great Toy Robbery* was paired commercially with Kubrick's *Dr. Strangelove* and proved to be a huge hit in the States. A year later, Lamb was invited to teach animation at Harvard's Carpenter Center for the Arts. He leapt at the chance. "When I went there in late '65, the building, which had been designed by Le Corbusier, was brand new. The faculty of arts and science really didn't know that they had a film programme, much less an animation department, so I was given years of grace to experiment with the students and discover what I should teach them," recalls Lamb. "Had I stayed at the Board, I would have become tunnel-visioned into animation. I discovered a great sense of connectedness with the world during those tumultuous times. Those were the years when the National Guard was on campus, when people were smoking dope, being radical, burning draft cards ... I had my eyes and ears opened while still making films and being around curious minds who wanted to take animation courses." During this period, Lamb discovered Caroline Leaf, Lynn Smith, Elliot Noyes and others; he also made *House Moving*, an intriguing experimental short.

Back in Montreal, at the Board, Kaj Pindal parlayed the success of the *Old Lady* into what remains his most individual work. Les Drew undoubtedly deserves credit for his animation in *What on Earth!*, but even a Martian could see the "auteur's" touch of Pindal throughout this piece. His cool, modernist style is apparent in overhead shots of the freeway with its perfectly positioned, colourful, yet nearly identical, denizens-cars. The conceit of the film is clearly in tune with the obsessively mechanistic side of Pindal. If the Martians landed here tomorrow, wouldn't they think that cars controlled the world, not humans? Observes Pindal: "No one had really questioned car culture before. A lot of people were talking about Ralph Nader (and his book *Unsafe at Any Speed*). I had always been pro-car. At the time, I drove an import, an old London cab; other friends had sports cars. But two things happened. I went to L.A. and saw the freeways which were pretty alarming and I found out that Copenhagen was considering putting a highway down the middle of the downtown area. Well, you could do whatever you want with other cities, but leave my Copenhagen alone!" *What On Earth!* did spark debates about the effects that automobiles have on the environment and, happily, Copenhagen did not build its proposed freeway.

The idealistic social environment that Lamb was participating in at Harvard affected Pindal and his cohorts at the Film Board – admittedly, in a milder way. Kaj moved from his satire on cars into a series of films depicting the hazards of cigarette smoking. A former smoker himself, Pindal plunged eagerly into the creation of a group of incisive and funny thirty-second spots and one short, *King Size*. Pindal gets to indulge his mechanical side in the best of these spots when a huge accordion respirator is made to replace the lungs of a determined smoker of the future. The media manipulations of the cigarette companies and their advertisers are fiercely satirized throughout because, as Kaj puts it, "If it (the spot) doesn't bite, it isn't doing its work properly."

Reaching an apex in his popularity at the Board, Pindal was next assigned the task of creating a vast animated lightboard piece for the International Exposition at Osaka, Japan. Using bold and simple graphics, Pindal created a piece that reflected the diversity of Canada. In it, the folkloric image of loggers in a vast Northern terrain is contrasted with scenes of workers moving through the bustling urban centres that so many Canadians inhabit today. A bravura scene of logs being moved by a typically extraordinary Pindal designed machine is a high point of this justly well-received multimedia installation. Pindal was disappointed that *The City (Osaka '70)*, the film version of his work, received poor distribution from the Board; it is presented here in its entirety.

Pindal left the Board after a triumphal visit to Osaka. He, his wife Annie, and the Pindal children moved to Copenhagen where Kaj took up a position as the head of a new animation department for Danish television. Never a natural administrator, Kaj soon grew restless with the bureaucracy in Denmark; remarkably, he found conditions for creating films to be far easier at the Film Board than in his homeland.

Returning to Montreal, Pindal was offered a contract by Rene Jodoin, an old colleague who was then the head of the French Animation Department at the NFB. A protege of McLaren, Jodoin believed in giving his unit a great deal of creative leeway in making their films. Pindal joined a group that included such outstanding talents as Bretislav Pojar, Co Hoedeman, Jacques Drouin and Pierre Hébert. Unfortunately, as Pindal wryly notes, perhaps he was "given too much freedom" by Jodoin. The films he made for the French unit, *Caninabis* and *Un cheval a toute vapeur*, lack the concise and sprightly power of his best work. An excerpt from *Un cheval* shows that his draftsman's skill had not deserted him; though the film, as a whole, lacks coherency, it does possess an erotic power, rare for Pindal.

In 1971, Derek Lamb left Harvard and became an independent animator. He began to do spots for Sesame Street under the aegis of a company, Imagination, run by ex-NFBer Jeff Hale. It was while visiting Hale in San Francisco in 1972 that Pindal and Lamb met again and decided to do work together. Both were freelancing, although Pindal did have steady work through Jodoin. Pindal created a "laughing dog" sequence for Lamb that Hale particularly liked; and so, their occasional partnership was rekindled. Over the next few years, Lamb wrote the Oscar-nominated *The Shepherd*, directed *The Psychic Parrot* and continued to produce short television pieces for PBS and the Children's Television Workshop in New York and San Francisco. Pindal freelanced in Montreal and, for a memorable period in London, England, where he worked for Richard Williams' famed animation company. Very little of either artists' work from this period is currently available; however, *The Last Cartoon Man* does indicate that Lamb's writing and producing skills were still finely tuned. What Lamb needed was a larger theatre in which to operate.

The opportunity came in late 1975. Wolf Koenig wanted to leave his position as executive producer of Studio A, the renamed English animation department where Lamb had received his start in North America. Though the novelist Thomas Wolfe has advised that "you can't go home again," Lamb, after some hesitation, did just that. He returned, hoping to revitalize the studio and ended up presiding over the finest era for animated film at the NFB.

"The Film Board has these peaks and valleys, and it was in a bit of a valley actually, a lot of a valley, when I came back," recalls Lamb. He had inherited a morale problem and "a wacky situation where half the people weren't coming in at all while others were living in the place. We had guys with their feet up, watching TV; I had to bring the exterminator in to take care of the mice." Reluctantly, he participated in the firing of a formerly gifted animator who was no longer capable of producing work. On a more positive note, Lamb brought in Diane Bergeron, a superb administrator, to act as his right-hand person. Lamb told her that he didn't "want anybody to ever come to me and say that they're over budget and didn't know about it. We found a fabulous assistant for Diane and told her to never leave the phones unattended. The Prime Minister could call during lunchtime. When you begin to put those sorts of demands in place, other things begin to take care of themselves."

One of Lamb's first productions upon his return to the Board was *The Hottest Show on Earth* (1977), a very funny combination of live-action and animation which dealt with, of all things, the subject of home insulation. Lamb co-wrote, co-produced and directed this award winner, utilizing among other top talents Kaj Pindal, Veronika Soul, Terence McCartney-Filgate and David Suzuki. A co-production with Energy, Mines and

Resources Canada, this NFB entry played on the CBC and became widely known for its hilarious opening scene which spoofs the entire genre: scientific documentaries.

The success of this hybrid rekindled interest in the animation unit. Over the next five years, Lamb was consistently able to garner funds from other federal agencies, including a large sum earmarked for national unity purposes in the period leading up to the 1980 Referendum crisis. These supplements to the normal allocation made by the Board each year to the studio allowed many more animators to keep on working during the Lamb era. By 1978, spirits had revived considerably at Studio A. That year, John Weldon and Eunice Macaualay's *Special Delivery*, which was produced by Derek Lamb, won the Academy Award. Caroline Leaf (*Interview*), Janet Perlman (*Why Me?*), Eugene Fedorenko (*Every Child*) and lshu Patel (*Afterlife*) were all working on pieces that would win accolades over the next two years. It was during this time that Kaj Pindal accepted an offer to teach at Sheridan College, a decision that diminished the "esprit de corps" at the Board, but proved to be truly advantageous for a new generation of Ontario-based animators. Lamb marked the passing of Pindal's presence in Montreal by producing a film about him, *Laugh Lines*.

Lamb emphasized the importance of narrative construction during his tenure at the Board. The many prizes won by Studio A in that period are a reflection of his insistence that animators cut back on their natural tendency to improvise, and rely instead on solid story principles. "Whenever I can," he said at the time, "I get the story onto slides. The history of animation is littered with films that didn't make it because of story problems ... if you can spend six weeks getting your story really knocked out, it's worth six months of time trying to fix it – or finding it can't be distributed." Lamb's major productions – *Why Me?*, *Every Child*, *The Great Toy Robbery*, *Karate Kid* – work so well because he is attuned to the audiences' desire to see a well visualized and conceived story on the screen.

Why Me? (1978), a black comedy about mortality, is one of the most offbeat films ever produced at the NFB. It is also tremendously compelling due to its emphasis on the main character's humanity and the outrageous, but apt, humour that runs like a current of electricity throughout the work. Nesbitt Spoon, a self-described "average man on an average day" is told by his doctor that he only has a limited time to live – five minutes. Over a period of time that is nearly twice that length (the film is actually nine minutes and twenty-two seconds), he goes through nearly every conceivable reaction known to humankind. Spoon moves from denial (it must be another Spoon), through self-pity (why me?), to anger (nearly demolishing the doctor's office), through to plea bargaining (take my car, my credit cards), resignation (vowing to go heroically "like John Wayne in *The Alamo*"), to love (of the doctor!) and acceptance (living the rest of his life "as best I can"). Lamb, who wrote the script, had read Elizabeth Kubler-Ross' *On Death and Dying*; the piece is so perceptive and psychologically accurate that it was purchased by many hospitals and crisis centres as a teaching tool. Thanks to Marshall Efren's brilliant performance as Spoon and Janet Perlman's marvellously cartoony interpretation of both him and the doctor, *Why Me?* is consistently funny, despite its potentially dire premise. As co-director and co-producer with Perlman, Lamb reached a level of profundity that few animated films have ever achieved. It is his – and their – masterpiece.

Lamb followed up that film with *Every Child* (1979). As executive producer of the Studio, he felt personally compelled to create a reply to the United Nations' offer to co-produce a film for the International Year of the Child. One of the U.N.'s major precepts for children is that they all deserve a name and a nationality. With the performance art duo of Les Mimes electriques, Lamb scripted a parable in which a baby is left on one doorstep after another as well-meaning people each come up with a reason for rejecting the child. Animator Eugene Fedorenko, hand-picked by Lamb for the film, created a pictorial design that is sufficiently comic to allow the audience a proper distance from the material. In the end, the child's carriage is rolled into a city dump where two artists, who transform into Les Mimes electriques, amuse the baby. This simple fable struck a chord worldwide: among its twelve awards were one at the Ottawa International Animation Festival and, of course, an Oscar.

That same year, Lamb produced *Laugh Lines: A Profile of Kaj Pindal*. A personal project, this film started when Lamb interviewed his old friend and colleague for twelve hours about Pindal's life, philosophy and working methods. Lamb recalls that even Kaj's wife, Annie, had "not heard in detail the story of his parents' split-up." This naturally reticent artist would not have been as candid if anyone except for Lamb and the Board had been the producers of the film. The resulting documentary is a fine portrayal of Pindal – one realizes that he is an artist who finds animation (and comedy) to be a very serious business.

By the early '80s, Lamb found that he was growing restless. Derek's efforts had been so successful that he found himself in the unenviable position of being judged against his own past hits. He and Janet Perlman decided to leave the NFB and start their own company. Their commercial house, Lamb-Perlman, produced a number of short commissioned works. The company's major series, the "Sports Cartoons," a Canadian–German co-production, was animated by, notably, Zlatko Grgic and Kaj Pindal. Many of these punchy, funny films proved to be quite popular on television stations in Europe. After a few years, however, none of the principals found these shorts to be artistically satisfying. Eventually, Lamb and Perlman closed up the shop and accepted offers to teach at Harvard's Carpenter Center for a session. Since Lamb's return to Massachusetts, both he and Janet Perlman have continued to make animated work mainly in Canada while teaching, on occasion, at Harvard.

Like Derek Lamb, Kaj Pindal found himself with a case of wanderlust in the '80s. He left Sheridan to pursue freelance animation in Europe and the United States. Thanks to a recommendation by Lamb, he animated a significant amount of *Twice in Time*, a George Lucas science-fiction feature. This stylistically interesting piece employed a talented, and extremely young, Henry Selick. Regrettably, the film suffers from a poorly constructed narrative line; one wonders what Lamb, who turned down the opportunity, would have done if he had been the director.

After the Lucas film was finished, Pindal proposed a project which the NFB accepted: to revive Peep and make a longer film about the chick and its barnyard friends. For the original *Peep Show* (1962), Pindal had used a technique harkening back to his days as a cartoonist and animator in Denmark. He had taken a spool of adding machine paper and drawn out a long, continuous strip of action which "storyboarded" what eventually became the tale of a chicken, *Chirp the Robin, Quack the Duck* and others who live on a farm. In 1962, Pindal had hoped that Peep Show's simple story and "cartoony" animation technique would work as a pilot for television, but the NFB showed no interest in creating an animated series at that time. Nearly a quarter of a century later, Pindal and Film Board producer Michael Scott discovered that *The Peep Show* continued to show excellent rental and sales results through their own distribution network. They decided to remake and elaborate on the first production. *Peep and the Big Wide World* (1988) resembles a television special intended for very young children: using a half-hour format, it relates three ten-minute tales of *Peep* and his friends. Part of the charm in these pieces is the marvellous narration by Peter Ustinov, whom Kaj recorded in Switzerland for this production. Although the film won awards in Ottawa and Chicago, the *Peep* project was again allowed to drift after its initial release.

As *Peep* was winding down, Kaj Pindal was called in by Michael Scott to meet Peter Dalgleish, who runs Street Kids International, an organization dedicated to educating and aiding homeless children throughout the world. Dalgleish wanted to enlist the Board's assistance in creating a film that would speak directly to the kids but also to adults, who might affect changes in the countries where homelessness and poverty are a way of life to so many people. Research indicated that animation, which can communicate to both kids and adults, was the preferred form for such a film. Scott suggested that Pindal, whose delightful style is so intentionally childlike, would be the ideal animator for the project. Both Kaj and Scott thought that Derek Lamb, well known for *Every Child*, would be the ideal producer of the film.

"Peter embodies what I love best about Canada," comments Lamb. "He has a great sense of the world. When I first met him, I saw Peter as a logical extension of what we had been doing at the Board. He wanted to give the public serious information in an entertaining way." Lamb pauses to recollect what happened after he and Pindal agreed to take on the project. "Peter had Kaj and I on a plane to Guatemala and Mexico in two minutes flat. It was amazing to be plugged into a world we had never seen before. We were, suddenly, with kids in Mexico City, riding up and down on subways, watching them survive. Kaj and I saw kids being rounded up, locked up for the weekends, dealing with the cops. There were thousands of kids in Mexico living in a kind of Dickensian world, sleeping under highways or in cardboard boxes. But they had great humour about who they were. Kaj and I took hundreds of pictures. Kaj would sit and draw Mickey Mouse for them and then do their portrait." The two came back ready to make the best film possible for Dalgleish and Street Kids International.

Karate Kids (1990) and *Goldtooth* (1994) represent a high point in the ongoing collaboration that Kaj Pindal and Derek Lamb have engaged in, off and on, throughout their working careers. The films deal with serious issues – the first with AIDS, the second with substance abuse. For Kaj, who has often dealt with the deadly effects of smoking, and Derek, whose "every child" had ended up at a city dump, these films are a culmination of the themes that have haunted their work. Kaj has used a simple design style to illustrate Derek's solidly constructed narratives in both films. Each has featured the Karate Kid, a strong but fallible street youth who experiences too many of life's hard lessons. Karate loses friends and relatives to the horrors of street life, but it is made clear that he and others survive and grow despite the adverse conditions in which they are forced to live. Both pieces are about a half hour in length and have been widely publicized and broadcast.

In the past year, Pindal and Lamb have been working on a project with Jeff Schon, an old friend and colleague, who now produces CD-ROMs for Random House's Living Books programme. Fittingly enough, it is a new adaptation of *Peep*. With Lamb as the producer and Pindal as the animator, the new *Peep* may well find an audience on the Internet and as a CD-ROM. For this duo, who continue to teach as well as animate and produce, *Peep* is yet one more chapter in careers that have taken them from Montreal, via animation, to places throughout the world.

Always philosophical, Lamb admits "I wouldn't even want to suggest that my life has gone the way I wanted it. Over and over again, out of the blue, a phone call has changed the course of my life, and the people around me, in profound ways. In retrospect, I could have planned things more coherently." Pindal, too, has been surprised by a life that could have easily led him, through his good friend Ward Kimball, into a career with Disney. Yet, as Lamb points out: "I'm enjoying life now and so, I think, is Kaj." He pauses. "How much more can you plan? The first option often isn't an option at all."

CHAPTER 9

A Taste of Tashlin (1998)

by Mark Langer

D IRECTOR JEAN-LUC GODARD HAILED him as the vanguard of a genuinely modern comedy style in the cinema. Critic Andrew Sarris con-
demned his work as "unabashed vulgarity," stating that "the problem of
Tashlin will remain a problem of taste."[1] Few figures in American cinema
have inspired such contrary evaluations as Frank Tashlin. In recent years,
appreciation of Tashlin as a pioneer post-modernist and seminal figure in
American cinema has increased. Although best known for his live-action
1950s comedies, Frank Tashlin had a long career in animation before he
went on to write or direct films featuring Bob Hope, Jayne Mansfield and
Jerry Lewis.

Born Frank von Taschlein in Weehawken, New Jersey on February 9,
1913, Tashlin's entry into the workforce was anything but promising, with
employment as a newspaper hawker and brassiere factory labourer. His
first job in the animation industry came in 1928 as an errand boy at the
Fleischer studio. Gradually, Tashlin worked his way up at a variety of New
York studios, including Paul Terry and Van Beuren, to become a story
man and animator, contributing cartoons to newspapers and magazines
on the side.

In 1933, events in Burbank, California would change the path of Tashlin's
career. When animators Hugh Harman and Rudy Ising left producer Leon
Schlesinger, they took most of Schlesinger's production staff, with the
notable exceptions of Friz Freleng and Bob Clampett. Schlesinger's studio provided animated films for release through Warner Bros. An urgent

DOI: 10.1201/9781003288022-10

recruitment drive filled the studio with new talent, including Tashlin, who worked as an animator and gag man on the *Looney Tunes* and *Merrie Melodies* series. Independently, under the name "Tish-Tash," Tashlin began a syndicated comic strip called *Van Boring*, in a parody of his former employer Amedee Van Beuren. Schlesinger insisted that he be given a percentage of the animator's income from the strip, claiming that Tashlin couldn't prove that he wasn't thinking up ideas for the strip on company time. In disgust, Tashlin quit.[2]

After a period of uncredited work at Ub lwerks' Celebrity Productions (whose film *Room Runners* [1933] anticipates work that Tashlin did later at Warner Bros. in *Porky Pig's Feat* [1943]), Tashlin moved to the Hal Roach Studio, where he worked as a gag man and screenwriter on the *Our Gang* series, as well as for Charlie Chase, Thelma Todd and Laurel and Hardy films. When director Jack King left Schlesinger to return to Disney, Tashlin was rehired, this time as the head of his own unit. His directorial debut with *Porky's Poultry Plant* (1936) was also the first film that former Disney composer Carl Stalling scored for Warner Bros. release.

Just prior to his return to Schlesinger, Tashlin discovered the writings of Soviet director and theorist V.I. Pudovkin. Based on Pudovkin's theories of optical retention and composition, Tashlin began to experiment with the use of montage and extreme camera angles. Films like *Porky of the North Woods* (1936) and *Porky's Romance* (1937) utilized montage sequences where shots were as brief as six frames or one-quarter of a second. In one scene of *Porky's Romance*, six and a half seconds contain ten different shots. Such use of editing was revolutionary in American animation of the period.[3] This also led Tashlin to remarkable experiments in cutting sound, such as the contrast of intercut musical leitmotifs linked to the pursuer and the pursued in */ Got Plenty of Mutton* (1944), where the music is keyed to the ardour of the pursuer and the increasing exhaustion of the prey.[4] Tashlin's use of extreme angles, quick cutting, his contrasts between kinetic action and stasis, and his fondness for emphasized key poses produced a unique sense of timing that makes the most hilarious moments in his movies (such as the "Well what do you know? The little light – it stays on!" gag in *Plane Daffy* (1944) almost impossible to convey to someone who has not experienced the films.

Along with his colleague Tex Avery, Tashlin was fond of foregrounding the very process of filmmaking itself, either through self-conscious allusions to boss Leon Schlesinger or by means of characters directly addressing the audience. In this respect, Tashlin's work in animation preceded the self-reflexive quality of his live-action films, such as *The Girl Can't Help It* (1956) where Tom Ewell introduced sound and colour, or *Will Success Spoil Rock Hunter?* (1957) where Tony Randall interrupts the film to remind the audience what they are missing by not being at home watching television or listening to the radio. Throughout many of Tashlin's animated films, there is a heightened sense of the obviousness of genre conventions, such as the over-conventionalized rush to the rescue in *Porky of the North Woods*, or the spoof of the stiff-upper-lip self-sacrifice depicted in such films as *Dawn Patrol* (1938) and *Plane Daffy*. As Will Friedwald notes, "Tashlin anticipates both Spielberg and Mel Brooks, using a given vocabulary of genre elements, and outdoes both of them in making you feel along with the characters, then pulling out the rug, reminding you that this is a movie."[5]

In 1938, following another disagreement, Tashlin left Schlesinger for the Walt Disney Studio, where he worked as a story director.[6] Tashlin contributed to the Mickey and the Beanstalk featurette that was later incorporated, in truncated form, as the Happy Valley segment of *Fun and Fancy Free* (1947), the "Peter and the Wolf" section of *Make Mine Music* (1946), and early development work on *Lady and the Tramp* (1956). His contributions to work at Disney were uncredited. Tashlin would later poke fun at Disney films through work like his scripted send-up of *Fantasia* (1940) for Clampett's *Corny Concerto* (1944). Nevertheless, Tashlin admired Disney and was quick to point out the debt that Warner Bros. cartoons owed to Disney's ideas and innovations. Tashlin's movement to Disney was inspired not by admiration, but by political action. As the director later told Mike Barrier, "One of the reasons I wanted to go to Disney's was to help the cause of the [Screen Cartoonists Guild] union ... I was vice-president, and we used to meet in cellars ... and it was tough going; everyone was afraid to join. That was the reason I went to Disney's; we couldn't crack them. I was able to make some inroads over there, and finally, we went on strike, and they had to join the union."[7]

Tashlin left Disney over the credit issue before the strike of 1941, establishing himself as a gag writer at the Screen Gems cartoon unit at Columbia. Within months, Tashlin became production supervisor, hiring striking Disney staffers, such as Bob Wickersham, Dave Hilberman, Zack Schwartz and John Hubley right off the picket line. What followed was a series of innovative films, beginning with Tashlin's *The Fox and the Grapes*

(1941) which set the model for the blackout gag structure later used in Chuck Jones' Roadrunner and Coyote cartoons. Although Tashlin infrequently received director credit on the Screen Gems cartoons, his leadership set the tone for the entire studio. Recalled John Hubley, "Under Tashlin we tried some very experimental things, none of them quite got off the ground, but there was a lot of ground broken. We were doing crazy things that were anti the classic Disney approach."[8] Tashlin's departure from Columbia brought the period of experimentation to a close, but the group of talents that he assembled went on to form the core of United Productions of America, where the continuation of the Tashlin-inspired experiments revolutionized American animation.

Returning to Warner Bros., Tashlin contributed to the Private Snafu series of films for the "Army–Navy Screen Magazine," with films like *The Home Front* (1943) that took advantage of laxer censorship standards for those serving overseas. Although Tashlin's earlier work often dealt with sex-obsessed protagonists, his work began to more aggressively push the boundaries of what was expressible in terms of risque humour in films made for domestic audiences as well, such as the gag about bisexuality in *Stupid Cupid* (1945) or the later breast fetish jokes in the features *The Girl Can't Help It* and *Will Success Spoil Rock Hunter?*

Tashlin's films featured most of the Warner Bros. characters, but he tended toward those featuring Porky Pig and Daffy Duck. Unlike Bugs Bunny, these are characters that lack control over their environment. Unlike the simple-minded Elmer Fudd, they are capable of articulating complex reactions to that environment. Under Tashlin's direction, Porky and Daffy became critical portrayals of the American male. Tashlin's Porky is a model of spineless civility – passive, speaking with inarticulate stuttering, and fundamentally emasculated. The director's Daffy was the yin to Porky's yang. An aggressive vulgarian, Daffy was the loud-mouthed avatar of patriotic platitude and bonhomie. Utterly oblivious of his lack of social graces, Tashlin's Daffy soldiers on in films like *Nasty Quacks* (1944) and *Plane Daffy*, confident of his charms that drive others to the point of murder. The obnoxious boosterism of Tashlin's Daffy makes him a caricature of the go-get-it ethos of middle-class striving. Compared to the work of his peers at Warner Bros., Tashlin's approach to his characters eschews the psychological identification of Chuck Jones or the rubberized artificial antics of Bob Clampett. Instead, Tashlin uses his characters as vehicles through which the absurdities of contemporary culture are examined.

In 1944, Schlesinger sold his studio to Warner Bros. New management headed by Edward Selzer was considered uncongenial by many of the employees. For example, Chuck Jones recalls a time when Selzer walked into a story session where participants were laughing over a newly-devised gag. "What the hell has all this laughter got to do with the making of animated cartoons?" asked Selzer.[9] Many key personnel left the studio – Tashlin in 1945, followed by Clampett the next year. Tashlin made two puppet animated films for release through United Artists and then returned to writing and gag work on live-action films, such as *A Night in Casablanca* (1945) and *Love Happy* (1948) with the Marx Brothers, *The Fuller Brush Man* (1947) with Red Skelton, and *Miss Grant Takes Richmond* (1949) and *The Fuller Brush Girl* (1950) with Lucille Ball. Screenwriting on the Bob Hope features *Monsieur Beaucaire* (1945), *The Paleface* (1947) and *The Lemon Drop Kid* (1950) created an alliance with the actor that led to Tashlin becoming a director and set on a career path in feature films that would last until his death of a heart attack on May 5, 1972.

Although often marginalized as a mere precursor to his later features, Tashlin's work in animation not only anticipates his live-action style but was a significant contribution to animation itself. Tashlin was at the forefront of those introducing quick cutting, extreme angles and a faster sense of timing to animation. His use of ironic juxtaposition, deliberately artificial characters, socially critical attitudes, and general alienation from contemporary American mores influenced artists in animation and live-action cinema. While Tashlin is one of a number of animators who also have directed live-action (including Gregory La Cava, Tim Burton, Jan Svankmajer and Terry Gilliam) he has no peers in his prominence in both media.

NOTES

1. Andrew Sarris, The American Cinema: Directors and Directions, 1929–1968. (N.Y.: Dutton, 1968), pp. 140–141.
2. Shamus Culhane, Talking Animals and Other People. (N.Y.: St. Martin's Press, 1986), p. 245.
3. Leonard Maltin, Of Mice and Magic. (N.Y.: Plume, 1980), pp. 229–230; Culhane, p. 139.
4. I am indebted to Greg Ford for this insight (Tous mes remerciements a Greg Ford pour cet eclaircissement).
5. Jerry Beck and/et Will Friedwald, Looney Tunes and Merrie Melodies. (N.Y.: Henry Holt, 1989), p. 55.

6. Tashlin was replaced as director and unit head by Chuck Jones at the suggestion of Schlesinger executive Henry Binder (Chuck Jones remplai; a Tashlin en tant que directeur et chef d'unite sur la recommandation de Henry Binder, membre de la direction du studio de Schlesinger).

7. Mike Barrier, "Interview," in Claire Johnston and Paul Willemen (eds.) Frank Tashlin. (Edinburgh: Edinburgh Film Festival, 1973), pp. 48–50. I Mike Barrier, "Interview," tire de'article sur Frank Tashlin publie dans le programme du Festival du film d'Edimbourg 1973, edite par Claire Johnston et Paul Willemen (Edimbourg, Edinburgh Film Festival, 1973), pp. 48–50.

8. Maltin, p. 214.

9. Ibid, p. 252.

CHAPTER 10

The Animation of MTV (1999)

by Kelly Neall

I N THE CONSTANT BATTLE to win the hearts and pocketbooks of the world's youth, MTV has effectively used artistically innovative animation as a persuasive tool. In doing so, the station has helped produce a wealth of quality work that has not only stimulated its viewers, but to some extent stimulated the entire animation industry. MTV's creative programmers have sponsored works of diverse styles and approaches to effectively present the viewer with lifestyle choices, world issues, and of course one of the most dynamic logos of all time. Animation on MTV has helped give the station its trademark style of exuberant incongruity that continually pleases the most jaded, attention-deficient audience. Most importantly though, it is used to sell the station itself, to reflect emerging cultural trends and present them in an accessible and fresh way.

Fred Seibert first began commissioning the famous ten-second ids right from MTV's beginning in 1981. Seibert has said that one of the reasons they had wanted to use animation was that visually, it seemed the closest thing to rock and roll: "We had grown up during the days of LP design and we wanted to make pieces that made the same impact on the video generation as album covers had been on ours. We wanted to create essentially the notion of the moving album cover."[1] The fast-paced syntax of MTV also developed from The Children's Television Workshop where

DOI: 10.1201/9781003288022-11

commercial-like animation shorts were interspersed throughout *Sesame Street*.

MTV's expansion into Europe added even more diversity to the animation, although Peter Dougherty, Creative Director of MTV Europe stresses that although some of the work may vary culture to culture, the vibe remains the same. MTV Europe, sometimes in conjunction with the U.S., put together a series of animated shorts that highlighted world issues and problems. The films were produced through competitions where animators were invited to submit storyboards to be judged by a panel. These animations on topics such as the environment, racism and unfair labour practices were often quite radical in approach and method.

In 1986, Abby Terkuhle came over to MTV (USA) from *Saturday Night Live* where he was the film segment producer. In addition to ids, Terkuhle began commissioning animation shorts. Henry Selick (*The Nightmare Before Christmas*) who had created ids and top of the hours for the station, produced *Slow Bob in the Lower Dimensions* in 1990. While some of these shorts would be programmed as interstitials, *Liquid Television* (1991), produced by Colossal Pictures opened up a new televised venue for independent animators. With this half-hour show began the propagation of animation into MTV programming time. Both *Aeon Flux* (Peter Chung, 1995) and *Beavis and Butthead* (Mike Judge, 1993) were expanded from *Liquid Television* shorts to half-hour shows. During this breakthrough period, MTV opened up an in-house studio, which would become one of the largest animation facilities in New York.

Other shows which have appeared on the MTV airwaves have been met with varying levels of popularity: *The Head* (1994 & 1997), *The Brothers Grunt* (1994), *The Maxx* (1995), *Daria* (1998), and most recently *Celebrity Deathmatch* (1999) and *MTV Downtown* (1999).

Animation has been an effective tool in MTV's constant quest to retain its hipness because it can present cutting edge design and ideas without seeming elitist. Because the MTV insignia must represent that which is ultramodern, the radically abstract, painterly, or just plain weird, ids are valuable cultural cache. Teenagers want what's new, but they also want something accessible – MTV's animation is the perfect solution.

The longform animation showcased in this programme demonstrates MTV's tap into emerging cultural trends and how it successfully translates them back for youth. While earlier shows, such as *Aeon Flux* and *The Head*, exhibit the influence of alternative comics, *Daria, Celebrity*

Deathmatch and *MTV Downtown* use animation in a less obvious way, interpreting current "reality" based entertainment.

While *Beavis and Butthead* presents a one-dimensional critique of juvenile inertia, spin-off show *Daria* presents a world that has real stories about teenage geek-dom. *Daria* creators Glen Eichler and Susie Lewis [Lynn] created an empathetic, intelligent female character that provides a running social commentary on her life in Lawndale.

Like *King of the Hill*, *Daria* can reach a greater level of realism because it is animated. The truth is easier to take when it comes out of the mouth of a cartoon. Chris Marcil, a *Daria* writer noted that: *"My So-Called Life* tackled some similar themes as *Daria* – you know, the girl who's not the most popular and isn't considered the greatest beauty – and it didn't last, ... I suspect it may have had something to do with the fact that it's hard for people to take something that's as real as that. The success of *90210* is that it is fantasy and everybody really is gorgeous and it's very easy to look at. With animation, it at least makes reality more palatable."[2]

MTV animation director Chris Prynoski wanted a vérité level of realism for his show *MTV Downtown*, recording kids on the streets of New York to help create naturalistic sounding dialogue. The animation, influenced by Ralph Bakshi and John Hubley, lends a funky, modern and very urban look to the series. MTV Downtown creates a different type of realism to Daria, it's not a world the (average) viewer knows, but it's a lifestyle they take voyeuristic pleasure in watching.

Celebrity Deathmatch again plays on the notion of "real" entertainment. Where can all this reality based programming lead the audience? Is *World's Best Car Crashes* far removed from the Roman Forum? *Deathmatch* plays out the viewer's fantasy of this ultimate "reality" based thrill.

Although wholly and happily commercial, MTV's use of animation is not without redemption for high-minded critics. Candy Kugel noted that "What [MTV] should be lauded for is that it has increased the visual sensibilities, the visual palettes of an entire generation. It's expanded how people see."[3] Henry Selick praises the creative freedom that he was given while doing work for MTV: "I got to continue where I had left off after doing experimental films at CalArts. It was good for me. Every single piece I did for them I varied the style and technique so that I got to explore things that I'd wanted to do."[4]

There is also no denying that MTV's social issue series was thought-provoking and inspired. Instead of being the usual public service announcement, many of these challenging pieces resist closure and leave the viewer asking questions. The animation, varying in style from piece to piece is dramatically different from anything else on tv. MTV's use of animation is effective on both an artistic and commercial level. It has provided a forum for ground-breaking animation while also providing a means to filter through the newest cultural ideas to its audience.

NOTES

1. Chris Robinson, "CTW and MTV: Shorts of Influence" *Animation World Magazine* (September 1997, Vol 2, No 6) p. 18.
2. Alex Kuczynski, "Daria Morgendorffer Speaks to MTV's Audience in Full Sentences" *New York Times* (May 11, 1998).
3. Robinson p.15.
4. Robinson p.18.

OTHER SOURCES

Harvey Deneroff, "MTV Animation: Putting Toons to Music" *Animation Magazine* (July 1999, Vol. 13, Issue 7, No. 80).

Mo Willems, "A Conversation with Arlene Sherman and Abby Terkuhle" *Animation World Magazine* (September 1997, Vol. 2, No. 6).

"MTV Downtown: A New York State-of-Mind" *Animation Magazine* (July 1999, Vol. 13, Issue 7, No. 80).

CHAPTER 11

Phil Mulloy

An Appreciation (2001)

by Richard Meltzer

W ELL, FOR STARTERS, I kinda think Phil Mulloy is the most enter taining – "interesting" – "engaging" – not to mention the most viscerally enjoyable animator since, oh, Tex Avery...okay?

His works are primitive in the very best sense of the term, and I'm not talking "neo"-primitive: I mean every bit as primitive as the Three Stooges. Simple? basic?...like a stick-figure version of Sam Beckett.

Phil is also a bloke who trucks in TRUE VULGARITY, and I'm not talking its Puritan mirror image (the films of Peter Greenaway, say). True vulgarity, like that of the Trashmen ("Surfin' Bird"), Sam the Sham ("Wooly Bully") or Bobby Bittman (remember him?), is not easy to come by, no no NO! – and ditto for its tag-team partner, the truly infantile. If you think Beavis and Butthead, those card-carrying infantilists, qualify as the real deal, I say PHOO: they're just a pair of flawed, dipshit hipsters – hipsters maudits, if you will. Phil Mulloy's real real deal leaves no room for hipsters, thank you.

When it comes to shitpissdoodooweewee – not to mention pustules, scuzz and scum – P.M. is a beacon in the night. The Ubu Gang? They're a pack of art school aesthetes – yuppie performance artists – Dada opportunists – by comparison. Pikers!

DOI: 10.1201/9781003288022-12

And then there's the consummate RHYTHM of his work – the timing and sequence of his anything proceeding to his anything else. A lot of the action feels improvised, or maybe that's the wrong word, uh, wrong concept – certainly not improvised in a real-time jazz sense. (Animation ain't instantaneous creation.) Ongoingly AD HOC – is that a bad thing? The simulation of real time, and the go-go-go of hot synthetic time. Some things feel inevitable yet gratuitous; others are total surprises that seem totally reasonable and totally, well, silly.

Man with a vacuum cleaner: have him use it to suck himself off. Drunk in the street with a bottle: make sure that after he's drunk it, it breaks... shatters. An old married couple who don't quite get along: have it turn out they're both gay. Waiters with trays on a staircase: have them wobble like, well, dumb cartoons. Use every opportunity to suggest the fragility of everything in this here life – and/or its cheesiness – and do so without it ever feeling preorchestrated.

When in doubt, have people in the next frame fuck. Gratuitously. (I mean isn't that what the meat-dance is? Isn't that its "context"?) Either that, or as a means of "explanation" – like how come the line for the men's crapper at the banquet in Sound of Music is so freaking long? Well, 'cause two guys are down on their knees (I forget now: are they employees of the banquet hall, blue-collar jackjoes?), committing an unnatural butt-act (hey: let those rich sumbitches WAIT!).

Or here's an idea: chop or shoot somebody's head off, or at the very least draw some blood – how ELSE to introduce red the COLOR? Or have humans, dogs or aliens piss, shit or puke.

GREAT MOMENTS IN FILMMAKING PER SE – When you've got actors, eh, maybe it ain't so e-z, so automatic, to get them to upchuck their lunch on the dotted line. "What's my motivation?" they'll probably ask – it's their training – and you'll then hafta bullshit 'em: "Sickness...uh.. .revulsion...perhaps you've swallowed a tainted rat or y'know, maybe..." Whereas with animation, see...ha ha ha HA.

Then he goes and toys with such material, "sends it up" – well, the fuck stuff anyway. Line drawings of persons poking each other can possibly (in time) get tiresome, so in Sex Life of a Chair the theme is CHAIRS fucking. Where the sendup, the fun, kicks in is the absurd lengths he goes to in sexually anthropomorphizing chairs, dig it, WITHOUT making any ref to them as seats for people's butts ('cept the potty seat for "coprophilia"). Extremely up to date – nothing if not contemporific! – he utilizes a CELL PHONE in the phone-kink segment.

Nor is he a slouch on the non-smut front: the wide world of non-ano-genital, non-scatological ideation & meaning. What the McKenzies might call "topic." (Did someone say "politics"?) Check out Advert Against God, Advert Against Science, Winds of Change, The Chain, Intolerance and answer me this: who on the fat bloody planet makes hotter anti-war, anti-state, anti-church, anti-crummy-ideas, screw-the-rich, pro-"diversity" films – hitting the nail on so many goddam heads – than Phil Mulloy? Who could ask for more from a single filmmaker?

Clearly he wouldn't do it for money, but if you pointed a gun at his head – and showed him f'r sure it was loaded – I could see him having no trouble NOHOW depicting former Governor G.W. Bush of Texas, execu-tioner of 130 or 140 or 150 (whatever the number ended up) mostly black death-row inmates, as a cold-blooded BUTCHER...but w/out the gun, no. He really ain't too big on PROPER-NOUN topicality – 's his preference, what're you gonna do?

Which is maybe just as well, eh, 'cause names've been known to trip him up. I know of ONE slip, and I don't mean to quibble, but in the advert for Sing Along With All Your Favorites ("Karlheinz Stockhausen...John Cage...Karl Maria von Weber") there is one name that flat-out don't belong. K.M. von Weber is a dandy dude to namedrop if you're talking melodi-ous overtures of the 19th century, but if it's 20th century CACOPHONY you're after, Anton Webern is your man. Webern is who he means, or who he'd better mean, or else he's just pullin' our fucking LEG, in which case, well, fuck HIM. "Recorded live in Nashville" – all right!

Last but by no means least, it might be edifying to compare our man Mulloy to the late great Edward D. Wood – Edward D. WOOD??? That's right. One of the great, great, GREAT directors of the previous century, an architect of sheer delight – far greater and delightfuler than (for inst) Cocteau. Or Douglas Sirk. Or Frank Borzage. Or Kenneth Anger. Mulloy's treatment of the planet Zog and its inhabitants (The Ten Commandments/ Number 3, Intolerance) is just REDOLENT of the space shtick you'll find in Wood's Plan 9 from Outer Space – if you don't believe me, go rent it. Take your time, it's a good'un, or fast-forward to the fabulous SOLARONITE scene...hoo wee!

"One of the strangest episodes in the history of the world was about to unfold" – okay, tell me, whose line is that: Phil's or Ed's? (Great men think alike.)

Hey, folks – I hate to sound like a rooter, but Phil Mulloy is my favorite living filmmaker.

CHAPTER 12

Rex, Epicurus and Me

The Search for Pleasure (2001)

by Chris Robinson

"Every being strives after pleasure, and it is in pleasure that happiness consists."

"Oh that was only our Vince. He shoots himself occasionally."

REX THE RUNT

What I love about *Rex the Runt* is not the absurdity or surrealist tendencies – *The Simpsons* occasionally provide a flicker of that as does my life in general – but instead the very mundane shrug of its protagonists. I mean these dogs (Rex, Wendy, Bob and Vince) live a life completely devoid of pleasure. They are barely satisfied with their basic passions: "Telly" and food. Now of course there's a little more to the show. Between channel surfing they've: used a shrink ray to travel inside Vince's brain; travelled back in time; drilled a hole in the centre of the earth and subsequently used the now deflated planet as a spaceship; formed a band (with the exception of Wendy, they have NO musical talent) so that they could enter a talent contest (they lost) and pay a 10 quid bill; and Wendy momentarily became a TV star after she was acquitted of shooting Vince (she did shoot him but he's plasticine). You'd think these adventures would provide a level of excitement and pleasure, but they don't. Their reaction remains the same whether they are entering a black hole or taking a piss. Not only are

DOI: 10.1201/9781003288022-13

they uninterested (even their voices are monotone and occasionally barely audible) but they also seem incapable of finding any sort of pleasure in life. It's this absence of pleasure that makes the series both funny (ala Buster Keaton) and disturbing (as a reflection of our own increasingly mundane lives).

If we believe Epicurus, pleasure is the key to a relatively pain free existence. Easier said than done of course, because most of us haven't got a clue what defines pleasure. For many of us one of the biggest obstacles in life is the ability to string together more than a few moments of pleasure. Generally those moments are self-gratifying individual or 'moving' pleasures. Moving pleasure is something you are enjoying while in the process but which leaves you unfulfilled. According to Epicurus, the more satisfying type of pleasure is 'static'. With static pleasure, you are left with no needs or wants, just pleasure. For example, compare 'playing' a hockey video game to actually playing hockey (street or ice). There is no comparison. The 'real' activity will pleasure you on both a physical and intellectual level. Generally, you will feel exhausted and fulfilled. A video game will not achieve the same level of pleasure. It will leave you a need.

In this way, *Rex the Runt* is a less a mirror of our current society than a foreshadowing of our eventual digression. The quartet have become so dulled that they are unable to differentiate between television and the real world. As such, when given the opportunity, their ability to experience lasting, meaningful pleasure has eroded. In *Too Many Dogs*, they travel back in time NOT to explore history and the foundation of the world, or even acquire any sort of knowledge, but simply to figure out who ran off with half their house. In *Adventures in Telly: Part 3*, they find themselves travelling in space. Rather than express any wonder or seek any knowledge about the universe they play ping-pong, complain of boredom, stop at a space service station, and basically just can't wait to go home.

It never used to be like that. As kids, we were genuinely enthralled by seemingly mundane stuff like gift-wrapping paper or even a manhole on the street. Everything was so new and the possibilities were boundless. Vince seems to possess all the wonder of a child. He has relatively simple needs and seems to enjoy shooting himself, having people travel in his brain, being shot, eating spaghetti, drinking, and saying, "Tuesday." However, Vince cannot discern between pleasure and pain; punched or caressed, it's all the same to Vince. He is, at least on a sensory level:

dead. Paradoxically, within the context of Epicurus' thinking, Vince has overcome one of the biggest obstacles of pleasure: the fear of death.

BEING VS BECOMING

Life today has become determined by wants and needs rather than an authentic and long-term feeling (physical and mental) of pleasure. Over time, our want of a simpler life has potentially gone too far and overtaken our ability to experience. We embrace THINGS rather than MOMENTS. Think about all the things that are fundamentally just selfish wants and how we've re-written them as needs. Let's take the phone for example (because Bell Canada interrupted my writing). There was a time when of course we didn't need phones (let alone faxes or internet). I love hearing people say, "I don't know how we got along without it." Well…you did, and you did it just fine. I digress. Now, it's not just enough to have a phone or, hell, even an answering machine. Let's get voicemail, dial display, extra phones in the house so you don't have to run ALL THE WAY upstairs. It's really insane and you know I sit here and listen to this poor woman on the other end try and convince me that I need these THINGS. Yes … I'm sure it would make my life a little easier if I had dial display because I wouldn't have wasted my moment of genuine fuggin' pleasure answering her damn call. (Bear with me, it's relevant) We've allowed virtually every aspect of our life to become easier and yet we're all still miserable (hence the increase in anti-depressants and alcohol, spousal and child abuse). When will we stop 'this crazy thing,' sit back and say, "ya know, these THINGS are not making me happy." We are, as Abe Spalding, the protagonist of the very excellent Canadian book, *Fruits of The Earth*, living FOR the moment rather than IN the moment. As Heraclitus said in another time, we never ARE because we are always in a state of BECOMING. This can be a positive thing, as Heraclitus likely meant it to be because it suggests something evolving. But today, basically it means we're all so god damn busy seeking THINGS rather than savouring MOMENTS.

And what happens when we get those THINGS? In *The Trials of Wendy*, Wendy becomes a famous and wealthy TV star (after being acquitted for shooting Vince), but she's utterly miserable (as are Bob, Rex and Vince) and when asked, returns to her former life without any hesitation.

Without realizing it, Wendy has stumbled upon perhaps the most important element of pleasure of the Epicurean notion of pleasure: friendship. Friendship, for Epicurus, is a great way of attaining pleasure. Friends provide security and comfort. Without them, life is lonely and full of uncertainties. Sure Rex and co. insult, shoot and hit each other, but they are always able to transcend their momentary differences for the sake of their friendship. Most importantly, they possess trust and treat each other as they would treat themselves (yes, Wendy shoots Vince, but Vince shoots himself regularly). Friendship keeps them from loneliness. Sure, they're miserable, but at least they don't suffer alone, and for some, it's better to go through hell with someone else than to go through it alone.

CHAPTER 13

Narrow Roads

The Wor (ks) (lds) (ds) of Taku Furukawa

By Tina Paas

LITTLE BOYS, OR NOTHING IS WHAT IT SEEMS

Taku Furukawa was born on the cusp of World War II, in the fall of 1941 in lga Ueno, a small town in the Western Mie, on the island of Japan. Within the narrow grids of streets were the remnants of the Ninja Yashiki (Ninja trick houses), rooms filled with secret passages, hidden doors, dark corners, mystery. Next door was the home of Matsuo Bashou, poet and travel writer of the late 17th c., whose journal, *Okuno hoso michi* (The Narrow Road to Oku) is considered one of the great masterpieces of haiku. At the time of his birth, the small, independently focused animation community (mainly producing folk tales) was amalgamating to create a slew of propaganda cartoons, projecting worrisome clear-cut ideas of good and bad, man and monster, black and white. Insulated within the tall castle walls of lga Ueno (the tallest in all of Japan), Furukawa gathered his own set of heroes (and villains), as he sat pouring over the images of the *manga no kami*, Osamu Tezuka, and imitating the sword-wielding Samurai in *Chanbara*.

DOI: 10.1201/9781003288022-14

The end of the war and, more specifically, the subsequent American occupation of Japan, brought about change that even the tallest walls could not keep out. As a 'spoonful of sugar' is said to help cure what ails you, a country recovering from the devastating effects of war was now given a taste of The Great American Cartoon. On a large scale, the allure of the well-established western animation studios, running with machine-like precision and proficiency, was too great for the struggling independent collectives or individuals. Toei Animation Studios, which opened its doors in the mid-50s, is the best example of these early attempts; the cogs and wheels of its big movie-making machines pumping out a feature per year. On a much more microscopic level, the American films made their way through the narrow streets of lga Ueno, landing in the lap of a certain little boy. Furukawa can pinpoint the very day, the "Memorial Day" in which his career path was decided: "My father was a teacher and one day, when I was eight years old, he brought back some press materials of Disney's *Snow White*. That was really the memorial day for me to wish to be an animator." A rather unexpected choice for a little boy weaned on the subtlest of poetry, but it in the end it came down to this: "I was enthusiastic about the character design of the 7 Dwarves." While his brother was more of a Tyo Story Head Spoon draftsman, copying the characters from the American magazines and newspapers, Furukawa's interests lay in the 'Illusion of Life', as they say, and he set to work putting the images in motion. Flipbooks. "Ombro cinema."

EXODUS

The formation of the post-war western-style studios did not necessarily lead to the destruction of the pre-war independent tradition in Japan. While it was slow going initially, the late '50s saw the creation of a new wave of independent Japanese animation. The post-war independents are a unique group; their histories entwined. Interestingly, their careers demonstrate the possibilities of a symbiotic relationship between commercial and independent worlds. This is all exemplified in the following pared down "family tree," presented to me by Furukawa:

Ryuichi Yokoyama: Pioneer of post-war independent animation. Made independent at a time when efforts were focused on assembling western-style studios.

Osamu Tezuka: The aforementioned *manga no kami*, influenced by the "DIV" attitude of Yokoyama; opened his own studio Mushi Productions after a stint at Toei; introduces Japan to the animated TV series with his *Tetsuwan Atom* (Astra Boy) series – inspiring Toei and numerous other studios to open their own branch for TV production; and after great commercial success, leaves commercial animation altogether in the '80s to focus on independent filmmaking.

Yoji Kuri: A disciple of Ryuichi Yokoyama; one of the first internationally recognized of Japan's independent animators, creating his own abstract, enigmatic films; opens Kuri Jikken Manga Koba in 1960 – a production company devoted to creating more independent-minded short films.

Taku Furukawa: After majoring in Spanish at University, studying illustration & design and working briefly at TCJ (Television Corporation of Japan, spawn of Mushi), Furukawa joins Yoji Kuri at his studio in 1964.

Rin Tarou: Starts at Mushi Productions at the same time.

Hayao Miyazaki: Starts at Toei at the same time.

They are all the same age.

Under the guidance of Kuri, Furukawa completed his first film, *Zuraw* for the 1st Tokyo Animation Festival in 1964. Furukawa credits Yoji Kuri with not only helping to expand on his earlier training at TCJ but also with showing him a path by which to live as an independent. Together they collaborated on various projects, sometimes even adopting the same soundtrack; as in Kuri's *The Room* (1967) and Furukawa's *Oxed Man* (1968) – an odd jerky pastiche of city sounds, clicks and pops, monkey screeches, and what appears to be a vigorous racquetball match. While *The Room* is more of a light-hearted, sometimes raunchy exploration of form, *Oxed Man* has an eerie and foreboding tone; as a bizarre man-beast who, upon falling from the sky, tries to "shake up" the orderly utilitarian lives of the citizens below, to no avail. Along with the story, the bold black and white graphic style, rhythmic cycles, and jittery, frantic animation form a sharp comment on the dangers of collective conformity.

Following in the footsteps of his animation forefathers, Furukawa resigned from Kuri's studio to form Takun Jikken Manga Box in 1970. Furukawa began making a film per year (sometimes two), films characterized by a Kuri-esque desire to explore the boundaries of sound and image. *Head Spoon* (1972) alternates at once between the human voice, shrieking feedback and a soft, meditative piano to accompany bizarre morphing forms, repetitions and cycles. In the opposite spectrum, *Nice to See You* (1975) is unique in its complete lack of sound and a contemplative study of the surface of one image. *Phenakistoscope* (1975) pays tribute to the origins of the animated film and *Portrait* (1977), one could say, to the invention of Polaroids.

The '70s saw a surge in the production of anime TV series; for every set of tastes, there was a corresponding series, a genre (and then some) for every age. Furukawa underwent an equally tireless exploration of techniques and stream-of-consciousness imagery. However, what set him apart from most of his commercial (and independent) counterparts was his awareness of the signs of the times and the messages they held for the future. He was fascinated (flashes of insight leading him to create) and disgusted (the need for change leading him to create) with power, speed and the effects of the slow progression of time. Perhaps it was his child-hood proximity to solitary poets and spies that enabled him to take a step back and cast a critical (and ever-watchful) eye. At a time when Japanese culture was succumbing to western influences, he responded with *New York Trip* (1970), a weary, bleary impression of America's megalomaniacal culture in the late '60s. The barrage of image and sound produce a similar effect as in real life – that with enough cacophony one eventually becomes desensitized (or downright bored). As a dewy voice proclaims: "When the moment comes what will I do, I have done everything." As time passed, buildings were raised, and money changed hands, Furukawa's films pondered the ever-changing face of culture and its subsequent effect on our desires: from the humorous *Coffee Break* (1977 – to the alert worker comes the promise of quality goods and plenty of them!) to *Bird* (1985 – the evolution of man's efforts to grasp the unattainable). Even the films targeted at a younger audience carry an underlying message: *Sleepy* (1980) tells the story of a dragon who, for all his good qualities, is always falling asleep as the world passes him by.

NOW AND THEN

In his paper "New Trends in Japanese Popular Culture," Tetsuo Kagawa writes: "the electronic collectivity either integrates individuals into a homogeneous 'fused' collectivity or emancipates every 'singularity' in the collective. Electronic media and the mass culture they cultivate have this dual potentiality." Kagawa focuses on the social ramifications of karaoke and the Walkman, but we can locate similar trends in Japanese animation of the '80s and '90s. While the Japanese animated series had been around for nearly a decade, inciting an underground following in a few European countries, it was not until the advent of the VCR and home video that the worldwide consumption of anime began. Conversely, the recent advancements in technology have heralded a new generation of independents: filmmakers, like Koji Yamamura and Koji Morimoto, who have the opportunity to break away from the collectivity of the large studios. Equipped with new inexpensive digital tools, they have returned to the home studio to make personal films. And, thanks to initiatives by television and web broadcasters, these animators now have access to a wider audience beyond the festival circuit. Furukawa is one such animator, creating various commercials for television, as well as a series of short films for children commissioned by NHK (Japan Broadcasting Corporation).

While these technological advancements have led to greater awareness and appreciation of Japanese animation, they can also be blamed for the disappearance of the country's diversity: The varied dialects and traditions found throughout Japan; subtle differences based on occupation, religion, sex and age, were quickly erased with the presence of television, radio and other forms of mass media. Furukawa's *Tyo Story* (1999), retells Ozu Yasujiro's live-action classic, *Tokyo Story* (1953) using this new language, which speaks of the fractured gap between two generations: those united by century-old traditions and those by this new "electronic collectivity." Furukawa's series of Bashou-inspired films, however inadvertently, also demonstrate the country's cultural homogenization and the world's shrinking boundaries. While Bashou's travel journals expanded on the minutiae of the Japanese landscape, ("Bush clover in blossom waves/ Without spilling/A drop of dew") Furukawa's 2D world necessitates the need to seek inspiration from outside sources. Both *TarZAN* (1990), an animated account of his trip to Africa, and his newest work in progress, *Himoko*, based on his travels with a tour group to Spain, feature frenzied photo-taking, attempts at capturing the last of the world's "exotic" locales. In its attempts to appear "exotic," the few cultural resources that are left in Japan have been quickly exploited; even the Ninja Yashiki of Furukawa's youth has been reduced to a simulated environment, roped in, encased in glass.

Thankfully, Furukawa has not suffered a similar fate. For nearly forty years, he has explored the shapes and forms of the animated film, using nearly every available technique and style, from abstract collages and computer renderings to tiny and simple comic characters. From his humble beginnings in the shadow of castle walls and western ideals to the evolution of his present-day studio (Takun Box Co., Ltd.), Furukawa has expanded on his experiences within Japan to reflect the state of our world today. Beyond his extensive oeuvre, he is equipped with a strong awareness of the history of his craft, deep respect for his predecessors and his peers, and faith in the new generation of Japanese filmmakers that will no doubt learn from him.

CHAPTER 14

Piotr Dumala

Notes from Underground (2002)

by Tom McSorley

All respectable ants begin with the ant-hill, and they will probably end with it, too, which does great credit to their constancy and their positive character. But man is a fickle and disreputable creature and perhaps, like a chess-player, is interested in the process of attaining his goal rather than the goal itself. And who knows (nobody can say with certainty/, perhaps man's sole purpose in this world consists in this uninterrupted process of attainment, or in other words in living, and not specifically in the goal, which of course must be something like "two times two equals four" – that is, a formula; but after all, two times two is four is not life, gentlemen, but the beginning of death.

"THE UNDERGROUND MAN" IN FYODOR DOSTOEVSKY,

NOTES FROM UNDERGROUND (1864)

There is a crack in everything.

That's how the light gets in.

LEONARD COHEN, "ANTHEM" (1992)

Piotr Dumala makes light out of darkness and darkness out of light. Within, as he calls it, the "alchemy" of animation,[1] he carves lines of light

DOI: 10.1201/9781003288022-15

and perception into the dark and obscure; he also smudges the light away to suggest the power, the danger, and the odd, paradoxical sanctuary of darkness itself. It is a potent alchemy. From the appallingly funny fatalist grotesques of his earliest films to the austere uncertainties of later works, Dumala's distinctive animated world of ticking clocks, ubiquitous insects, distant footsteps, eyes wide open, existential dread and profound solitude registers that something has gone awry in the world we inhabit.

Like his literary influences, chiefly Fyodor Dostoevsky and Franz Kafka, all of his animation creatively and forcefully presents the world as cracked, as broken, as unfinished. This is not all bad. Such a state of things contains possibilities. There is anxiety and dread everywhere, but there is also desire and, most important of all, imagination. As Dostoevsky's Underground Man later observes, an observation which echoes throughout those exquisite silences and strangely mobile stillnesses of Dumala's later work, "I agree that two and two make four is an excellent thing; but to give everything its due, two and two make five is also a very fine thing." Faced as we are in the 21st century with a soul-destroying grid of materialism, technology, and realpolitik, two plus two had better equal five, at least once and a while. Indeed, in a world seduced by systems of thought and technological instruments that admit only the goal and never the process, the end and not the means, the brave, tough-minded, imaginative animation of Piotr Dumala is more relevant, more necessary, than ever.

Born in Warsaw in 1956, Dumala grew up in a nation that, despite being dominated politically and economically by the U.S.S.R. during the Cold War, also created one of the most dramatic and influential indigenous political movements of the late 1970s, Solidarity. In film, the sophistication and accomplishment of Polish cinema during the 1960s, 1970s, and 1980s is also remarkable, with the emergence of such auteurs as Roman Polanski, Krzsyztof Zanussi, Andrej Wajda, Krzsyztof Kieslowski, Jerzy Skolimowski, to name a few. Political repression did exist; in spite or because of it, Polish film artists worked with and around the system to show that two plus two can equal five. As in other countries in the former Soviet sphere, Poland's polychromatic, protean cultural strengths and traditions outweighed, outwitted and outlasted a monolithic and imposed political formula.

In animation, following such early 20th century pioneers as Feliks Kuczkowksi, Stanislaw Dobryzynski, Ladislas Starewich and Zenon Wasilewski, there came after 1956 the impressive artist-driven animation of Jan Lenica, Walerian Borowcyk, Piotr Kamler, Miroslaw Kijowicz, Stefan Schabenbeck, Witold Giersz, Zbigniew Rybczynski, Jerzy Kucia and others. Influenced by trends in contemporary Polish graphic arts, this "Polish school" in the 1960s and beyond tended toward dark-toned images, absurdist humour and subversive social satire. Its narratives are preoccupied with exploring themes of individual alienation, existential angst and the limits of expression.

When Piotr Dumala arrives with his ferocious first work, *Lykantrophia* (Lycanthropy, 1981), follows it with the pitch-black humour of *Czarny Kapturek* (The Little Black Riding Hood, 1983) and then the atrociously amusing *Nerwowe Zycie Kosmosu* (The Nervous Life of The Universe, 1986), it is clear that he belongs in the Polish animation tradition. He connects with the surreal strangeness and corrosive social critiques of his distinguished predecessors while pursuing his own forms of animation and, significantly, while also experiencing the end of the Cold War and the painful transition from a state-run to so-called "free market" economy. Dumala's work does conform to what critic Giannalberto Bendazzi calls Polish animation's "poetry of pessimism," yet the transcendent power of Dumala's best animations undoes pessimism's more passive positions by suggesting intensely private, imaginative strategies for escape and action. For example, with all its lunacy, anger, drab scatology and raucously sad hilarity (imagine a set of very, very twisted early Fleischer cartoons), the recent series *Nerwowe Zycie* (Nervous Life) offers dozens of brief vignettes about our agitated, absurd world which affirm that although humans are trapped within systems of their own devising, they stubbornly, even stupidly refuse to be defeated by them. It is the imagination, however deformed and corrupted, that defeats closed, formulaic, mindlessly repeated thoughts and deeds.

If this kinetic, frenetic and, yes, splenetic material – animated in spare and simple line drawings – represents one aspect of Dumala's work, the other, beginning with *Latajace Vlosy* (Flying Hair, 1984) and continuing through to *Crime and Punishment* (2000), is a startling, densely textured form of drawn animation reminiscent of detailed metal engraving or woodcut prints. Rendered with elegant restraint – here like the drawings of Daumier and Odilon Redon, there like those of Gustave Dore – these films continue the exploration of themes of absurdity, alienation and individual isolation. They also constitute a rhythmic counterpoint to Dumala's others, as in these films the amount of actual motion is pared down considerably. Now there is only the slight movement of an eye, a fluttering leaf, an insect crawling, the hands of a clock, an unexpected figurative transformation or a sudden gesture. As a result of this aesthetic distillation, each instance of motion acquires more concentrated dramatic significance, more meaning, perhaps, and more ambiguity. Dumala's images linger. They give us time. In an uncanny way, they invite us to look through them, to penetrate the darkness they contain in order to see past the conventions of representational art and animation and, by extension, to see past the accepted "normal" surfaces of the world as it has been constructed.

This unmistakable style (a technique of paint on a plaster plate upon which Dumala draws/engraves with needles directly under the camera) begins in *Flying Hair* a visually and sonically layered tone poem involving a man, a mysterious woman and a night of intense rain. As the slashes of rain are transformed into hair into rain into needles, the couple finds shelter under an umbrella. Based on a text by Dostoevsky, *Lagodna* (Gentle, 1985) elaborates on this style. While a clock ticks, the relationship between a young woman and an older man deteriorates as he attempts to keep her from the outside world. It is the story of desire, possession and, as ever in Dumala, the quiet, devastating awareness of time passing. The flies which crawl on the face of the trapped, immobile woman (which buzz again and again in Dumala's films) evoke the "Furies" sent by Greek gods to mock humankind's hubris; of course, they are also symbols of decay and mortality which no amount of human will or desire can prevent.

Despite the apparent hopelessness and fatalism, in Dumala's work the imagination itself affords us some measure of energy, some claim to individual agency, some defiant dignity which, from all our undergrounds and enclosures, compels us to say that we will resist "two plus two equals four." In the haunting and brilliant *Sciany* (Walls, 1987), we have the tale of a man entombed in a dark cell. He seeks to define his space, to identify it and to find a way out. He fails, and yet there is the sense in the lonely figure that there exists something beyond his and our vision. In the more playfully surreal but equally serious, *Wolnosc nogi* (Freedom of the Leg, 1988), a man's body parts leave for an evening of reverie. All the parts return but one leg. Consequently, he must chase it all over the city. Playing with perspective and notions of "reality," Dumala slyly reveals that the world is not always under our control and maybe that is not always such a bad thing.

Two other artists who recognized the fissures between the self and the world, for better and for worse, were Fyodor Dostoevsky and Franz Kafka. As mentioned, each has had a considerable influence on Dumala's sensibility, and they are the inspiration for his two most recent works. *Franz Kafka* (1991) is a stunning, masterful examination of existential literature's most tortured participant–observer. Combining moments in Kafka's life with imagined images of his interior reaction to these events, the film weaves together Kafka's poetic mixture of natural, erotic and fantastic worlds. The many extraordinary images in this work culminate in a breathtaking final sequence that expresses precisely the awareness of Kafka's (and our) entrapment in the world and the sublime, lonely power of the imagination to escape from it.

And yet there are limits. Always limits. Indeed, Dumala's next film is an adaptation of Dostoevsky's fabled novel concerned exactly with the limits of individual liberty, however courageously imagined. Many years in the making, *Crime and Punishment* (2000) plays with the original narrative structure of the novel to render more complex Raskolnikov's urge to kill without remorse and to emphasize the inescapability of his conscience before, during and after the act. No romanticized existentialist solitude here, but rather a vivid, absorbing meditation on mortality, time and the possibilities of redemption in a seemingly irredeemable world.

Piotr Dumala has written, "I am only concerned with films in which the author takes himself, his subject, and the viewer very seriously."[2] This is not to say that his work is unremittingly heavy and humourless; it is not, as his *Nervous Life* and various commercial spots will attest. As an animation artist of the highest order, Dumala is dedicated to the serious challenge of how to identify ourselves in that troubled space between the way the world is and the way it should be. The world tells us one thing, but we sense another. We know there is more. Perhaps we are all underground in some way, Dumala's work insinuates, but we can see the cracks and the traces of light. Our eyes are open. We are alive. Our clocks are ticking. We can count to four. Or five. And we can imagine.

ACKNOWLEDGEMENTS

Although most of the thanks are due to Piotr Dumala for his extraordinary work, I'd also like to thank, for various and different and occasionally overlapping reasons, Frank Taylor, Tom Knott, Chris Robinson and Ben Jones. Thanks also to Midhat Ajanovic Ajan's insightful article, "Radiant Shades of Darkness: Piotr Dumala's film animations" (Goteborg, Sweden, May 2001).

NOTES

1. Piotr Dumala, "The Philosophical Stone of Animation" Animation World Magazine (January 2001, p.32) Translated by Michal Klobukowski.
2. Dumala, ibid, p. 32.

CHAPTER 15

Janie Geiser's Uncanny Silence (2002)

by Barry Doyle

Silence is so accurate, words can only paralyze the viewer's mind and imagination.

MARK ROTHKO

Mark Rothko wrote this in reference to visual art, generally, and to his own abstract expressionist works specifically. His point reflects, of course, an abstract moralizing, but more importantly it denotes the limits of language to describe conscious states, ideas and the depths of human thought. However, silence is not a vacuum, and it doesn't exist as some kind of empty space. For any absence calls forth a presence: the very presence of the absence itself. And sometimes silence or a lack of language creates more noise than all the talk on a season of Oprah. This abundance is exactly what Rothko wanted the viewer to experience: the creation and process of meaning, and the unexplainable compulsion to make meaning without the aid of language or a clear narrative path. It is this process that gets called forth in Janie Geiser's work by her insistence on repudiating language and emphasizing impressions, leaving only traces of fractured narratives. Within this chaotic and discombobulating world, the viewer is left with an overabundance of images and the compulsion to make meaning out of seemingly meaningless cinematic tableaus.

DOI: 10.1201/9781003288022-16

Janie Geiser – with a background in puppeteering, theater, film and animation – is probably best known for her short film work of the last decade. Portraying characters and situations that highlight our essential aloneness in the world, Geiser's work has a deep foundation in the complexities of psychic knowledge and, conversely, the untenable notion of ever knowing anything about our interior selves. Her work about the states of consciousness and finding a way to probe our psychic worlds is rich with Spiral Vessel iconic and whimsical imagery and impressions that leave viewers at once completely disoriented and strangely comforted. Her films are fraught with a tension of knowing and unknowing for subjects and viewers; a tension that allows Geiser to question the very idea of a stable narrative or meta-narrative. Geiser weaves tenuous threads through these unstable narratives, producing richly complex and atmospheric works that compel viewers to an almost endless series of questions about their content.

One thread is the overriding gothic tendency in Geiser's film work. I'm specifically referring to her shorts The Red Book, Lost Motion and The Fourth Watch. Within these works there are apparent and veiled themes that point to The Fourth Watch gothic. Foremost, is the notion of the uncanny and the ensuing terror that is produced by something that is familiar to us and simultaneously can be seen as foreign and deeply troubling. In Writings on Art and Literature, Freud laid out the idea of the uncanny (or in German, unheimlich, which literally means unhomely, or not of the home, unfamiliar) as something that "is frightening – to what arouses dread and horror; equally certainly, too, the word is not always used in a clearly definable sense, so that it tends to coincide with what excites fear in general" (193). He also went on to complicate the idea by stating: "the uncanny is that class of the frightening which leads back to what is known of old and long familiar" (195). It is here that I want to point out the importance of "what is known of old and long familiar" in Geiser's work: the space of the domestic, the home, the house. This site serves to create the potent terror and uncanny in the above works. Needless to say that there are a multitude of themes and movements in Geiser's work, however I will focus only on domesticity and the gothic, and ever so briefly.

Geiser ends The Red Book with an amnesiac woman in an apartment, and, in a frightening moment, the cityscape falls away. In a literal sense, the city burns, and inevitably the domestic space inhabited by the amnesiac will dissipate as well. The space is familiar as a living area with its windows looking out at the cityscape, but it is barren and devoid of memories and emotion. It is as though the room is the amnesiac's torture chamber, but the torture is, in a way, self-inflicted by her illness. That space of living becomes the harrowing space of instability.

And what to make of the man with the house on his shoulders, the house that floats on the screen and the woman who seems to give birth to a house? Literally, the domestic – its pleasures (familiar comforts and routines) and darkness (abuses and rigidity) – is always with us in our habits and psyche. But also the familiar domestic psychological freight we carry with us is so embedded in our identities that we cannot distinguish it or isolate it. The scenes with the houses seem to be an attempt by Geiser to at once show the domestic as separate but inextricably attached. The woman giving birth to a house exemplifies this simultaneous movement: like a mother of a child, the woman giving birth to the house realizes the domestic is part of her, familiar to her, but it is also separate, foreign, even threatening.

Lost Motion begins with a male toy figure set in a kitchen; we are immediately put into the domestic. But this domestic space is so uncanny: a male figure is the lone character in a barren kitchen. The dappled light and the pinhole camera perspective add to a mood of isolation. Shots of maps, stamps and trains hint at travel; the male figure could be a traveling salesman (?), which adds to a life of alienation. And Geiser keeps returning to the kitchen with shots of the male figure, or an empty kitchen chair, or the kitchen devoid of anything, reinforcing aloneness. We are at once familiar with this setting (we've all been in kitchens) but estranged from it as well (this kitchen is very creepy).

Midway through, the film takes a dramatic turn in tone – a turn that bolsters the uncanny Gothicism of the first half – in terms of soundtrack and setting. The soundtrack changes to dark, foreboding synthesized music. The setting alternates between the kitchen and an unidentifiable toy mechanism, the lighting becomes darker. Then in repeated scenes there appears a menacing, and truly frightening, decapitated head of a doll lodged in the toy mechanism. The male figure is shown negotiating the toy mechanism: does the toy mechanism represent the male figure's unconscious or memory? Does the doll's head represent the earlier terror of childhood for the male figure or for some other figure? Then we are presented with a female nude toy figure (sexual forays of the traveling salesman?) interspersed with the doll's head, giving us a darkly charged sexual atmosphere. Interestingly, we are presented with, in the final shot, the kitchen and the lone chair: back to the locus of domesticity but clearly not the same after the haunting images of the doll's head, the harsh toy machinery and sexed nude figure. The familiar becomes, and is, strangely distant; the canny becomes, and is, the uncanny.

A prosaic and harmless tin dollhouse provides the setting for The Fourth Watch, easily the most intentionally haunting of the three films, and the one that uses a wide variety of gothic devices. It opens with a slow, wavering piano piece that hangs on three repeated notes. The use of shadow and mottled light is used liberally on the dollhouse setting. Silent film actors are projected, with their movie backgrounds, onto the various rooms of the doll house. The movie backgrounds are bedrooms, kitchens, doorways and hallways. These settings almost serve as a ghostly doppel-ganger for the dollhouse. The actors find themselves in situations familiar to the gothic: various faces filled with apprehension; a somnambulist; a boy in a bed with fear washing over his face as a door opens slowly reveal-ing the darkened face of a man; a woman engulfed by a shadow; a woman creeping tentatively along a hallway. All of the actors are isolated in their settings and in their fear. All of them appear in the uncanny location of the home; the place where all is familiar and filled with terror.

It is no mistake that Geiser chose silent film actors for The Fourth Watch. What better characters, than ones that don't speak, can be used to project our fears onto? Their silence, as with the silence of all the characters in the three films, is our license to construct our own narratives of fear or whatever takes our fancy, to create meaning out of that profound absence of language. Rothko spoke about privileging the accuracy of silence over the paralyzing effect of words. However, the silence that Geiser provides to viewers is much more than a tool of accuracy. It is the genesis of mean-ing and interpretation itself, a force that crushes any notion of accuracy. Geiser's use of silence is at once rich and rewarding, and at the same time the excess can be bewildering and haunting in certain ways. Haunting because one is plagued by the question of "what does it mean?" Despite the "familiar" in her work, one is left disoriented, estranged and wondering. It is truly uncanny.

CHAPTER 16

The Fecal and the Feral

John Kricfalusi, Theme & Variation (2002)

by Richard Meltzer

I HOLD THESE TRUTHS TO be self-evident:

- That without *The Ren & Stimpy Show* you don't get *Beavis and Butt-head* or *South Park*...am I right or am I right?
- That by setting his nose to the toon-table grindstone a dozen years back and freaking out and going ape and laying down a thick, heavy seminal dose of the kinda stuff you're "not supposed to show on TV," *heh heh*, John Kricfalusi made the jerkoffs of cable realize there was indeed an audience, a mega-audience!, for some really fucked up shit on the home screens of middle-class N. America, for "puerile humor" till you puke ... and since then the rest has been HISTORY.

Which makes him *what*, the Eisenstein of Bathtub Fartwater Animation? The D.W. Griffith? Well, yeah ... or somethin'.

"The Absolute unfolds itself"-Hegel said that. Inevitabilities, y'know, inevitablize. But who's got forever, eh? Not you, not I-and without Johnny as the auteur-in-chief of this here operation we might *still* be waiting ... diggit.

DOI: 10.1201/9781003288022-17

For which we should of course be GRATEFUL. We should kiss his royal Canajun ass, or slap it fondly yet royally, and extend our own hind parts for his reciprocal thwack...we should behave towards his person in a generic manner not unlike the butt-directed behaviors of characters in his toons. We should – I truly mean it – 'cause if not for Johnnyboy, pshaw, we would only have our own tub to fart in: no toon tubs Writ Large...no way! And who am "I"? (Funny "you" should ask.) A mere conceit, the cheesy fabrication of a Lower 48 hireling's wretched self-conscious. I will say no more.

There are themes and themes and THEMES in the works of John Kricfalusi (obsessive love-hate; the pathology of misplaced enthusiasm; mammality vs. humanity; the anthropomorphization and neuroticization of subhuman sentience; pecking orders of self-loathing, both species-generic and personal; the weirdification of normal; the provisionally unreal vs. the existentially not-real-nohow; excrement as metaphor and substance; the primacy and glory of ultra-stoopid), but none as obsessively front & center as *same-gender interspecies cohabitation.*

A male dog and a male cat are bickering bedmates throughout the run of *Ren & Stimpy.* "Me-Yowww!," from Kric's earlier gig, the Bakshiproduced *Mighty Mouse: The New Adventures,* flirts with cohab (and codependency) 'tween a steroided M.M. and Derf, a dumb-feeb alleycat. At toon's end, Derf ends up bunked with a bulldog.

Delving deeper into prehistory, "The Ice Goose Cometh" features Mighty's resurrection of '40s loon star Gandy Goose (frozen in a glacier) and the latter's reunion with cat bud Sourpuss-homage to the ORIGINAL *non*-mutually-enamored boy-boy slumber pair.

And some enamor too. Couple-three episodes for the '88 revival of *Beany and Cecil*: an adorable homo sap and sea serpent share a mattress but *don't* let it fuck with their friendship.

PRETTY IN PINK.

The Kric loves the color, sheez...couldn't do without it. But for a bawdy born-and-bred BEAVER-Canuck, he scrupulously avoids the one mainstream application the unwashed masses might be likeliest to topically "associate" it with: female pudenda, esp. the welcoming sight of pudenda, *spread.*

"Pussy."

Y'know?

Instead you get tongues, stretched out and wriggling like giant squid tentacles from *20,000 Leagues Under the Sea*, and great massive gobs of abandoned Bubblegum.

"Boo Boo Runs Wild" begins with Ranger Smith defiling the forest with tacky proscriptions: "Do not feed the bears." "No shedding." "No loafing." "No bulgy, veiny eyeballs." "No grunting." Yogi's pal Boo Boo can take it no more: "I was born a bear, and I'm going back to my bear roots."

Sounds swell, but after a token bit of bark scratching and basket raiding, all that really springs from so promising a premise – the archest expression of ursine atavism we're given a dose of – is a protruding tongue and a pool of drool. Boo Boo slobbers on Yogi's gal's hind paw, which seduces her into slobbering too. (Yogi himself is too starched a Republican to join the fun.) At their most protuberant, the two bear tongues stretch a couple-three meters, covered with flies.

"The presence of God is in His absence" – Meister Eckhardt said that. In the video for Björk's "I Miss You," the Icelandic crooner's primary organ of love is relentlessly implied, fiercely alluded to, but never audio-visually delivered...nor, for that matter, are her nipples.

Allusions galore: noses as nips as throbbing/squiggling penises, asses as flaming rocket exhausts...inflated condoms as (of all things) falsies...guns firing, a chicken torn in two by our singer in heat...but zero mammary-genital payoff. 'Cross the gender divide, guest stud Jimmy the Idiot Boy, for the record, DOESN'T HAVE A DICK.

Anyway, a plethora in pink – Björk in pink mini-dress, a pink shower cap, lavishing and writhing in pink bubble bath, her nipples and cunny covered in pink cartoon foam (at one point she powders her tongue) – as the center of grav for a no-quit, full-court-press erotica that is ultimately infantile, gratuitous and top heavily toon-y.

Toon-y as cutesy; coloration as concept: the reduction of Björk (musically, rock-historically speaking) to bubblegum status, exiling her to cultural beaches balmy and bland enough to harbor the B-52s, Britney Spears and Madonna. By vid's end, "bubblegum" qua concept and "cartoon" qua concept are inextricably – here comes trouble! – one & the same.

Cartoon as *imitation of life*; imitation as *lame simulation* – if not outright *sham*.

Trouble...

(Didja know, by the by, that even *Fantasia* – the Beethoven's 6th sequence – has uncovered crotches and breasts?)

A masterpiece! ein Meisterstück! un chef d'oeuvre! (Two ways of lookin' at it.)

The Mighty Mouse blockbuster "See You in the Funny Papers" is (a) the G-G-GREATEST commercially produced psychedelic cartoon ever and/ or (b) the MOST PSYCHEDELIC a commercial toon, by hook or by crook, has ever managed to be. This includes any of the nuttier Betty Boops, and Warner thingies like "Dough for the Dodo" w/ Porky Pig ... believe it.

Wow.

'Cause like a minute into this one, jeepers, there's this runaway Elvis balloon, a fat Elvis balloon – fat balloon of the mid – '70s fat Elvis, but which is fatter, him or the balloon? Hard to say. And the sideburns are very ugly. The balloon breaks free during some kinda parade and is headed for the PIZZA CONVENTION (that's right), where it ignites and bursts into flames... HEY! Jus' like The *blimp*! The *blimp*!...y'know, Captain Beefheart. "The King has burst into flames!" – Jesus – "Worst disaster in human memory"...absolutely.

At which point *just imagine, kids,* if you'd smoked reefer or dropped "L" before tuning in! – and it just gets more surreal, and more cubist, and more dada, and more German expressionist, and more futurist, and more pop art and op art and plop art, and oodles 'n' poodles of art for art's sake (imagine: if this was later Kricfalusi, post-*Ren & Stimpy* 'stead of pre, there would also no doubt be fart for fart sake!) – y'ain't never seen such an ongoing sendup of High-Booty Art...like fucking *wow*, folks.

So anyway, anyway, it's a good'un, a *mighty* good'un: arguably the greatest achievement (any genre) by a Euro-Canadian, on a par with "Snowbird" or Stompin' Tom's "To It and at It"...or Marcel Pronovost's discovery of nitrogen.

It's that good, people!

The world hath never seen the self-conscious, self-referential like of "The Man from Next Thursday," starring the fab, fearsome Ripping Friends ... verily, it hathn't.

And I'm not even talking about that fart in the tub of wet cement, or the litter box of Tomorrow that teleports catshit-de rigueur references to the Kricfalusi *oeuvre*.

I'm talking 'bout plot. I'm talking 'bout dialogue. I'm talking voice overs. I'm talking script, I'm talking TEXT, I'm talking what the lit-theory claptrappers would call "fictive space" – a space which in this case rarely leaves square one...and I don't mean page one. All this toon does is TALK ABOUT ITSELF.

It is more self-conscious, more self-referential, than *Six Characters in Search of an Author*, more than all the films of Henry Jaglom and Ross McElwee, more than *Tristram Shandy* or a 30-hour monologue by Kim Fowley.

It is probably the most textually baggaged, verbally burdened animation ever wrought by god, man or beast...you could look it up!

"Man's Best Friend," the kink-thriller that finally got him CANNED by the jerkoffs at Nickelodeon, is the closest J.K. gets to um, uh (what should we call it?), actual non-allusive libidinal sex? The representation (or even signification) of getoff?

"It's discipline that begets love," snarls George Liquor at designated underlings Ren & Stimpy, and then slam, bang, wham, *phwang*...until EVERYONE is reduced to infantile goo-goo-ga-ga: the primal bliss of diapered submission.

This uncompromisingly nifty S&M-o-ganza could easily screen with select scenes from *Lawrence of Arabia, Five Graves to Cairo, Midnight Express, The Fountainhead, L.A. Plays Itself*, and *Sick: The Life & Death of Bob Flanagan, Supermasochist*. It could in fact be the CARTOON BREAK (before the Rodney King newsreel) ... what an ole-fashioned "day at the movies" that would be! (Check out also the neato-coolo top/bottom "man's best friends" reversal riff in Hubert Selby's *The Room*.)

"You're the top!" Cole fucking Porter said *that*.

An anagram for JOHN KRICFALUSI:

HI, I JACK ON FURS

(Who would put it past him?)

CHAPTER 17

Ominous Beauty

The Animation of
Jean-Francois Laguionie (2003)

by Tom McSorley

IN THE FILMS OF Jean-Francois Laguionie, ominous things are about to happen. A bomb is about to go off. Noah is going to "find" a woman for his ark. The devil is about to reveal his – or her – true identity. An actor is going to try to find his real self in a mirror. A man will fall hopelessly in love with a mermaid. A man and a woman are going to cross the Atlantic Ocean in a rowboat. On the surface, all is seemingly calm and ordered, but in Laguionie's deceptively simple and mischievously designed films, what we are looking at may not be what we are actually seeing. His animated worlds, consistently beautiful and pleasing to look at, are filled with all manner of distant early warnings, intimations of dire consequences and subtle threats of apocalypses now and soon.

Born in 1939, Jean-Francois Laguionie attended the Centre d'art dramatique with the intention of becoming an actor. While studying performance, he also did a lot of drawing. In 1963, he discovered animation when he was introduced to the legendary French animator, Paul Grimault. So impressed was Grimault by Laguionie's work, he loaned the young Laguionie his animation equipment and, from 1965 onward, Laguionie has been producing some of the most elegantly rendered animated films in French animation. He has also been producing the films of other

DOI: 10.1201/9781003288022-18

animators, has worked in live action cinema and has written several collections of short stories.

Laguionie's paradoxical work examines familiar myths and uses fairy-tale narratives to explore the often-dangerous differences between reality and illusion. As he once observed, "I like false realism. I like trompe l'oeil, false perspectives and everything against which one could break one's face, but which also displays a sincere intention to represent reality." What one sees and what it means, in other words, contains much complexity, considerable trickery and a dynamic admixture of artifice and authenticity. This double perspective, this sense of the presence of the ominous in the beautiful, is the aesthetic and ideological energy of skepticism which powers his animated films.

In the brilliant Cold War parable, *Une Bombe Par Hasard*, a man arrives in a deserted town where an unexploded bomb lies in the town square. The man restores culture and order to calm the fears of the townsfolk assembled up on a nearby hill; for his trouble the people return, descend into venality and violence, boot him out of town, and then, of course, the bomb goes off. Was he tricked, or did he trick them into self-immolation? If so, why? Similarly, the "devil" in *Le Masque du Diable* gets the protagonist into all kinds of trouble thinking he knows who the devil is; just when we think we know what is going on, Laguionie turns the mask on us, revealing our mistake. In *Potr' et la Fille des Eaux*, the obsessive love between a man and a mermaid leads to a cruel reversal of their physical states, and love won't conquer all. In *L'Arche de Noé*, meanwhile, Noah dutifully collects all those birds and animals, two by two, but then realizes he needs a woman. So, he goes out and violently abducts one. This brute is the "hero" who saved the world from a watery grave? The sexual politics of this myth are revealed, upended and demolished in concise and, as always, attractive, even serenely stylish animation.

In his multiple award-winning 1978 film, *La Traversée de l'Atlantique a la Rame*, there is a moment that captures the subtlety of Laguionie's approach to apocalyptic narrative and to the rich contradictory powers of his animation style. A young couple decides, against their parents' wishes and, perhaps, against their own better judgement, to row across the Atlantic Ocean with only themselves, their love and some musical instruments. In a haunting and beautiful sequence, one night out on the rowboat they watch the doomed Titanic slip by them. The next morning, some survivors of the disaster drift toward the rowboat. Without warning, the woman clubs them viciously with an oar, keeping the couple's romantic floating sanctuary free from human misery. The savagery of this gesture is as shocking in its suddenness as it is deeply unsettling in its implications. So is this what romantic love can engender: bestial narcissism? It is the most concentrated and compelling example of how Laguionie's work constantly forces upon us a reevaluation of the warm, almost comforting, aesthetic surfaces we witness in his animations.

It is in this profound tension between the surface and what lies beneath it that the dark dramas of Laguionie's films derive their sinister powers. Animation historian and critic Giannalberto Bendazzi rightly observes that Laguionie's animation style is a combination of "both naïf painting and Magritte." There is a delightful sense of play and the naive in his work, but beneath it are suggestions that all is not as it seems, much like the mysteriously troubling work of René Magritte. As these six exquisitely designed and animated works reveal, Jean-Francois Laguionie is a fearless explorer of the tales we tell ourselves, the tricks we play on ourselves and others and of the sometimes strange and unpleasant realities which lie beneath the apparently beautiful. Be careful. Look closely. The end may be near.

CHAPTER 18

The Wage Of Mersh, The Fart Of Art

Oscar Grillo In The 21st Century (2003)

By Richard Meltzer

I T CAME TO ME in a dream jus' now: *The opposite of wine is milk, the opposite of east is west, the opposite of Phil Mulloy is Oscar Grillo.*

* * *

In an alternate universe, or even this one, Oscar Grillo's calling card could verywell read:

"I...ANIMATE...THE...WORLD. Come and git it!"

We've all seen, no doubt, knowingly or un-, four score and more of the gentleman's snap-happy adverts for Bud Light...Cheetos...Kellogg's Mini Wheats...Ruffles...UPS...Perrier...Hamlet cigars...limey investment crap... Heinz beans...Frank Sinatra best-ofs: goods/services many of us could very well live without, charmingly sold to us (with ultra-profit aforethought) on dotted lines we cannot resist 'cuz they all just *look so damn nice.*

Eclectic and glib from merry pillar to merry post, calling on, referring to and/or "appropriating" images, icons, geometries and techniques associated with everyone from Ralph Bakshi to Ralph Steadman to Betty Boop to Mister Magoo to R. Crumb to Ludwig Bemelmans to Picasso – and

DOI: 10.1201/9781003288022-19

even, possibly, to whatsems of his own origination – mixing and matching and stitching in the most seamless manner that ever wuz, Oscar's commercials are fine, fine, SUPERFINE exemplars of animated art, of the state of THE Animated Art, leading us w/ polish and flair, and w/out an *iota* of shame, by our goddam nose in a manner we cannot help but DIG – but one question mus' be axed:

Is there *anything* – any theme, product, corporate concept, vested vanity wrinkle, real or metaphoric carcinogen – he WOULDN'T animate?

Would he have animated, if called upon (and adequately compensated), the Bush buildup for the Iraq War? Would he willingly and willfully have breathed color, face and *appeal* into it for not merely the "rubes," but also the "yuppies," the "liberals," the "intellectuals," the "indifferent," bozos and their uncles who listen to alt-rock or tend organic gardens or surf porn sites or read Goethe to pigeons...thus leading too many among us to our *doom*, to our own not-so-merry *undoing*? Would Oscar Grillo have done THAT?

See, heh, I'm only *asking* – 'cause I really dunno...won't somebody tell me?

Hey, folks. This dude is an "enigma."

* * *

For those living, breathing or otherwise who value the VAST TALENT of Linda Eastman McCartney, Oscar has got a carload – a truckload – a boatload! – of videos-4-U. For those who don't...well...um...a viewing of his Linda vids (if you bring an *open mind* to it) will prove my-t-educational...an instructional GOLDMINE, betcha by golly.

In case you've wondered, as I have, if anything in the annals of recording has ever (in fact) been cheesier, twinkier or MORE SUPERFICIAL than the waxings of Paul McCartney w/ Wings, a sit through the "Seaside Woman" vid will flat-out TELL YOU, but you gotta be patient – please! – you will hafta wait for the end credits to supply you a nametag for it: *Linda McCartney w/ Wings*.

Linda the singer doesn't have the existential reverb of even a Melanie, a Sting, a Mr. Pat Boone. She is, in point of fact, *unlistenable*. Emotional content? *C'mon*. Nada. To meet the nada where it lives, breathes and shits, Grillo paces his eclecticism, intelligent to the nth, so as not to alter or interfere with the *sub*-superficiality of the audio-lyrical gestalt...his restraint is one for the ages. (Uh...*bravo*.)

The vid for *Wide Prairie*, meanwhile, will provide a swift and decisive A to the Q: *What, if anything, could be cheesier, twinkier and/or more superficial than Linda McCartney w/ Wings?*

Linda *w/out* Wings (natch)...maybe you guessed. Didja know she once tried her hand, her pipes, at country, hoo weee!, or let's call it faux-country singing? I didn't either. "I was born...in Aaa-ri-zooo-nuh"...believe it. Makes you wanna play the Fugs' "I Feel like Homemade Shit." Oscar, up for the task, delivers horses, horses, running, running...across the prairie. Images of "city" and "country" are dealt deadpan, in no opposition worth mentioning, 'cause in this here tune, well, they ain't. Ain't opposed.

And then – is this getting boring? – the answer to...hey, *enough* o' that. "The Light Comes from Within" (Linda, no Wings) begins with a Grillo CARTOON of a frog, kissed by a chick, who becomes not a prince but a man-size frog who is an ASSHOLE. "I need a sense of calm,/Wanna smell the flowers./You need complete control,/You wanna build more towers" – I kid you not (wds. by Linda). Imagine having *that* to work with...christ...w hat a fucking *courageous* sonofagun.

And then, and THEN! – are you ready for *Shadow Cycle*? I would have someone tie you down first...this one CALLS FOR bondage. No lyrics this time, as the musical moment showcased is Ms. Eastman's handiwork as a COMPOSER. Of ponderous New Age clang-dang. "Scenario by Paul McCartney and Oscar Grillo" – OK, this time you hafta blame, or half-blame, the animator. Babe in a crib grabs at miniature horses. A surrogate gramps type takes the kid's pic, the kid waves, gramps waves back. The kid, older, flies, enters a looking glass, swims with endangered species. Cowboys and saucers and trains. An apparition with blue nipples. When in doubt, send in more horses; in *serious* doubt, send in a duck. The sacred, the profane, horses in *human* utero, all the groovy colors of a suburban dining room.

Makes you kinda wish for a good Kellogg's commercial.

* * *

There are those who will insist that working in Hollywood did Faulkner in...blunted his effectiveness at writing the Good Stuff...used up his last serviceable riffs, licks and chops.

All the freelance Linda work might well have done in a lesser bloke than Oscar Madison – excuse me – Grillo.

Yet not only did he live to tell! the! tale!, he's lived to paint his frigging masterpiece: "Parker's Mood."

From the musical equivalent of wet cardboard (mashed turnips) (sand in the vaseline) to a signature performance by *the* greatest musician, period, ever to record. Dig it: *five takes* of a Charlie Parker song, three of them absolute *mindblowers,* run verbatim (with decent-enough visuals) in a simulation of unfolding drama at the session of 9/18/48. Drama? More like an exhale of musical *fire.* A *viable* simulation. Really. It's quite amazing. Hottest cinematic use of music since *Help!* and *Hard Day's Night?* Easily.

The secret (and what a secret!): delirious beauty not-fucked-with sonically nor impinged upon visually. (Speaking of restraint.)

Hey. Grillo performs as important a role in the bringing of aural magic to an under-knowing world's attention as has ever been pulled off. People who know nothing of jazz except the Ken Burns horseshit will think Louis Armstrong was the whole show, but Parker was/is AT LEAST seven times as important as Louis, and as great, and eleven times as magical (for you Canucks: he was Rocket Richard AND Wayne Gretzky) (AND Gordie Howe) (AND Doug Harvey). Grillo does something Clint Eastwood, in his travesty, *Bird,* did not: he messes not with sound nor with history nor common sense. Hardly ever do the images get stupid (Bird as King Kong?), and only once, during take 2, is there show-&-tell footage that feels basically *wrong* (while John Lewis solos, OTHER PIANISTS – Thelonious Monk, Al Haig, Dodo Marmarosa – are pictured and named...uh, why?).

I quibble. "Parker's Mood" is arguably *the* landmark exercise in "applied music" (the Mad Peck's term) since...oh...the "Memo from Turner" scene in *Performance*...wait, no! Since "Rock Around the Clock" over the opening credits to *Blackboard Jungle.*

* * *

High Art, High Fart, or Blow, Oscar, Blow...

Beavis and Butt-head...South Park...Ren & Stimpy. What izzit about farts that makes animators LEAP to the subject?

Not a fart 'toon *per se* but an artsy-fartsy tale of suffering humanity, Grillo's "Monsieur Pett, or The Man Who Couldn't Help It" is something you could kind of imagine Beavis and Butt-head, the characters, watching with a smirk but getting few true giggles out of...something they'd consider *way* too hi-falutin', way too non-gratuitous. In it, farts are touchstones of embarrassment, not amusement, and we're faced with the "problem" of

FLATULENCE, with farts as an "issue." What the bloody hell should we make of it?

Claudia Jaffee of farts-r-us.com tries to 'splain it:

"We all, of course, fart. I personally *like* the way it feels to let a good one loose. The colon is extremely sensitive to pressure. Its sensory organs don't respond well to it...ugh...*very* uncomfortable. Pressure is *no fun*.

"As a parent, I encourage my daughters *not* to hold it in, and this goes for burping and pooping as well. The digestive system can be *merciless*. I encourage them to let it *all* out – anywhere, anytime. Poop in a pot, though...don't soil your panties."

Animation? Well, a fart can be handled strictly as a *sound effect*. No graphics are required, which can make an animator lazy. *South Park* may be Fart City, but it's a terribly lazy enterprise to begin with. 'Monsieur Pett,' on the other hand, is the baroque end of things...the bipolar opposite. *His* nightly farts send the wife and cat ten feet in the air – graphically. His *terminal* farts – what a wonderful notion! – *transform the world*...fart as illumination and *nova*.

"Think of *Monsieur Pett* as the high pressure of high art, *needing to fart*. If you screened it in the same room as *South Park*, they would cancel each other out, and the world would for a moment go black. Art would leave the pedestal, and we all would live *happily ever after*."

Now wouldn't *that* be neat?!!

CHAPTER 19

Miyazaki Magic (2004)

by Mark Langer

C HE IS ONE OF the most influential cinema artists of our era, and director of films that have garnered the Academy Award, the Golden Bear from the Berlin Film Festival, and countless other honours. "Not a day goes by that I do not utilize the tools learned from studying his films" said Pixar's John Lasseter, director of *Toy Story*, *A Bug's Life* and *Monsters Inc. Mulan* creators Barry Cook and Tony Bancroft claim that he "is like a god to us." Other admirers have included directors Akira Kurosawa (*The Seven Samurai, Ran*), Guillermo del Toro (*Chronos, Mimic*) and Tsui Hark (*Once Upon a Time in China, A Chinese Ghost Story*), designer Jean Giraud (*Alien, The Abyss, The Fifth Element*), and video game creator Shigeru Miyamoto (*Super Mario Bros., Legend of Zelda*). *Salon* magazine calls him the "Japanimation godhead" and "acknowledged master of the form." So honoured is this director, that a museum in Tokyo is devoted to his work.[1]

The object of this praise is the modest and unassuming Hayao Miyazaki, animator and co-founder (with Isao Takahata) of Studio Ghibli. His most recent film, *Spirited Away* (2001), broke every box office record in Japan, and is the third most successful non-English language film of all time.[2] Now, in advance of the release of Miyazaki's latest feature, *Howl's Moving Castle*, the Ottawa International Animation Festival is pleased to present a retrospective of work by this Japanese master.

Miyazaki was born in Tokyo in 1941, into a family involved in the aircraft industry. His privileged childhood sheltered him from many of the privations of the war, and a sense of guilt about this became a factor

DOI: 10.1201/9781003288022-20

129

in his later political thought as a Marxist sympathizer and union leader. Miyazaki was educated as an economist, but began his career in 1963 at Toei Doga, working as an inbetweener on a series of animated children's shows. It was there that he met Takahata, whose career trajectory closely followed that of Miyazaki. At Toei Doga, Miyazaki became active in the union, rising to be its head. Miyazaki progressed to writing and animating for feature films, most notably on the Takahata-directed *Horus: Prince of the Sun* (1968), which was created as a collaboration among its creative staff at a time of labour unrest in the studio. Takahata and Miyazaki left Toei for Nippon Animation, where Miyazaki began to direct projects initiated by others – first with TV production such as *Future Boy Conan* (1978) and then with feature-length films, such as *Lupin III: The Castle of Cagliostro* (1979). Based on the success of a *manga* (graphic novel) that Miyazaki created, the animator adapted his own work to the screen in the "eco-fantasy" feature *Nausicaä of the Valley of the Wind* (1984). *Nausicaä* was so successful commercially that Miyazaki and Takahata were able to persuade the manga publisher Tokuma to support the founding of Studio Ghibli.

Japanese animation or *animé*, crossing various media from television, direct-to-video and cinema, has more than any other factor reversed the fortunes of a Japanese film industry, which had been in an economic decline since the 1960s. Studio Ghibli is an exception to much of the animation produced in Japan, in that it is aimed neither exclusively at the hard core *animé otaku* (fanatical fans), nor is it part of a kiddie-oriented marketing franchise, like *Sailor Moon* or *Hello Kitty*, where the brand is marketed across media platforms and as toys, clothing and other products.[3] Instead, Studio Ghibli films follow a strategy the former Ghibli head, Toru Hara, once called a "3H" approach – High Cost, High Risk and High Return.[4] What this means is a quality product, based more on the auteurial insights of Miyazaki and Takahata than on audience research and marketing experts.

Miyazaki's films stand on their own as artistic experiences directed towards a broad demographic, eschewing the focus on a youth audience or ancillary product tie-ins. The director's works are a bundle of contradictions. Although intensely personal, his films also draw on a broad range of world culture, evident in the Tenniel homage in the design of Yubaba in *Spirited Away*, the use of the Paris Commune anthem "Les Temps des cerises" in *Porco Rosso* (1992), the tribute to Winsor McCay and John Ford through the form of characters and environment in *Laputa: City in the Sky* (1986), or the Swedish-inspired location of *Kiki's Delivery Service* (1989). While Miyazaki's stories increasingly are deeply imbedded in Japanese myth and culture (despite nods to such authors as Jonathan Swift and complaints by Japanese critics that the director's work is Eurocentric[5]), his films have developed a huge following among all classes and age groups internationally.

Miyazaki meets his acclaim with reticence. After the success of *Kiki's Delivery Service*, the director wanted to close Studio Ghibli because he was afraid that it might lose its touch, and was only persuaded to stay in order to train the next generation of animators.[6] A later attempt to retire and turn direction over to a younger protégé, Yoshifumi Kondô, failed with Kondô's tragic death. This resulted in Miyazaki returning to direct the forthcoming *Howl's Moving Castle*.

Hayao Miyazaki exercises a high level of control and has been known not only to write and direct, but to personally draw up to seventy percent of the frames of his movies.[7] Miyazaki's animation is refined, yet typically Japanese in its style. As David Kehr has pointed out, *animé* films "hang on to the jerky, discontinuous movements that have characterized the earliest work in the field." While this can be explained in part in economic terms or by reference to an earlier tradition of *ukiyo-e* (woodblock prints) where motion was conveyed by still drawings, others like Kehr point out that "Japanese animators are more interested in capturing single expressive gestures, or in evoking a particular mood through the careful use of color."[8] In contrast to this pared-down and suggestive use of motion, Miyazaki places great emphasis on highly detailed and evocative backgrounds. According to the filmmaker, "the background in anime isn't an afterthought. It's an essential element."[9] American animation typically emphasizes its characters as autonomous, self-motivated entities through the use of the detailed movement inherent in personality animation. In Miyazaki's work (as with much *animé*), the emphasis is on significant gestures and poses in the context of detailed backgrounds. This means that the director's interest in his characters is more in relation to their physical environment and society. Miyazaki's characters always exist in context.

Never following fashion, Miyazaki often created *animé* that contrasted with what others in the industry were doing at the time. For example, the science-fiction *Nausicaä of the Valley of the Wind* used organic imagery in a period when *animé* features were dominated by the high-tech look of *mecha-animé.* After what Jim Hoberman has called the "apocalyptic pan-theism" of *Nausicaä*,[10] the filmmaker went on to base his reputation on the success of childhood parables and then turned to overtly political subjects. Miyazaki's films take many forms, from the simple, child-oriented tales in *My Neighbor Totoro* and *Kiki's Delivery Service*, to the historical epics of the Muromachi era or early fascist Italy portrayed in *Princess Mononoke* and *Porco Rosso*, from the anti-war sentiments and "parallel universe" 19th century Wales of *Laputa: Castle in the Sky* to the toxic futuristic wasteland of *Nausicaä of the Valley of the Wind*. Despite their diversity, these films consistently display qualities of "Miyazakiness" that add up to a consistent vision, not only of the animation medium, but of the world.

One Miyazaki hallmark is his fondness for flying sequences, with an emphasis on the sense of freedom and liberation that flying gives. A life-long aviation buff, Miyazaki creates fanciful model airplanes in his spare time. In *Porco Rosso*, even a gunfight between air pirates and the pilot hero is shown as exhilarating and not perceived as frightening even by the little schoolgirls caught in the crossfire. Such sequences inform almost all Miyazaki films, from the flight that Satsuki and Mei enjoy with the Big Totoro and the Catbus in *My Neighbour Totoro* to pirate Dora's flappers in *Laputa: The Castle in the Sky*. Even Miyazaki's preview done for *Little Nemo* (a project later realized by American director Bill Hurtz) fea-tures this most characteristic action in a night flight tribute to cartoonist Winsor McCay's "Dreams of a Rarebit Fiend."

Miyazaki's films center on characters around the age of today's tech-nologically savvy Japanese *animé otaku* demographic, which is mostly late childhood or early adulthood. These are people in the process of leav-ing childhood to develop independent lives. This is a stage that Miyazaki characterizes as "tragic" because all children are "born with infinite pos-sibilities, and really the process of childhood is about cutting off many of those possibilities."[11] Miyazaki's protagonists are caught between fam-ily ties and a new relationship with the outside world beyond their fam-ily unit. While sometimes this change is seen as part of the passage to adulthood, as in Kiki's honouring of the witch tradition by moving from home, it is more frequently the result of a tragedy – the mother of Satsui and Mei is a tuberculosis patient at a remote hospital in *My Neighbor Totoro*, Ashitaka in *Princess Mononoke* leaves his native village because of a fatal illness, while Chihiro's parents are transformed into pigs in *Spirited Away*.

There is another cusp or transition point that interests Miyazaki. The filmmaker's life spanned the period of the older traditions of Imperial Japan and those of post-war, industrialized democratic Japan. *My Neighbour Totoro* is set in the 1950s "economic miracle" period, just outside of Tokyo. The rural area in which the story is located is now the Tokorozawa suburb of Tokyo where Miyazaki lives, and the farms depicted in the film are now suburban housing and shopping centres. As the film progresses, we see more and more evidence of the introduction of urbanization, as gradually we see buses, then trains, then hydro-electric towers intruding into the rural landscape. This is in part autobiographical, as Miyazaki has been involved in preserving the few natural areas of this suburb. But it also reflects Miyazaki's larger concern about the interaction of nature and industrialized society, as well as the relationship between a traditional, spiritually-oriented culture and a modern scientific, industrialized one. Many of his films are situated at historical turning points where nature-based civilizations become industrialized ones. *Princess Mononoke* is set in the period when firearms technology transformed warfare in Japan, while *Laputa* takes place late in the European Industrial Revolution.

While not a practitioner of religion, Miyazaki reflects on the passing of humanity's relationship with nature, and with the spiritual values embodied in the natural environment but overlooked by science. These values are often represented by nature spirits such as the Shishigami of *Princess Mononoke*, the Totoros of *My Neighbour Totoro* or the entire panoply of deities in *Spirited Away*. Children and young adults are portrayed as being in the interstitial zone between nature and urban society, or between spirituality and science. Five-year-old Mei, for example, is the closest to the nature spirits in *My Neighbour Totoro*, as she is the one who first discovers and befriends the Totoros that adults like her father cannot see. Princess Nausicaä reconciles humanity with nature in the remains of a world destroyed by a technological apocalypse. San, a human adopted by forest gods in *Princess Mononoke*, rejects humanity, yet accepts Ashitaka and reaches an accommodation with technological civilization. Through such characters, Miyazaki critically examines some of the basic myths and beliefs of Japan, and often deliberately violates cultural conventions. In many of his films, he questions the value of the emphasis on high technology that is so prevalent in contemporary Japanese culture and shows the importance of maintaining links to nature. And, he does this with female protagonists.

Women, particularly younger women, have a privileged position in regard to nature in Miyazaki's work, although not an exclusive one. Yet, Miyazaki doesn't seem to present a Manichean "nature good/industrialization bad" or gender-biased attitude towards this – he doesn't deal in simple oppositions. For example, the robots in *Laputa* are weapons of mass destruction, yet also tend a natural environment. Lady Eboshi, ruler of a technological community in *Princess Mononoke*, ravages nature and destroys the old gods, yet establishes the egalitarian Irontown which benefits the outcasts of society. Miyazaki appears to see both sides in a universe where simplistic distinctions between moral opposites is impossible. Miyazaki's comment about *Spirited Away* could apply to any of his films: "this story is not a showdown between right and wrong, but one where the heroine is thrown into a place where good and bad dwell together and where she will experience the world."[12]

NOTES

1. Cited in Janet Maslin, "Waging a Mythic Battle to Preserve a Pristine Forest," *The New York Times*. 27 September 1999, Sec. E, p. 1; http://nausicaa.net/miyazaki/miyazaki/impact.html; Dave Kehr, "At the Movies," *The New York Times*. 20 September 2002, Sec. E Part 1, p. 6; Andrew O'Hehir, "Spirited Away," *Salon*. Wednesday 25 September 2002.
2. Andrew Osmond, "Anime Magic," *Sight and Sound*, v. 11, no. 11 (November 2001): 24.
3. This is not to say that no such marketing of Studio Ghibli property exists. In Japan and other locales, there is a brisk trade in such things as Totoro toys, books based on Studio Ghibli films, DVDs, etc. But these are desirable byproducts of Miyazaki films, rather than symptomatic of an integrated marketing strategy that preceded the films. They pale by comparison to other marketing efforts. For example, Sanrio's *Hello Kitty* began as an image on a plastic coin purse, but now exists as a TV program, comic books, audio recordings, DVDs and videotapes, as a Sega video game and in two theme parks in Japan. The character also is used to market a wide variety of products (many sold in a chain of dedicated "Hello Kitty" stores) from children's toys, electronics, cosmetics, clothing and fashion accessories to non-child-oriented products like *Hello Kitty* appliances, laptop computers, feminine hygiene products, toilet paper and vibrators.
4. Osmond: 25.
5. Mitsuyo Wada-Marciano, email to the author, 19 June 2004.
6. Yuri Momo, "Studio Ghibli blocking out new approach to business," *Nikkei Weekly*. 3 February 2003.
7. David Chute, "Organic Machine: The World of Hayao Miyazaki," *Film Comment*. v. 34 no. 6 (November/December 1998): 62.

8. Dave Kehr, "Anime, Japanese Cinema's Second Golden Age," *The New York Times* (20 January 2002), Section 2: 22.

9. Hayao Miyazaki, quoted in Richard Corliss, "Amazing Anime," *Time*. v. 154 (22 November 1999): 70.

10. Jim Hoberman, "Metaphysical Therapy," *The Village Voice*. (2 November 1999): 133.

11. Hayao Miyazaki, quoted in Elisabeth Vincentelli, "For a Japanese Animator, Grown-up Messages Are Kid Stuff," *The Village Voice*. (2 November 1999): 144.

12. Miyazaki, quoted in David Pilling, "Japan's Cartoon Hero," *The Financial Times*. (23–24 February 2002): 7.

CHAPTER 20

Robert Breer

Dadanimator (2004)

by George Griffin

THE ARC OF ROBERT Breer's creative life is so anchored in the fine art world of painting, sculpture and avant-garde film that to savor it fresh again, at this festival, is to be reminded of the deeply complex lineage all animators share. Having completed his latest film in 2003, 50 years after his first, Breer continues to demonstrate and embody the vitality of experimental animation, even as that term undergoes reappraisal.

Born in 1926, Breer grew up building model airplanes and drawing cartoons in Detroit where his father was one of the principal engineers at Chrysler, chiefly responsible for introducing aerodynamics to automobile design. As an undergraduate art major at Stanford he was attacked for painting like Mondrian, instead of following the social realism of his teachers. In 1949, Breer came to Paris and studied on the G.I. Bill at the studio of Ossip Zadkine. He immersed himself in the hard-edged abstraction of Neo-Plasticism, producing and exhibiting elegant canvases of flat, angular shapes which seem in retrospect ready to slip into motion. He began a series of film experiments in 1952, and in 1955, made "Image Par Images," the first fine art edition flipbook for the influential Le Mouvement exhibit, the first show of kinetic art (which included Duchamp, Calder and Tinguely, among others). By 1956, Breer had exclusively moved to

DOI: 10.1201/9781003288022-21

("backed into," as he says) filmmaking and, upon relocating to New York in 1959, broadened his work to include kinetic sculpture and mutoscopes. The shift to animation involved a radical reinvention of accepted practice. Instead of merely dissecting and rearranging his formal designs as a temporal collage, Breer intervenes during shooting and editing – spontaneous, playful actions resembling jazz improvisation. There is a pervasive feeling of randomness colliding with order; structures and relationships appear and recede slyly, subverting expectation. Design, like his sense of timing, becomes compressed, a shorthand. Challenging the cinematic mandate for narrative continuity, Breer creates a cinema of discontinuous, saccadic angularity, formal yet brimming with personal reference and wit.

Like Emile Cohl (the caricaturist who reverted to stick-figures), whom he consciously mimes in LMNO (1978), Breer undergoes a kind of regression from the established elegance of painting to the more primitive, intimate gesture of the sketch, often with blunt markers and crayons on index cards. Like his friend Jean Arp, who famously tore up his canvas and flung the pieces on the floor to discover a more satisfying design, Breer often employs chance procedures in sequencing to create a wide range of visual experience – from collisions of disparate sequential themes to suggestions of simultaneity.

It is impossible to see Breer's films without being reminded of the art world movements and ideas that influenced him: Dada's anarchy, Abstract Expressionism's action, Pop's appropriation of fun, Minimalism's severity. Yet, this heady mix is often tossed up with snatches of cartooning as children, rats, pocket knives, cats and nudes tumble through the timescape. How do we interpret these icons? Are they aspects of a personal narrative, breathing the complications of familial life and love? Symbols of a footloose nation teetering nonchalantly between war and peace? Illustrations of what art critic Harold Rosenberg called the "anxious object"? Or, as William Carlos Williams put it, "no ideas but in things"?

Breer's "things" take on a loaded intensity in *Recreation* (1956) which features a fragmentary voice-over text delivered in an affectless monotone which may or may not be a description of the cascade of images to follow. The mechanical tempo of the voice, the propulsive staccato of the individual, unrelated frames yields a vision of hallucinatory intensity: the viewer struggles to impose order and meaning, only to be tripped up by the sudden appearance of a toy chicken. Unlike *Form Phases IV* (1954), the series of spatial games which are clearly extensions of Breer's painting concerns, *Recreation* represents his effort to construct a stacked collage in time, a series of "unrelationships," similar to the mutoscopes and wall-mounted flipcard constructions to come. As further evidence of symbiosis between filmic image and object, Breer enlarged every frame to 35 mm and mounted them between sheets of Plexiglas to "recreate" a composite window for installation.

The other film from the 1950s, *A Man and His Dog Out for Air* (1957), composed of squiggly ink lines that cavort on a white field, is dedicated to his young daughter. It takes the form of a busy, abstract doodle which ultimately resolves into its eponymous scene, redolent of Calder's circus.

Using innocent names like "creepy," "rug," or "float," Breer has, since the 1960s, created kinetic sculpture in a dazzling array of scale and multiplicity. Designed to resemble overturned teacups, crumpled sheeting, or other vaguely utilitarian detritus, they meander automatically at a snail's pace, altering direction when obstructed. In all of Breer's constructions, we see both a keen attention to engineering, materials, and craft, like other minimalist and serial sculpture in vogue at the time. But Breer's work tends toward the unexpected, the parodic – playfully out of control. The date films, like 69 and 70 on the program, are elegantly designed extensions of the sculpture: precise, hard-edged, repetitive, formalist studies in line and shadow, intended for a gallery space inhabited by floats.

Sound plays a critical role in Breer's work: largely absent, intruding casually at curious moments, often imitating machinery, random ambience, snatches of conversation or radio. The tracks owe much to John Cage in their refusal to organize the visuals into a dramatic narrative. *Fist Fight* (1964) is one of the few examples of continuous music which might shape the animation. Not only does Breer subvert the music of Stockhausen (itself already the epitome of "difficult") by using a muffled microphone and including the audience's extraneous post-concert chatter, he plays Satie-like tricks by offering one false start and climax after another.

The other anomalous example is the music video *Blue Monday* (1988), a commercial collaboration with Weimaraner artist William Wegman for the techno group New Order, in which the musicians take delight in thumbing through Breer's flipbooks.

During the 1970s and 80s, as Breer's work becomes more complex in technique and personal associations, it also seems to achieve the level of poetry. He has in a sense found a groove: an effortless language balancing mimesis and abstraction, photography and drawing, object and image, sexual desire and the domesticity of family life. Home movies loosely rotoscoped in crayon collide with mythic American icons of baseball, airplanes, telephones and, well, take your pick. The mysterious objects of Recreation, the eccentric rhythms of perception, the witty scribbles, all have now taken on the familiarity of streetcorner argot, graffiti for the mind, and while still open to multiple interpretations, one feels able to speak more of content and meaning than mere form.

To call Breer an experimental animator correctly places him in the family of Richter, Fischinger and Lye. Yet regardless of the tools we use, all animators can learn from Breer's gift: his mischievous spirit of inquiry, neither heavy nor aerodynamic, which conveys delight in discovering simple truths.

CHAPTER 21

Transforming Realities

The Work of Co Hoedeman (2004)

by Barry Doyle

I N ADULTHOOD WE SOMETIMES forget the power of fairy tales. Their transformative magic allows a metaphorical retelling of some fundamental conditions that we all face. This transformative magic is a door that opens to other realities or reinterpretations of some common reality. Most fairy tales deal with death, aging, the limits of our existence and creative ways to get around those limits. Pretty heady stuff for tales that are supposedly aimed at children. But then, we should trust kids in terms of dealing with these issues and reinterpreting reality in a creative way. We should remember that fairy tales are just as much for adults as for kids; perhaps intended even more for adults than we allow. The audience for fairy tales is broad, as is the audience for animation. Similarly, we often hear animation being dismissed as kids' stuff, juvenilia, too popular for the critical eye. However, there is so much animation deserving of critical discussion, even though it appears to be aimed at children. Co Hoedeman makes films that fit the category: transformed realities, creative, deal with death and aging, and appear as though they're intended only for children. Hoedeman, a former National Film Board animator for close to forty years, makes films that have been constantly categorized as "children's films." He has won some 80 awards for his work, the most famous (at least on this side of the Atlantic), but not necessarily the most personally important, being an Oscar for his 1977 film, *The Sand Castle*.

CREATIVITY

Creativity and creative solutions are the driving forces in the film *Tchou-Tchou* (1972). A village of vibrantly coloured wood blocks is inhabited by a boy and girl (as well as a ladybug, caterpillar and bird) built from the same material as their surroundings. They play hopscotch and a dragon appears, forcing the boy and girl to hide in a mini fortress that magically assembles itself. The dragon passes and they go back to playing games. The dragon returns and the boy tries to chase it off by throwing blocks at it, but the dragon becomes enraged and destroys the block structures, leaving wreckage throughout the village. The girl, although slightly hurt from the dragon's outburst, helps the boy make a sign to point the dragon away. The dragon appears again and follows the sign, only to be frustrated by another sign that points in the opposite direction; the dragon, confused and angered by this game, destroys the sign. After nightfall, the boy and girl find the sleeping dragon and insert wheels into the body of the wood block dragon: a perfect example of transforming their reality. Dawn comes and the dragon awakes, transformed into a train (thus the title). The boy and girl, having used their creative and fantastical energies, enjoy a ride on the dragon train. Here we have evil transformed to good, fear to fun, insecurity to safety. In a final whimsical touch, the bird, ladybug and caterpillar board the train as it rides through the village. Every scene in this film employs the creative impulse to change the limits of the characters: the mini fortress assembling itself; the magical signs appearing; and the playful altering of the dragon.

A wonderfully creative film, *The Sand Castle* (1977) is set in the shifting landscape of a desert. A sand creature that roughly resembles a human comes up from under the dunes. This initial sand creature forms a family of other varied creatures and, in turn, the created become creators of other beings. The first creature draws a diagram and gestures to his progeny. Just as they have constructed themselves, they build several sand structures within a walled area. Each creature performs specific tasks: torso-less and leg-less sandmen act as plows; a goose-like creature regurgitates piles of sand where needed; sandstars smooth surfaces; and a tripod creature builds paths. The creatures celebrate the completion of their small village with a dance, which is interrupted by a sandstorm that partially destroys their outpost in the desert.

This cast of sand (a basic element in kids' lives) creatures provokes the viewer to question the process of creativity. The process follows a creator (the initial sand creature) creating other creators, who create more creators, who create the sand structures. Behind the whole process is the god within the machine: the animator as creator. But Hoedeman doesn't seem to be saying, "look at how clever I am." He is really pointing out the creative impulses in us all, and our ability to transform reality. Hoedeman animates the subjects in this film as a child would animate scenarios in the sandbox or at the beach. He is telling us that creativity is not the film animators' domain, but available and fundamental to all of us.

DEATH, AGING AND THE LIMITS OF EXISTENCE

Charles and Francois (1988) is a film of adulthood and childhood, youth and aging, death and existence. It opens with Charles (the grandfather) and Francois (the grandson) rounding up a chicken. Charles cuts the head off the chicken while Francois looks on in shock. In the next scene, Charles complains of being "too old to chase butterflies." Francois suggests a fantastical game that involves no running, in which grandfather and grandson swap heads. They see each other's desires, fears, dreams, sadness and hopes. Then Francois grows older, leaves home, gets married, and grandfather and grandson drift apart. Francois and Charles see a puppet play that is acted out by Francois's wife. In the play, the two characters are Charles and Francois; they act out their differences, loneliness, longings. The character playing Francois asks the character playing Charles, "Call me your wonderboy." Charles responds by saying: "Words like that have a hold on me. Childhood sticks in my throat." It's as though Charles can't let go of childhood, but it's suffocating him at the same time.

The film tackles large issues: How do we grow (old)? How do we live? If there is an afterlife, then what is it like? Do we keep loving after we're dead? These themes are apparently for adults, and yet, childhood is an integral part of understanding death and aging. What four-year-old doesn't ask about death (if not out loud, then to themselves), or what happens to us as we age? The film opens with death (Francois witnessing the slaughter of the chicken) and closes with death (Charles's lonely walk down the path to the house where he will die). In between we get a meditation on aging:

a young man catching up on his grandfather, the mental chasm of age difference narrowing with each year. The questions about death in childhood (where do we go when we die?) become similar in old age: Charles asks: "Do we keep loving this earth when we die?" This question reflects the concern about the limits of existence. Where do we end? When does death begin? The film doesn't answer the questions – nor should it – but poses them in a creative, stylized way.

Four Seasons in the Life of Ludovic (2002) gathers the four Ludovic films together. Ludovic, a plush bear figure, is a character that speaks an internal monologue. In the films, Ludovic seemingly reflects the life of a three or four year-old. Ludovic deals with death in *Visiting Grandpa* by interacting with his grandmother's magical portrait, which transforms her into a benign ghost. Initially, Ludovic isn't quite sure what happened to his grandmother. None of the adult characters "tell" him what happened, but Ludovic does the math. After touching and smelling her shawl – out of sight of his grandfather, of course – he reaches to take a candy but reminds himself he isn't allowed. However, grandmother gives a nod from her portrait and Ludovic takes the candy. Later, when grandfather is outside having a nap, Ludovic dances with his grandmother's ghost in a touching scene of longing, transformation and possible acceptance. The grandfather witnesses Ludovic's dance but doesn't interrupt it. Ludovic, through the dance, is searching for a creative way to get around the limits of our existence; to reach across the chasm between life and death and start a process of healing. Perhaps the grandfather learns something from Ludovic: the final scene shows the grandfather and the ghost of the grandmother dancing.

If we turn to fairy tales to find meaning, then we should turn to Hoedeman's films as well. They offer a transformative effect in terms of seeing reality anew. There are the immense creative impulses of the characters within the films and Hoedeman's own creative energy propelling the stories. Other films not mentioned earlier – like *Garden of Ecos* (1996) and *The Sniffing Bear* (1992) – deal with death and the limits of existence. Others – like *Odd Ball* (1969), *Matrioska* (1970), *Masquerade* (1984) and *Ludovic: Magic in the Air* (2002) – explore creative ways to push our limits. On the surface, the solutions Hoedeman provides may seem facile, but the blunt realities of everyday life – death, aging, our limits – often call for apparently simple approaches: imagination, magic and creativity from the vast mind of a child.

CHAPTER 22

Animating Pee-wee's Playhouse (2005)

by Chris Robinson

A LTHOUGH I WAS 19 years old when *Pee-wee Herman's Playhouse* (which aired from 1986 to 1991) first came on TV, I was a fairly devoted follower of the kid's show. A few years earlier I'd worked at the Airport Drive-In. We got to see movies for free. *Pee-wee's Big Adventure* played during the summer of 1985. I must have seen the film about 15 times. For a teenager, Pee-wee was a strange but familiar character: a half-man, half-boy with the mind of a child, but the tongue of an adult. In a way, he was reflective of that so-called 'me' generation of the 1980s. Pee-wee was a single-minded, selfish little boy obsessed with materialism.

Pee-wee Herman's Playhouse was/is different from anything else on TV. Pee-wee (Paul Reubens) lived in this fantastic playhouse. It was filled with an assortment of talking toys, creatures, robots and furniture. Each day Pee-wee was visited by a mélange of strange friends like the magical genie, Jambi, Reba the mail lady, the crusty Captain Carl (Phil Hartman), the lavish Miss Yvonne, Cowboy Curtis (Laurence Fishburne) and, of course, the King of Cartoons. The show reached kids and adults because it encouraged all of us to find that rich imagination within us. Through Pee-wee, the adult characters like Reba, Captain Carl, Miss Yvonne and Cowboy Curtis, embraced that inner child.

DOI: 10.1201/9781003288022-23

145

Unlike so much garbage manufactured for children by sanctimonious adults, *Pee-wee Herman's Playhouse* was a no-holds-barred celebration of the beautiful chaos of childhood. Pee-wee continually encouraged kids to let loose and enjoy themselves, even if this meant jumping or running around the house, screaming the "secret word," or just being plain silly. And yet underneath it all, Pee-wee was teaching kids to cook, to read and to learn about different cultures; in short, Pee-wee taught kids to embrace every crumb of life and to get off their asses and be imaginative, inquisitive, naughty, hyper and curious: like real kids are supposed to be.

Complementing the rich scenarios and characters was a wide array of striking set designs and multi-media segments. The design of the show was easily the most striking and imaginative of any television show. Fusing 50s and 60s kitsch with the raw "scribblings" of graphic artist Gary Panter, the show's camp tone went in the face of most shows and, in doing so, embodied, a punk spirit (Panter was one of a number of "cutting edge" artists who worked on the show). Accompanying the live-action scenes were vintage educational films, old cartoons, puppets and a supply of innovative animated sequences by noted animators like Dave Daniels, Nick Park, Richard Goeslowski and Craig Bartlett.

Critics and adults loved and hated the show for its subtle play on sexuality (and not-so-subtle – as when Miss Yvonne gets off on the rocking horse) and its multicultural characters. In the white as snow world of Reagan's America, *Pee-wee Herman's Playhouse* was a defiant "scream real loud" against an increasingly stifling and politically correct society.

PAUL REUBENS ON PEE-WEE

Interviewed by Chris Robinson

Before you did Pee-wee's Playhouse, you made the film with Tim Burton, but even before that you did a theatre production, The Pee-wee Herman Show. Both of these were more adult in nature. Was it difficult to make the transition to doing a kid's show? Were you surprised when CBS approached you?

Paul Reubens: The stage show was conceived as an homage to kids shows of the 50s and 60s. I always wanted something that kids and grown-ups could both enjoy. So I tried to make it speak to both groups. We did matinee performances of the so-called "adult" version for kids. My theory was if there was a double entendre it would go over the kid's heads. On the other hand, if a child understood it, then that would be based on them having some knowledge that we didn't teach them. I felt like originally we took a kid's show and added some adult elements. In *Pee-wee's Big Adventure* there was some similar thinking as far as having appeal to both kids and adults. The film is rated PG but I never viewed it as a kid's movie. CBS approached me at the premiere of *Big Adventure* to do an animated *Pee-wee* show. My preference was to do a live-action program. It was conceived as a kids show that adults would be watching too.

Did you ever have problems with the network? Did they ever want you to censor anything? Also, on average, how long did it take to make an episode?

PR: It took about a week to do each episode. Judy Price, who was the head of children's programming at CBS, told me to do whatever I wanted. I'm still amazed that they not only said that, but they totally lived up to it! The very first note I received said, "you can't stick pencils in a potato." Check out episode one, there I am sticking a potato with a pencil. I think in five years they gave us a total of five notes. There's an episode that includes Pee-wee in the bathroom and off-camera you can hear him peeing. CBS asked that I put a little musical score over it and lower the volume of the trickle. I did what they asked. It was supposed to be taken off for the DVD release but someone made a mistake, and it remains. It will be gone for the special edition with all the bonus materials. One other change that was made after an episode aired was in the "Fire in the Playhouse" episode. Miss Yvonne tells the fireman "I have a smoke detector in my bedroom, over the bed." The network received a letter about it. One letter. When the episode re-aired, we dubbed her saying "I have a smoke detector in my kitchen, over the sink." It was put back to her bedroom in the DVD. CBS was incredible – they were completely honorable and wonderful to work with. I doubt I'll ever have another situation like that again.

How did Gary Panter become involved in the show?

PR: Gary's work was all over Los Angeles. He did posters for some of the big punk bands, and he had a cartoon in The L.A. Weekly. I kept seeing stuff of his and was a fan. When I decided to do the show, I contacted him and asked if he'd come see my short Pee-wee stuff at The Groundlings, the improvisational group I was in. Afterwards, I asked him if he'd design a poster for a full-length Pee-wee show and he said, "okay, but I'd like to design the sets and puppets too." They don't get any more brilliant than Gary Panter. I would work with him on anything I ever do. We're working on an animated Pee-wee show and a Playhouse movie script together. He has unbelievable projects of his own as well as his light shows and painting career.

Why did you decide to use animation on the show?

PR: I was influenced by *Captain Kangaroo, Mickey Mouse Club, Howdy Doody* and local cartoon shows with a live action host. I liked the idea of mixing animation with live action. At the time, Saturday morning kids' television was entirely animated – there were no live people on the national level. The animation was mostly conceived during the script-writing phase. We would suggest what any given sequence was supposed to be and then Prudence Fenton (animation producer) and I would discuss it in way more detail. We'd usually storyboard after that and then have another discussion and make changes. Prudence had a lot of freedom in figuring out who she wanted to execute the ideas. She's tapped into so many people and has an incredible knack for putting the perfect person with the right idea.

There seemed to be less animation in the later years (although you did add "El Hombre"). Was this a budget issue, or had I just lost my marbles after watching 45 episodes in a few weeks?

PR: Some shows had more animation than others, but budget certainly played a part in the last two seasons.
I hear that you plan to bring Pee-wee back.

PR: There are two Pee-wee movie scripts. One, *The Pee-wee Herman Story*, is what I call the dark Pee-wee movie. It's about fame and how it doesn't agree with Pee-wee very well. Valley of the Dolls Pee-wee. The second script is a movie version of *Pee-wee Herman's Playhouse*, an epic adventure story originally written by me and Gary Panter. The DVD release was very successful and I am now working on the special material for the deluxe version. I think it's possible that the series could continue, there have been some recent discussions about it but nothing to report yet.

CHAPTER 23

Bob Clampett at Warner Bros. (2006)

by Mark Langer

OB CLAMPETT'S CAREER IN animation spanned decades, but arguably his most creative period occurred when he directed at Warner Bros. Clampett was born in San Diego, but his family moved to Hollywood when he was quite young. He grew up by the Chaplin Studio. His boyhood interest in puppetry and movies was encouraged by his mother, who helped him make hand puppets to put on shows for the neighborhood. Clampett was also an enthusiastic cartoonist, and managed to get his work published in local papers while still in his teens. Employment at the *Los Angeles Examiner* and studies at the Otis Art Institute gave the young artist a solid grounding. Clampett also manufactured Mickey Mouse dolls with his aunt, in cooperation with the Disney studio. As a result of this, Clampett was able to tour Disney's facilities to see how animated films were made.

After leaving high school, Clampett approached Leon Schlesinger, head of Pacific Art and Title. Schlesinger was producing cartoons made by former Disneyites Hugh Harman and Rudy Ising for release by Warner Bros. The young artist was hired and put to work on the first "Merrie Melodies" cartoon. Some time after Harman and Ising left Schlesinger, a new unit headed by Tex Avery was set up to produce cartoons in a decrepit wooden building on the Warner Bros. lot that the animators dubbed "Termite

DOI: 10.1201/9781003288022-24

Terrace." Clampett was assigned to this, as were later WB luminaries like Chuck Jones. While in Avery's unit, Clampett worked on the first Daffy Duck cartoon, *Porky's Duck Hunt* (1937). At night, as an independent venture, Clampett also worked on a test reel for a projected series "John Carter on Mars" which was based on the character by Tarzan creator Edgar Rice Burroughs. The project foundered when MGM, which was to fund it, opted for a Tarzan series instead. When Clampett was promised a production unit of his own in the near future by Leon Schlesinger, he opted to remain with Warner Bros. After working under veteran Disney animator Ub Iwerks on a couple of productions, Clampett was promoted to director in 1937.

Of the "big five" Warner Bros. animation directors (Tex Avery, Chuck Jones, Friz Freleng, Frank Tashlin and Bob Clampett), Clampett is perhaps the least known and appreciated. This is regrettable, although not surprising. Many Warner Bros. animation directors were influenced by Disney in depicting psychologically coherent characters. For example, Chuck Jones' Bugs Bunny or Daffy Duck would frequently be in psychological conflict, either with each other, or with characters like Elmer Fudd. Jones' approach to his characters leaned heavily upon establishing sympathy between them and the audience. Jones' Daffy Duck has touches of pathos. His Daffy is basically a supporting actor in a starring role – somehow never quite up to the demands of the part, but unstinting in his efforts. Daffy's grasp always exceeds his reach, but he perceives his shortcomings in terms of social injustice – the ultimate self-rationalizer pitted against a harsh world in which other characters, such as Bugs Bunny, effortlessly prevail. Richard Corliss has pointed out a scene from Jones' *Rabbit Seasoning* (1952) where Daffy, hiding with Bugs in a burrow, is asked to stick his head up to see if Elmer is near. When Daffy does, he is shot in the face and drops back into the burrow, croaking "Still lurking about!" States Corliss: "The voice is broken, but maniacally chipper, defeated but indomitable." Similarly, Jones' Bugs Bunny represented the kind of character that audiences aspired to be, and whose actions were morally based. Jones' Bugs tended to be innocently conducting his life before the intrusion of some hostile force (most often in the person of Elmer) forces him to take defensive, just and retaliatory action. The Jones interpretation of these characters was consistent with the conventions of stardom, and suitable for today's character franchising which has helped to canonize these portrayals. This moral and psychological approach, taken up by other Warner's animators, like Friz Freleng or Robert McKimson became the standard version of Warner Bros. characters.

Clampett took a different approach. Daffy was developed by Warner Bros. director Tex Avery and writer Ben "Bugs" Hardaway as a foil to Porky Pig, and the same creators made Bugs Bunny (named after Hardaway) in the same mould. Not completely realized personalities, the early Daffy and Bugs were simply bundles of comic attributes in the same spirit as a later character written by Hardaway – Woody Woodpecker, who shared their manic "hoo-hooing" and frantic movements. While Avery did alter Bugs and Daffy in a manner that initiated the later Jones psychological refinements, Clampett remained truer to the characters' origins. In the case of Bugs Bunny, Clampett rarely showed the character in a positive light. While Jones' rabbit is provoked into action (typically stating after a provocation "Of course you realize this means war."), in such films as *Wabbit Twouble* (1941), Clampett's Bugs initiates conflict with a persecuted Elmer who only wants a "weel good west." In *Tortoise Wins by a Hare* (1943), a vengeful and stupid Bugs is repeatedly outwitted by Cecil the Turtle. Such contrasts apply to most other characters as well. Clampett's Tweety (a character the director created) in *Gruesome Twosome* (1945) stands in contrast to the passive innocent later portrayed by other directors and is a vicious participant in mayhem, slapping a bee around before slipping it into the horse suit containing the two feline antagonists, and later bashing the dog Spike over the head with a bone.

While Clampett claimed to be concerned with the personalities of his starring characters, it was secondary to other preoccupations. When characters speak to the audience in Jones' films, it often is to elicit sympathy. When Clampett's characters talk to the audience, it is to denaturalize the narrative by rupturing the diegesis. For example, in *Wabbit Twouble*, Bugs addresses the viewers with lines like "I do this to him all the way through the picture" or "Funny situation, ain't it?" In *Gruesome Twosome*, when a female cat is left alone on screen, puckered up for a kiss, a dog pops up out of nowhere and announces "Ladies and Gentlemen, I don't belong in this picture. But I can't pass up a chance like this!"

Clampett's films portray a world of illogical metamorphosis and emotional extremes. In the case of Daffy, his malleable mallard is a character in constant plastic variation, from the inflatable iron lung victim of *The Daffy Doc* (1938), to the elastic-legged runner in *Baby Bottleneck* (1946), and the startled zoot-suited scat singer who turns briefly into a giant eye in

Book Revue (1946). The integrity of characters like Daffy was less important to Clampett than taking recognizable cultural icons and myths and
restating them in hallucinatory form, as exemplified by Daffy's frenetic
imitation of Danny Kaye, careening among caricatures of big band personalities while playing out a jitterbug variation of *Little Red Riding Hood*
in *Book Revue*, or Daffy as Duck Twacy, fending off wildly exaggerated
Chester Gouldish villains with names like Pickle Puss and Neon Noodle
in *The Great Piggy Bank Robbery*(1946). Clampett's Daffy is less a psychological figure than a rubberized absurdist participant and commentator
on the cliches of contemporary culture.

It is this emphasis on contemporary culture that obscures much of the
humour in Clampett films. They are chock-a-block with references to
comic books, novels, advertising slogans, radio and movie stars, and lyrics of songs, that can render them indecipherable at times. While *Coal
Black and de Sebben Dwarfs* (1943) is superficially a racist re-reading of
the traditional fairy tale, this text acts simply as a framework for a dense
series of references including *Citizen Kane*'s Rosebud, Jimmy Durante,
Cab Calloway, the wartime rationing of consumer goods such as tires
and sugar, and then-popular songs (such as "Chattanooga Choo-Choo,"
"Blues In the Night," and "Old Man Mose"). *Kitty Kornered* (1946) makes
reference to Capra's film *Arsenic and Old Lace* (1944) and comedian
Jerry Colonna and Orson Welles' "War of the Worlds" broadcast. *Baby
Bottleneck* brings in Jimmy Durante (as does almost every Clampett film
of the period), Bing Crosby, Eddy Cantor and the Dionne Quintuplets,
and ends with perhaps the most perplexing cultural reference for today's
audience in the film's final line: "Mr. Anthony. I have a problem." This
refers to pioneering relationship guru John J. Anthony, whose radio program "The Good Will Hour" on the Mutual Broadcasting Network was
the prototype of today's pop psychology programs. Clampett was more
preoccupied with his contemporary popular cultural context than his
contemporaries, and this makes the full appreciation of Clampett's films a
challenging task for today's audiences.

The primary reference in Clampett's work is to Walt Disney. The narrative of *Coal Black and de Sebben Dwarfs* spoofs Disney's *Snow White
and the Seven Dwarfs (1937)*, *Tortoise Wins by a Hare* refers to *The Hare
and the Tortoise*, *Baby Bottleneck* spoofs *Dumbo* (1940), and *A Corny
Concerto* pokes fun at the pretensions of both *Fantasia* (1940) and *The
Ugly Duckling* (1938) with a brief jab at *Flowers and Trees* (1932) thrown

in. Within almost any Clampett film will be some irreverent allusion to Warner Bros.' Burbank rival. Walt Disney said "We like to have a point to our studies, not an obvious moral but a worthwhile theme." Consequently, Disney films were invested with normative ideological meanings, endorsing middle-class values. Clampett appears to have declared war on those values.

A Corny Concerto is a full frontal attack on Disney's attempt to go highbrow with Fantasia, beginning with casting Elmer Fudd in the role of Fantasia's culture maven narrator Deems Taylor. Elmer's starched shirtfront keeps popping up in the air. In tucking it back into his waistband, Elmer keeps running his hands suspiciously low into his pants' crotch. Later in the same film, Bugs Bunny's hands are pried off his chest by Elmer and a dog, to reveal that Bugs is wearing a brassiere, which the rabbit ties around the heads of the two other characters before pirouetting off in a tutu. Coal Black restates the good taste and attempts at elevating the art of animation seen in Disney's Snow White and the Seven Dwarfs, as a jazz-themed celebration of African-American culture and patriotic endorsement of the war effort. In all these cases, Clampett infuses his films with an overt sexuality that would have made Disney blush, from Coal Black buying off Murder Inc. with sexual favours, to the competition between two libidinous male cats who have the hots for a female in Gruesome Twosome, or the oversexed reactions of both male characters to the book The Cherokee Strip, or the female characters swooning like bobby-soxers to Sinatra in Book Revue. Good taste forbids discussion here of the placement of Porky's face at the end of Baby Bottleneck.

Perhaps the supreme example of the sexual subversion of the Disney ethos in Clampett's work is in a film not in this retrospective. At one point in An Itch in Time (1946), the dog protagonist sustains an injury to his naughty bits and drags his genital area and behind along the carpet in a manner emulating the one the wolf used after falling into a pot of boiling turpentine in Disney's The Three Little Pigs (1934). In the Clampett film, the dog stops midway in his action, turns to the audience panting heavily and says, "I've got to stop doing this. I'm getting to like it." How Clampett got this past the censors is still a mystery.

Clampett also lampoons Disney techniques. Corny Concerto takes the Disney convention of having characters move on the beat of the music (dubbed "Mickey Mousing" in the animation profession) to absurd levels through exaggerated synchronization techniques and Elmer's voiced appreciation of the artistry of the convention – "Isn't that *wovely*?" This is in keeping with Clampett's propensity to always push the envelope in terms of exaggerating techniques. For example, Disney perfected the use of the take – a way of showing a character's reaction to some stimulus through strong facial expression and bodily movement. Eyes would pop out; the character's head would spin from one direction to another to register surprise. The purpose of this in Disney films was to emphasize the psychological reaction of the character to increase audience identification with the cartoon star. Clampett typically takes this Disney technique and subverts it. In *Book Revue*, Daffy's take when he realizes that the wolf is about to bite his leg results not in an exaggerated expression, but in Daffy transforming briefly into a giant eye. In *Kitty Kornered*, Porky's take when he discovers men from Mars in his bed is multidirectional and prolonged far longer than usual. In both instances, the subject is less the audience's emotional empathy with the characters but the convention of the take itself.

Clampett left Warner Bros. in 1946 to begin his own company. While his Warner Bros. period was not the only achievement of his career, it forms a coherent body of work that is distinct in some ways from his later efforts. Clampett later directed the first of what was to be a series of animated films for Republic Pictures, but Republic could not sustain the production. Turning to the new medium of television, Clampett left animation and returned to his love of puppetry with the pioneering "Time for Beany" show. Originally a local Los Angeles production, it soon went national, and was followed in 1962 by a hit animated version sponsored by Mattel called "Matty's Funnies with Beany and Cecil." The "Beany and Cecil" episodes, although done in limited animation, used more sustained narratives and greater playfulness with language than the Warner Bros. cartoons but shared characteristics with Clampett's earlier work, particularly in their heightened pop-culture consciousness and references to Disney. Although targeted to a juvenile audience, they became a cult hit with adolescents and young adults. Later in life, Bob Clampett was honoured with tributes in such venues as the Museum of Modern Art in New York and the Cinematheque Francaise in Paris. His studio remained active and, with his wife Sody, he created television commercials. Clampett also profited from the syndication of "Beany and Cecil" in various international markets. In 1984, while in Detroit on a promotional tour for the video release of "Beany and Cecil," the animator died following a heart attack.

Although Bob Clampett is not as much of a household name as Chuck Jones or Friz Freleng, his influence among today's animators is particularly strong. One only need look at the playful violation of taste norms, hip references to classical animation, and use of stretchable-bendable characters by directors like John Kricfalusi to see a Clampett sensibility. Although almost seventy years old, Clampett's Warner Bros. works, seen in the context of films made in 2005 and 2006 shown in competition at this year's Ottawa International Animation Festival, can be startlingly modern in their sensibilities.

CHAPTER 24

Showing Scher (2006)

by Richard O'Connor

THE TABLE WAS ELEGANTLY set, the meal from butcher's finest cuts, the guests all light-hearted and charming as if transported from an 1880s London drawing-room to a New York City dinner party. The host, however, was becoming visibly unnerved. With every moment he grew tenser, with each word he flinched. After a seeming eternity of Jeffrey Scher rhapsodizing on the brilliant simplicity of a local television commercial – how it might look upon first glance to be one of hundreds of cheaply produced ads for late night TV that, in fact, this one was *special* – after all this, and before Mr. Scher could say more, the host erupted: "All right, who told you?" Unwittingly, Mr. Scher had found himself in the presence of the *auteur*. Bonnie Siegler, the designer whose company, Number 17, regularly finds its work featured in $30 design magazines and who finds herself as Jeff's steady date, leapt to his defense, "He's not kidding. He's obsessed with that commercial. He flips through the channels late at night hoping that it'll come on."

Once the guests were sworn to secrecy, our host revealed the circumstances of the commission. It was essentially a good deed done for a neighbor. The artist decided to place an array of restrictions on himself as a sort of creative obstacle course to keep himself interested. He disregarded "fluidity" of motion in favor of implementing a number of short cuts. These short cuts became the graphic shorthand that had Jeff mesmerized.

DOI: 10.1201/9781003288022-25

Animators make fetish of motion. Many go as far as to scoff at certain techniques or films which value other elements above movement. Some might even discount Jeff Scher's work for its heavy reliance on rotoscoping and his dismissal of traditional film form. Instead of basing films on scripts and storyboards, his films are graphic realizations which eschew narrative for visual form and loopy editing which only finds linear meaning in the Rorschach of the Kuleshov Effect.

Cunning Stunts, for example, is a piece I first saw in a bar in Flatbush, Brooklyn, at a time when I only knew Jeff's commercial work. We had both worked on pieces for an HBO special, *Goodnight Moon*, and he had done an opening for Angelika Film Center, which had replaced one done by my former studio, as well as work for the New York Film Festival and the Sundance Channel which I had seen. For *Goodnight Moon* he created a title animation inspired by *Little Nemo in Slumberland*. Instead of tackling McCay's tight painting and drafting, Scher applied his own style – a loose watercolour based heavily on rotoscoped footage. The majority of his commercial films utilize split screens and multiple projections of the same image. Films in the great extended family descended from Pablo Ferro and his Burlington campaign of the late sixties. At the time, I first caught *Cunning Stunts* out of the corner of my eye in a bar blissfully free of animators, I did not know he was – in addition to being a painter/artist/filmmaker/animator – a pornographer. It even took a few moments of peripheral viewing to realize what was on screen.

Is pornography when traced and quick-cut still pornography?

Apart from the humour intrinsic in the film's concept, there is little scintillation in *Cunning Stunts*. The non-stop sexual activity, which parades across the screen, is abstracted to its purest graphic form. Shots are selected for their shape and power, and – here is why this is amongst Jeff's most successful films – the graphic interest of their motion. Men and women move as machines. The mechanical, matter-of-fact presentation absorbs the shock value. Dirty deeds done with clinical perfection. It all comes down to the visual impact of the frame.

If a painted-over pop shot is no longer porn, what becomes of a cartoon when it's recut and rotoscoped in watercolour? (Thankfully) it's no longer a cartoon, as *Lost and Found* demonstrates. Tracing over and repainting old rubber hose animation using pastels and watercolours, the picture throbs with energy. It also elicits questions around art and animation.

The artwork in an animated cartoon is commodified by its place in the production of a particular studio; the authorship of this artwork is regularly ascribed to the producer – Walt Disney, Max Fleischer, Walter Lantz. When he removes scenes from their original context and repaints them, Jeff Scher is reclaiming the material as an artist. He removes the angry marching bulls in *Lost and Found* from the ashtray by the coat check and puts a signature on them.

Cunning Stunts is a collage film unified through a singular technique. *Lost and Found* does the same thing. In many of his pieces, Scher will pull material from multiple sources and tie them together by painting in the same palette. Some films dissect a single source through frame-by-frame counterpoint, creating what is essentially a collage within a single source that alienates the content/action from the clip and turns it purely visual. This mindset has produced some films which are monomaniacal in their adherence to their self-imposed strictures – *Grand Central*, an Expressionist look at human figures and shadows as architecture in the train station, or 1985's *Area Striata* which rapidly moves through hi-con patterns and 1997's *Trigger Happy*, a silhouette film somewhere mixed up with Lenica, Lotte Reiniger and a handful of caffeine pills.

Amongst Jeff Scher's thirty or so films, spanning from the mid-seventies, when the New York native first picked up a camera, to today, my favorite is – on the surface – unlike his other films. *Sid* is a single perspective film made up of two or three continuous shots. No painting, no rotoscoping, no multiple projections. The only cinematic gimmick is an overcranked camera about halfway through when the stock goes from black and white to colour. In most of his films, Scher speeds up events. Here, time slows. In this film, a bug eyed dog plays with a steak shaped chew toy. The whole film is shot from the human's perspective as the dog grabs it and is spun repeatedly through the air.

The external signifiers all differ from his usually kinetic approach, but the internal logic is true to form. The foundation of the film is the graphic image of a goofy looking dog. The film proceeds from that starting point. I imagine sometime Jeff was playing with this dog – spinning it around, wrestling over its toy – and said to himself "this is one crazy, funny-looking animal" and he ran for his Bolex to capture it on film. A magical thing then happens – film becomes a medium for sharing an unshareable private moment. Instead of telling us at the dinner table how his dog can do

360-degree turns while holding onto a plastic sirloin, he has shown us, in a way we can fully share, the experience. With this film, made with no preparation almost as a "throwaway," a pure emotion is captured, the transcendent joy of play.

The short films filled with little boxes made from watercolour and pastels demonstrate an obsession with form as a way of showing. The essence of Jeff Scher's film work is this "showing." Bowls of fruit, human portraits, fellatio – paint it, put it on screen, people will look and see it's special.

CHAPTER 25

Bawdy Politics

The Animation of Joanna Quinn (2007)

by Tom McSorley

T HERE'S THIS WOMAN NAMED Beryl. She's loud, large, passionate, a bit insecure, more than a bit of a drinker and more than a bit of a party animal. Beryl likes to get out of the house, away from the telly, go have a drink and a gab with the gals and do things like snatch leopard skin thongs from the swaying genital bulk of male strippers. She also loves parties and weddings and takes her video camera to one wedding and straps it onto her dog's back while sloppily spouting film theory slogans from Leni Riefenstahl, Dziga Vertov and Sergei Eisenstein. You know, the usual. She's no wallflower, Beryl, and she's not averse to moving her own body on stage, either. She works out, as she knows she is on the hefty side and not getting any younger, but, hey, she can dance and she knows how to have a good time.

Memorable characters in animation are legion. Beryl is one of them. She is also award-winning British animator Joanna Quinn's muse, the principal and prodigious figure in a filmography that wittily and cleverly explores ideas of identity, representation, body image and gender politics. In the animating hands of Quinn and through her irrepressible Beryl, such explorations have never been so perceptive while being so funny. Her distinctive line drawing animation style playfully interrogates how the

DOI: 10.1201/9781003288022-26

body is represented and, by extension, how cultural biases and stereotypes distort how we see our own bodies as well as the bodies of others.

Born in 1962 in Birmingham and now based in Cardiff, Wales, Joanna Quinn's distinguished career as an animator is based on a love of the deceptively simple act of drawing lines. As she mentions in a recent interview, her career in animation began as a passion for drawing. "I always loved to draw. I was an only child, so I spent quite a lot of time alone and just drawing, drawing, drawing. I didn't really plan to be an animator. It wasn't until I went to Middlesex Polytechnic and did a graphic design course that I was introduced to animation. Then of course it just seemed so fitting. When everyone else was going, 'Oh my God, how many drawings?' I was going, 'Yippee, thousands of drawings!' It just suits the way I work."[1] Having trained at Middlesex, Quinn expanded her passion for drawing into a career, which includes extensive work in commercial advertisements, as well as in her own independent films. That career began with, to Quinn's joyful surprise, the extraordinary success of her first film, *Girls Night Out*, in 1986, which unleashed upon an unsuspecting world, the indomitable, unforgettable figure of Beryl. With her producer-writer partner Les Mills, she relocated to Cardiff and has been producing impressive and idiosyncratic animation ever since.

From designing and animating advertisements for chocolate, cat food, airlines, and toilet paper, to adapting a literary masterpiece by Geoffrey Chaucer, Quinn's versatile work is anchored in a respect for the subjects she animates. There is anarchy and satire here, certainly, but no contempt. In the midst of the considerable chaos and comedy of her work, there is an adamantine core of dignity, based on a recognition and a representation of what is actually there, and not what one wishes was there. This is especially true of the human body – the female body in particular – around which almost all of Joanna Quinn's best animation revolves, and where its politics finds expression.

Quinn's works are filled with the body's bumps and eccentric bulges, its flatulent eruptions, its intractable processes of expansion and erosion, its vast and ever-changing array of desiccation, decay, and carnal delight. Part of this is a nod to traditions of English humour, which often locates its comic effects in the lower regions of the human form, but an equally important part of Quinn's "body consciousness" is precisely her argument that the body must be seen, heard, even smelled (ah, if only we could smell animation) and not idealized. These are the tangible, messy politics of the body. In the case of this animator, that body politic is primarily female. Indeed, when it comes to women and their representations in popular culture and the endless gallery of idealized body imagery foisted upon them, Quinn – like her boisterous champion of the first, second and third waves of feminism, Beryl – takes no prisoners.

While the loveable, antic figure of Beryl does dominate the animated dramatis personae of Joanna Quinn, she is by no means the only strong woman to be found. There is the Wife of Bath in Quinn's exquisite adaptation of that particular story in Chaucer's *The Canterbury Tales*. She is cunning and clever and easily confounds the knight who searches for the solution to the unanswerable question: what do women want? Further along, there are two lively and licentious women who, literally and figuratively, take control of their own representation in an artist's studio, in *Elles* (1992). There is also the political powerhouse, for better and for worse, of Queen Victoria, in *Britannia* (1993), who, in various carnivorous and canine incarnations of imperialism, witnesses both the ascension and withering away of the British Empire.

Ultimately, though, it's Beryl who rules Britannia, and Joanna Quinn's animation. After all, even Quinn's and Mills' production company is called Beryl Productions International Ltd. Her character is at once a riot of malapropisms and aimless energies, as well as a proud and perceptive woman fearlessly fighting for self-respect and acceptance, whether it's during a night out with the girls, in *Girls Night Out*, or entering a dance competition in *Body Beautiful* (1990). Beryl will not, and cannot, be denied. In the masterful, award-winning *Dreams and Desires: Family Ties* (2000), she takes her video camera to her friend Mandy's raucous wedding, and somehow produces a record of the event worthy of Luis Buñuel. As Beryl gets drunker and the images become less inhibited, shall we say, the hilarity mounts as does the satirical critique of British society. Beryl argues that her work "could have been a triumph in the wedding video genre." Actually, Beryl, it is and, like you and the animation artist who drew you into being, it is so much more.

NOTE

1. Interview with Stella Papamichael, published, 25 May 2007, www.bbc.co.uk.

CHAPTER 26

Dušan Vukotić

A Canonical Modernist of Animated Film (2007)

by Hrvoje Turković

A T THE VERY BEGINNING of 1950s, Vukotić was a full-time cartoon-ist at *Kerempuh*, a satirical newspaper published in Zagreb, which printed caricatures, humoristic and satirical texts in the spirit of early socialist politics, although he contributed his caricatures to other maga-zines and newspapers too. However, when Fadil Hadžić, then the chief editor of *Kerempuh*, initiated a short-lived production of animated films (Kerempuh production and Duga Film Company, 1951–52), Dušan Vukotić readily joined the enterprise. His first animated films, as well as the films of other animation pioneers, were made under the influ-ence of the predominant paradigm of the time – the short films by Walt Disney. Importantly, Vukotić's films were done in the satirical manner of *Kerempuh*. The first film, *How Kićo was Born* (1951), was an anti-bureau-cratic satire, and the next was a blatant anti-Soviet, anti-propagandist political satire *The Enchanted Castle in Dudinci* (1952). In these first films, Vukotić didn't display ease with realistic Disneyesque animation. His ani-mation and drawing skills were not up to the well-adapted classical draw-ing and animation style of his colleagues – brothers Walter and Norbert

DOI: 10.1201/9781003288022-27

Neugebauer and Borivoj Dovniković. It was possibly just this maladjustment to the classical style of animation that was helpful in his succeeding stylistic and thematic innovativeness. Namely, Vukotić later on played a key role in the articulation of a distinctive modernist cartoon-film style in Zagreb animation.

When Zagreb film animation production was initiated, Vukotić, in cooperation with Nikola Kostelac, produced a series of animated commercials (1954–55: *The Big Race, A Visit from Space, The Blind Mouse*, etc. – about thirteen commercials in total), which became the starting products for the newly established [Zagreb Film] Studio for animated film and a stylistic template for the future production. Producing commercials quickly and economically, Vukotić and Kostelac maximally schematized a drawing and flattened the represented space in the style of modern graphic design of their time, encouraged by the new movement of neo-geometric art in Croatia (the EXAT '51 movement). Animation phases in these commercials were reduced, and the figures were only partially animated – in the style of today's television animation. It seemed that this advertising context opened up Vukotić's mind to the drawing and animation possibilities quite different from the Disney paradigm.

When Vukotić started producing autonomous animated films, he did not jump right into the modernist graphical canonization. The initial number of his succeeding animated films were made according to the traditional idea of the basic purpose of animated film. Namely, the animated films were conceived as "films for children," with the task of presenting recognizable, stereotypical stories in a comical, gag-like manner, with the three-dimensional, perspective scenery, rounded figures and with 'full,' realistic animation. The film stories Vukotić chose were mostly parodies of common genres – science fiction (*Naughty Robot, Cow on the Moon*), horror movies (*The Big Scare*), and fairy tales (*Abracadabra*) and popular western (*Cowboy Jimmy*). Parody supplied the recognizable situations that Vukotić could play upon, exercising his animation and gag imagination, testing different visual effects and playing with the spatial nature of scenery. Moreover, his films were not aimed at pure entertainment (as American children's cartoons), but in accordance with the socialist pedagogy of the time; he guided exposition to an obligatory *message*, the concluding moral thought that, ironically, branded the imaginative "escapism" (the children's uncritical imitation of western heroes, losing oneself to the horror story world, enchantment in fairy tales with wizards, the infatuation with science fiction...).

With *Cowboy Jimmy* (1957), and especially with three films all produced in 1958 – *The Big Scare, The Avenger, A Concert for a Machine Gun* – Vukotić introduced a new, more radical artistic style. Graphic flatness already pervaded *Cowboy Jimmy*, the bodies were often animated in an "unrealistic" manner (horse's legs 'curled' instead of moving in joints like biological horse legs; there were frequent leaping transitions of figures from one position to another). All of this became quite pronounced in *The Avenger*, where the spatial flatness of scenery, and it's occasionally almost abstract presentation, combined with the occasionally highly stylized animation, were particularly impressive. The trend reached its most radical peak in the *Concert for a Machine Gun*, where the characters and the scenery were systematically geometrized (reduced to basic geometrical shapes), completely flattened (non-perspective), and animation programmatically nonrealistic, mostly rhythmically "choreographed."

Although these films – with the exception of *The Avenger* – dealt with parody (*The Concert for a Machine Gun* was made as a parody of a crime story), Vukotić's work took a thematic turn from children films to adult films (*The Big Scare, The Avenger*, and *The Concert for a Machine Gun* no longer featured children). *The Avenger* was particularly important because in it he freely adapted a notable literary work focused on the psychological satirical characterization (the story was made after the Chekhov's story), and in *The Concert for a Machine Gun*, he turned to allegorical themes – the film was not just a parody of gangster film, but a global critical characterization of the distortions of the contemporary capitalist and urban civilization. In *Piccolo* (1959), he traced a characteristic escalation of hostilities from petty neighbors' intolerance to a global confrontation; *The Game* (1962) featured a transformation of a game into a cataclysmic war (both films were inspired by the Cold War atmosphere of his time), while *Surrogate* (1961) presented the contemporary world as a place of absolute surrogates.

The entire thematic shift retained one mark of his children's films – the tendency "to make a point," but now the pedagogical message was replaced by a philosophical one about the state of human nature and of contemporary civilization. He kept to the traditional view of animated film as a humouristic kind, but previous comical and gag-like elaboration of actions and situations was replaced by the satirical and allegorically intoned elaboration, with an emphasis on the graphic based gags – gags that played with graphic aspects of the film.

In fact, these two – the thematic turn and the focus on graphics – were interdependent. The best way to deal with the abstract, symbolic and metaphorical ideas was to use the abstraction and stylization potentials of animated film. The reduction of forms and animation and their stylization served these symbolizing purposes. The characters were more important as symbolic figures than realistic ones – they were presented in geometrical distortions; their limbs were not animated as bodily extensions with organic and psychological expressiveness, but as mechanical, detachable appendices, just symbolizing the general nature of the movement and typicality of character's reactions. Action scenes often became simple motives for rhythmic toying with Modrian type or Klee type geometric patterns. In fact, tracking the "story" of a film ceased to be of main importance – film stories were ultimately simplified because the whole point of this graphic game was to stimulate a comprehension of an abstract, philosophical and primarily moralist point of the particular film.

At that period, Vukotić's fertility and authority canonized this modernist style and turned it into a general approach in the Studio of animated film and among his colleagues. Vukotić was not the only cartoonist in Zagreb Film [Studio], not alone in the described stylistic enterprise. He was accompanied by a fertile creativity of the stylistically individual but philosophically close opus of Vatroslav Mimica and of other authors that were influenced by this new impressive and successful style (Kostelac, Dragutin Vunak, Ivo Vrbanić, Vladimir Tadej, Zvonimir Lončarić, etc.). Even when Vukotić and Mimica turned from animated films to feature films in the mid-sixties, their canonical example remained influential among the "second wave" authors of Zagreb's animated films in the mid-sixties and on (e.g., Borivoj Dovniković, Aleksandar Marks, Vladimir Jutriša, Zlatko Grgić, Boris Kolar, Nedjeljko Dragić, etc.); it remained influential even when they questioned some premises of the "first wave" author's world.

The animated opus of Zagreb film in the 1950s and 1960s was perceived as an extraordinary group deviation from the prevailing tradition of animated film that ruled the world cinema and international festivals at that time. This deviation was so much in the spirit of the growing modernist sensibility of the international cultural milieu, that it was immediately recognized as paradigmatic for the "art" branch of world animation. The festival critics singled the Zagreb group out by christening it "the Zagreb school of animation," and festivals awarded their numerous films, which featured their fertile and versatile but stylistically recognizable output. Although the socialist politicians in ex-Yugoslavia felt a certain unease when faced with the "abstract humanism" (and "abstract graphism") of these films, they tolerated it because of its general international success. The films were used as a showcase of the liberal variant of the socialist Tito's politics.

The world success of the "school," and the canonization of the role of Vukotić in it was sanctified by the most famous award – the *Oscar* for animation film of the American Academy of Motion Picture Arts and Sciences that was given to Vukotić's film *Surrogate* in 1962.

CHAPTER 27

Saul Steinberg and Animation (2007)

by George Griffin

EBRUARY 2007, THERE ARE three Steinberg retrospectives on view in New York City, complemented by the publication of a handsome art book, rich in biographical content, all focusing on the artist's cartoon work.[1] This graphic wealth demonstrates Steinberg's unique position in the second half of the last century as the mercurial immigrant/translator between high and low culture, between the private life of the mind and the hubbub of public experience. Like Tocqueville, Steinberg brought a European sensibility, conservative but acutely perceptive, to create an extended portrait of an American culture he clearly loved, using drawing, as he often put it, as a form of writing.

Although he exhibited drawings and sculptures in galleries, he will forever be associated with *The New Yorker* magazine which published covers and innumerable line drawings from 1941 to his death in 1999 (and continues to publish them posthumously). His popular and often plagiarized cover, "View of the World from Ninth Ave," aptly demonstrates a comic truth about the parochial perspective of the city dweller, as well as it renders an architectural record of startling accuracy that seamlessly gives way to a reduced landscape of codes: multiple perspectives, bird's eye

DOI: 10.1201/9781003288022-28

view, detail and vacant impression, all bound within a human line. His first collection of drawings (1945) was titled "All in Line."

If Steinberg's genius can be outlined, it might go something like this:

1. There is no Steinberg "look," no Steinberg line or flourish. His drawing style is so varied, as if invented for each concept at hand, that his work can be said to be "styleless," even about drawing itself. And yet one can always identify his work; it has a conceptual signature. It was, as he put it, "a way of reasoning on paper."

2. Steinberg asks us to look at things, then to look at our observing selves and our descriptive language. Automobiles, cats, war, businessmen, women, masks, cowboys, parties, the city, tourism, monuments, the artist, baseball, Mickey Mouse, the street and, above all, architecture; don't forget maps, signatures, handwriting, rubber stamps. This partial list of subjects, squeezed through Steinberg's pen, becomes reduced, abstracted to essential, emblematic shapes, part of our all-consuming cultural river.

3. Steinberg is the only cartoonist whose work is *sui generis*, partaking in both fine art history and the vulgar realm of comics, never comfortable in either world. Primarily a doodler, he redefined cartooning from the satirical commentary of Hogarth and Daumier by using a Modernist scalpel to peel away illustrative ornament. He could just as easily wrangle his vast repertory of technique (photography, collage, sculpture, mechanical drawing, caricature, painterly watercolour) to his experimental practice. If he had any need for a philosophical underpinning it would be existentialism, as filtered through Buster Keaton.

Steinberg's background as a Romanian Jew who emigrated to Milan to study architecture and publish satirical cartoons, barely escaping fascist racial laws (possibly forging documents along the way) to land in New York City during W.W. II, followed by military service in China and Europe, would seem to lead him towards a democratic, left-liberal critique of American culture. But, in fact, his work always retains a social reserve even while pushing caricature into formalist abstraction. A man drawn with a soft, ambiguous pencil might share a room with ink-lined curlicued women whose faces resemble their pointillist dresses, or a crayon-scribbled baseball player, or an organization man with a thumb-printed face, all of them studying the same indecipherable abstract painting. We are never meant to think of them as members of a political party, having ideas about Communism or racial integration. Only after the disturbances of the chaotic '60s and the rise of underground comix do we detect a more disturbing Steinberg view of the city: monstrous women entirely composed of legs and head, screaming sirens, machine-gun-toting mice, the menace of garish duplicity.

ANIMATION AND DESIGN

A condensed dialectic of animated cartoon history starts with Cohl's stick figures and McCay's comic naturalism synthesized to Felix and Mickey, composed of hose limbs and abstracted body, easy for a studio team to draw. This metastasizes into a storybook illustrated "realism" in design matched by a "baroque" choreography of squash and stretch. This aesthetic cannot endure market and labour stress and thus evolves into hard-edged "modernistic" design and limited animation, the chief catalyst being UPA. So ends the first half of the last century.

Amid Amidi writes in *Cartoon Modern* that Steinberg was one of the chief influences on this new designer-driven animation in the late '40s and early '50s. He even designed two Jell-O TV spots for the UPA commercial unit in New York in 1955. As the director of those commercials, Gene Deitch recalls just visiting Steinberg's studio and seeing his clocks and rocking chairs "set his young blood surging." The housewife-on-treadmill concept seems almost too literal for the mature Steinberg, but the unfilled linearity, disembodied hands, and screaming baby floating in domestic space, all suggest a fractured graphic style, radical for 1955. We may find the animation a bit generic, but don't forget this was the dawn of animated advertising, just barely removed from educational and industrial films.

Steinberg-inspired character design took many forms. The line became less curvilinear, more angular; anatomy became more abstract, more symbolic, more schematic. Hands could drop their silly paw-concealing gloves and assume all five digits, or even disappear altogether until needed. It became fashionable to reduce the figure to just lines and to place it in a purely linear scene. Flat shapes of colour or texture might float fore and aft to suggest depth, but the overall impression is a kind of compressed anti-pictorialism. By denying a character any shading or colour, its line took on an increased burden of expression. It's no surprise that cartoonists like R.O. Blechman, Robert Osborn, Jules Feiffer and William Steig, who inscribed psychological states through lines both subtle and flamboyant, came into their own in the '50s, a period of redefinition.

Even Disney designers felt the winds of change and sprang on board with the Oscar-winning *Toot, Whistle, Plunk, and Boom* and the earlier, less-known, *Melody*, both *Adventures in Music* directed by Ward Kimball. These literal educational illustrations, complete with corny voices and overbearing, cute characterizations seem far removed from the austerity of a Steinberg vision, but the flavour can be tasted in countless design touches. The opening title, a Calder mobile, is the sort of modern interior that Steinberg would use to imply a kind of sophisticated wink to the middlebrow audience (like the textbook entitled "Freud"). The flattened main characters and stylized backgrounds are UPA-derived, but in the various illustrations and wall charts, e.g., "Homo Sapiens" and chalk drawing stick figures, we see diagrammatic linearity that builds to a *tour de force* climax of stylistic heterogeneity in the finale.

THE ANXIETY OF INFLUENCE

Animation (the business between the frames) and Design (the business within the frame) have always occupied an antagonistic seesaw. When cartoon studios were Taylorized in the '20s, both functions split up with directors positioned as arbitrators. And since character and background design weren't particularly dynamic or innovative during the "Golden Age," authorship tended to be attributed to animators and writers.

The new paradigm introduced by UPA consciously referenced the world of art, literature, dance and music. This shift reflected a broader change in the post-war visual environment of print culture as Bauhaus-influenced graphic design (Paul Rand, Herbert Bayer, Saul Bass, Alex Steinweiss) meshed with the hard-edged comic work of so many anonymous commercial illustrators, like the Columbia record jacket artist Jim Flora. At UPA and other modern production studios, animation, as such, took a back seat. Not only did repetitive cycles, held torsos, gratuitous pan backgrounds and separated mouth actions increase the animator's productivity, this "limitation" was rarely seized as a creative challenge to fashion a temporal equivalent to "angular" design. As a result, many viewers, uninterested in design or underwhelmed by sophisticated subtlety, may have felt cheated.

As independent animators broke with the studio division of labour to meld design with the direct processes of sequence drawing and layering (collage, slashed reveals, and other paper tricks), we often consulted Steinberg's paired down vision: only backgrounds that really mattered, replace detailed drawing with a borrowed appropriation, and above all edit, edit, edit. Of course, Steinberg wasn't the only model for cartoons drawn on one level, floating in white limbo, reduced to the barest essentials of ink and paper, but it helped to drop his name whenever a client wanted too much colour, modelling, or decoration.

Did Steinberg hold the animator's art in as low regard as cartooning was in the art world? It is certainly no secret that cartoonists and illustrators, whose principal affinity is for the printed page, commonly have difficulty adapting to animation design. They often need to stop and examine a single arbitrary frame without respecting the demands of rhythm, tempo, and pacing. How many animators have watched a pencil test with a designer screeching "Wait! Wait! Stop! What's THAT?"

Would Steinberg have been any different? Aside from the Jell-O spots, his brush with film was limited to background illustrations for Alfred Hitchcock's droll *The Trouble with Harry*, and the artist's hand in *An American in Paris* (which he walked away from in a huff over conflicts on design and usage). Another unrealized project was the Eames Studio plan to animate Steinberg's panorama drawing, "*The City*" which was exhibited in the pivotal MoMA "14 Americans" show of 1946.

The first animated film to consciously translate a Steinberg design was also Candy Kugel's first independent film. *Inbetweening American* was based on a *New Yorker* cover illustration of 12 mythic American personae. When she showed Steinberg the workprint, he seemed to like it and even suggested future collaboration (he insisted on seeing it several times, running the moviola forward and backward, stopping often along the way). But when it was completed with music in 1977, he refused release permission without explanation. Was he jealous? Did he hate it? Did he have his own plans for an animated film? Was he worried that it would somehow diminish the huge retrospective planned for the Whitney Museum later that year? By far the animated film most faithful to Steinberg's design, it was eventually released after his death 24 years later and then only after Steinberg Foundation board members relented. Perhaps the curmudgeonly elitist egotism which kept him from working with animation was simply a part of his promethean creative engine.

STEINBERGIAN ANIMATION

More than being merely an interesting cartoonist whose designs or stories might be animated, Steinberg's work impacted the art of animation conceptually, indirectly, but profoundly, by broadening the grammar of cartooning, by portraying a new awareness of self-conscious psychology, and by constantly reexamining the codes and icons of our waking, living, modern world. He was a sponge and a filter, a condenser of cultural wisdom, whose values meshed with both affluent snobs and low-life, boho/info wonks who saw his work as a kind of meta-parody.

The *"View from Ninth Avenue,"* for example, boldly borrows a 19th century cartoon convention of the exalted urban viewpoint to tell a story of individual consciousness, of the delusion that our place, our particular utopian arcadia (or shopping mall), is the center of the universe. It's the hubris that denies the worth of the other, yet also confesses self-conscious complicity with its arrogance.

This random jumble of Steinberg themes and techniques to which he often returned, each time with a subtle accretion or rueful twist, could be re-imagined as a schematic diagram to be filled in with specific cultural referents that never seemed too topical nor too dated.

Though not an obvious influence, Steinberg is the artist I always cite as my primary inspiration, a habit formed early in life when I discovered what pictures caused my architect father to chuckle to himself. These were pictures of definitions and distinctions, where wit found parity with humour, where irony gently jostled the foundations of sentiment, where scribbles crashed the uptown party of gallery paintings. This was an alternate universe: a cat with a human face that never grinned, a building inscribed by its formal language, a car in squiggly splendour owned by a wizened cowboy, a photograph of dressy partygoers wearing paper bag masks. Sometimes the simplicity verged on the childish (though his work would never be identified "for children," whom he often drew as wistful miniature adults). He said, "I don't set out to make art, but to be clear." He was a "draftsman of ideas" yet also a collector who recycled his vast trove of ephemera (ticket stubs, receipts, candy wrappers) as if to fill in the unconscious cracks in our visual culture.

Steinberg drew every day, keeping sketchbooks, mapping his quotidian routines with clever numerical notations, even tracing the architecture of his daily quest for morning coffee, newspaper and observations of his favourite tree in his Manhattan neighbourhood. Jonathan Hodgson's

Feeling My Way (1997) takes a hand-held, live-action walk to work, down bustling London sidewalks and lanes, and layers on drawing and text to compose a dense meditation on life, time, and space. That his workplace destination was Paul Vester's Speedy Cartoons adds yet another layer of significance to this travelogue.

Nedeljko Dragić's *Diary* (1974) is a record of his trip to New York. The spiritual affinity of a Balkan artist to that of a Carpathian may be too elusive or vague to argue, but it's quite clear that Steinberg's immigrant view coloured the Yugoslav's impressions, with perhaps a touch of Fellini thrown in for good measure.

Everything is a Number (1967) is Stefan Schabenbeck's homage to the early Steinberg of linear, Pythagorian landscapes. Its ascetic monochromatism accents the spirit of menace found in much Polish animation of this period, as if the mysterious Schabenbeck were also channelling Kafka. Daniel Szczehura's early piece, *The Diagram* also plays with a human figure trapped in an oppressive maze of unreasonable, arbitrary linearity.

While Steinberg's tone was always cosmopolitan, skeptical, and parodic, it lacked the particular feeling of dark desperation often found in Soviet-Bloc animation, where "little men" were at the mercy of vast bureaucratic abstractions, voracious women, or pitiless fate. When the Wall showed evidence of crumbling, the gloom shifted and a more complex social critique began to emerge. Priit Pärn's *Dejeuner sur l'Herbe* could then be seen as more Steinbergian in its virtuosic shifts in style and hopeful elevation of art as a healing enterprise, even if artists were being censored. In retrospect, perhaps Steinberg appealed to Americans in the '50s precisely because he brought the mordant stain of European tragedy to our sunny shore, somewhat as Freud thought, on his first trip to the States, that he was introducing the "virus" of psychoanalysis. Steinberg then could be seen as the answer to Rotarian boosterism: writing pictures that said obliquely, "not so fast, Mack."

Even though Steinberg's essential mandate was that he "didn't have to be funny," his followers clearly had other ideas. One of the more prolific is Mo Willems, whose personal and commissioned work show a strong graphic indebtedness, both directly and indirectly through the '50s mimics at UPA.

Another Bad Day for Philip Jenkins collage is a spare set with actual newspapers as the hapless Jenkins (whose affectless face sports a distinctly un-Steinbergian nose) enacts repetitions of dead-pan disaster.

Pavel Koutsky's *Curriculum Vitae* (1986) extends a favourite Steinberg conceit of personal authentication via the grandiose document. A life chronicle is imagined in symbolic status icons which transcend culture.

Evert de Beijer's *The Characters* (1986) portrays a wacko couple madly pursuing their frantic interests in what appears to be a medieval castle. But soon enough we witness these characters in surreal interactions with other "characters" of a distinctly Steinbergian provenance. One particularly lusty scene with a transparent (clear plastic?) "E" would never have made it through Steinberg's decorous self-censorship.

This particular devotion to good taste may have resulted from Steinberg's early dependence on commissioned work for mainstream media or even his innate personal reserve. But it is consistent with the flattened mysterious introspection of his "characters." Many of the films mentioned here would probably have horrified him as too broad, too active, too entertaining. We may need to wait for a new generation of shipwrecked animators, or a new medium of meditative presentation to translate his vision into graphic performance. His art rejected "graphology and false bravado" by creating meta drawings which achieved the privileged state of being slightly annoyed they were just drawings.

NOTE

1. "Saul Steinberg: Illuminations," by Joel Smith. Yale University Press, New Haven. The source of many of the quotes in this article.

CHAPTER 28

Don't Throw Out Your Television

The Works of Christopher Mills (2008)

by Jerrett Zaroski

I'M SORRY TO TELL you, but ignoring popular culture isn't the solution. You might try to get rid of the crap that's on TV by pulling the plug, cure the theatres of trashy films by limiting yourself to film co-ops, but the world just goes on without you. There's another option, but it's a daunting task to sort through everything out there. For every hundred hours of trash TV, there's at least one hour of inspiring art to be gleaned from the massive pile of commercials, shows and music videos available. MTV is probably up to about 10 different stations by now, and damned if I know which one actually plays music videos.

We know of a few directors and animators to look for when channel surfing, but just like those great indie bands that gain an audience purely by word of mouth, you pretty much have to stumble across them by accident. Christopher Mills' work makes a great starting point and will let you kill two birds with one stone; it's a combination of quality animation and great music you may have never seen or heard before. Mills' resume is

DOI: 10.1201/9781003288022-29

stocked with videos, commercials, films, drawings and even a colouring book. Best of all, he's not trash TV.

Mills grew up in the far suburbs of Toronto and spent a good chunk of his youth playing with a video camera, an unlikely toy for kids at that time. A string of homemade horror movies made him and a friend real-life producers when their films were shown on the local cable access station (where he later landed a job, which, as Mills puts it, "seemed a pretty cool thing to do at 16"). He joined the A/V club after hearing about a guy who "would play records on the school PA system while he missed geography class." It was during this crucial time that Mills began to create his first music videos.

A year at Sheridan, a video cooperative out West in Winnipeg, and a number of videos and live projections later, Mills moved back to Ontario. His employment at a record store in downtown Toronto provided plenty of opportunities to film some pretty famous artists, "documenting the many in-store appearances and performances they had there... Ozzy, Mariah Carey, Oasis, Outkast, Yo Yo Ma, Marilyn Manson, Stereolab, Yo La Tengo, Fugees, etc."

So where do you go from there? Mills is pretty succinct: "Went to Ryerson. Took Media Arts again to try to build a reel. Found out that if you drop classes early enough, they refund your OSAP [student loan] with a cheque. I dropped most of my classes, and bought a camera, a computer and a big bag of 'shrooms." With such potent inspiration, more music videos followed and, as it sometimes happens, someone noticed his work: "I started attracting directors and production companies. I hooked up with one of 'em, and started doing videos 'by the book.'"

All this time, Mills hadn't yet played with animation, but like many animators early in their careers, the medium he started out in became frustrating. Live action video and film simply had too many constraints. Animation allowed him to remove a lot of those limitations and let his ideas roam.

After playing around with After Effects and getting an animation gig where he found himself clearly over his head, Mills buried himself in an instruction manual and barely slept for a month straight. His first video released after this experience is a claustrophobic flee through a Big Brother dystopia, for Interpol's *PDA*.

Each video led to more – more job offers, music videos, commercials, production companies. Currently working for the Toronto-based Vision

Film Co., Mills has so many videos under his belt, both live-action and animated, that it's too many for him to count: "I'm building new shelves as soon as I get some time off. It's mostly music videos (they're generally my favourite thing to do), but sometimes I get to do other things, too...projections, commercials, short films... I have yet to grow up and do a feature."

"I've started making documentaries about bands," he adds casually. His various videos for Canadian rock legends, The Tragically Hip, evolved into the animated documentary *Macroscopic*. Originally invited to prepare live backdrops to their shows, Mills' work led to an experiment in musical performance, a collision of behind-the-scenes soundcheck footage, live tour performances and animation. He's also worked on various forms of visual art, such as his collaborative sculptures featuring drawings encased in enamel blocks resembling ice. Other sketches were gathered into a colouring book for friends and left out during art shows for audiences to play in.

101 Uses for a Sparkler is a selection of Christopher Mills' music videos, a genre of film where it's clear his heart lies: "My ideas literally, always come from music... The exploration is usually about finding a certain truth in the imagery that falls out of music for me. I usually try to go with my gut when a strong image comes out of a song." The program opens with a video for the Ottawa-based band The Acorn, entitled *Flood Part 1*. Mills sets the mood right away, as your eyes follow an airborne penny, drifting slowly until it suddenly slams into a glacier, setting off a chain reaction of epic proportions. Pretty soon, we're taken on a fantastic voyage with our protagonists fleeing a massive flood as they travel across land, sea, air and space. It's a thrilling and vaguely spiritual setup to the rest of the program, a lifelong work-in-progress that Mills refers to as "the ultimate mix-tape.".

Perhaps the best way to describe Mills' technique is "mixed media," as broad as that term is. There's the familiar glint of After Effects present in his music videos, but it's likely the most reliable tool in his vast and ever-changing arsenal. His use of 3D animation to create landscapes is particularly curious and hearkens back to the days of early medical models, virtual reality and flight simulators. Rendered in low-res textures, oceans, buildings and fields overlap edges or split at the seams, and lack both in framerate and polygons. Mills' use of 3D comes across as quite crude, but his almost exclusive use of it for landscapes suggests a view of a rigidly structured yet fragile world. 2D objects and photos, often embracing their flat and retro "sprite"-like qualities, populate the 3D worlds in a way that strikes one as both fitting and unnatural. Not limited by digital artistry, Mills also draws by hand in a manner that is highly detailed but often monochromatic – cut-outs in a cut-out world. His blend of animation with live-action presents a complex relationship, where the two dichotomies are easily interdependent. Through the power of the green screen, people are rendered in jarring 2D and tossed around by Mills like the rest of his objects. His experience with film and video is evident; experiments with analog and digital feedback, pixilation and speed manipulation are prevalent. With such heavy use of technology, it's fascinating how Mills' worlds, teeming with life and discovery, feel far from mechanical.

This may be, in part, due to Christopher Mills' repeated efforts throughout *101 Uses for a Sparkler* to break down technology. Toys, phones and machinery are taken apart and examined as a collection of parts. His mixed-media construction extends this concept to the creation of the video itself: "I tend to think that seeing different materials and pieces brought into the making of one thing makes [it] continuously interesting with repeated views." Nested arrays of objects and their parts are densely layered, and with each viewing the music videos offer new details to discover. "On one job," Mills offers, "we made 10,000 drawings, then cut them out with scissors, then blew them against a house with a giant wind machine..." The effect, seen in The Tragically Hip's *Vaccination Scar*, is breathtaking.

I'll admit, it's hard not to be overwhelmed by some of Christopher Mills' videos. Objects spin, dance and soar within a world of severe spatial depth. Sometimes the virtual (and real) camera has such a wide lens, and objects are pulled so close into the frame, you might turn fish-eyed yourself. To be up-close and personal with the subject and still able to see so much of the landscape can be both claustrophobic and liberating (Mills attributes this look to spending "too much time staring into ViewMasters" when he was young) – now, just imagine it on the big screen. While his animation itself tends to be highly kinetic, this energy is compounded by the camera, which flits back and forth, shaking and careening in a constant exploration of the world he's created, as if it's always seeing it for the first time.

With so much visual complexity and continuous action, Christopher Mills' videos practically beg to be watched again. Fortunately, the entire genre of music videos thrives on this form. In an industry where repeat viewing is king – especially when it's voluntary – it's not hard to see how he's been turning heads both in the animation industry and in the art world. When I asked Mills why he thinks his particular works give him commercial appeal, he replied "I don't mean any harm, and I like having fun. In a past life, I would've enjoyed being a cuckoo clockmaker. Who doesn't like cuckoo clocks?"

No one, that's who. He would have made a killing.

CHAPTER 29

There's a Party in My Tummy

The Yo Gabba Gabba Revolution (2008)

by Chris Robinson

> *Every being strives after pleasure, and it is in pleasure that happiness consists.*
>
> —EPICURUS

> *There's a party in my tummy!*
> *(So yummy! So yummy!)*
> *Carrots in my tummy!*
> *(Party-Party!)*
>
> —BROBEE THE GREEN MONSTER

A S A PARENT AND the Artistic Director of an animation festival, I get to see a lot of TV animation for kids. Sounds pretty enviable, doesn't it? Well, it is when you stumble upon godsends, like the shows *Yo Gabba Gabba* or *Jack's Big Music Show* (okay, Jack is only animation in spirit). Otherwise, it's a pretty hellish experience being forced to hear god-awful

DOI: 10.1201/9781003288022-30

music and watch screaming adult-voiced kids, bad animation, idiotic storylines, annoying dialogue, writing and plots that read like they're were made by a factory of Ned Flanders clones. Trifles, "that are nothing at all, yet a nothing that's everything." They lack an "overflowing abundance, that *je ne sais quoi* which might even be the soul."

Yo Gabba Gabba is something completely different. It's a fresh and inspired crash of generations and cultures that fuses retro sensibilities, dance culture and, incredibly, fun. Not since *Pee-wee's Playhouse* has there been a show that is so cool and fun and different that it appeals to both adults and children. *Yo Gabba Gabba* also has elements of vintage *Sesame Street*, UPA, and *The Electric Company*. Viewers are approached as though they have minds. They are allowed to engage on their own terms with the show's various segments.

Moderated by a bright orange attired and wigged DJ named Lance, *Gabba* (a nod to The Ramones) is like taking ecstasy and going to a rave (something I never did. Too much happiness scared me). Along the way, you meet a quartet of friendly monsters, learn to draw from a guy from the new wave band Devo, do some dancing with Elijah Wood and other kids and watch some strikingly original animation (done by the likes of Joel Trussell, Nick Cross and other indies). In short, *Gabba* is about joy. Sure, there are lessons learned about life, but they are not hammered into the child (or parent). The characters don't shout at you like you're an idiot. The obnoxiousness of so much kids' TV is nowhere to be found in this paradise.

As there was with *Pee wee's Playhouse*, there's something refreshingly naïve and innocent about *Gabba*, and that's why it's so successful. It's not consciously trying to be hip. It's just made by people who are having fun and making things they enjoy and love. And that's the THING. You watch this show and realize what a joy it is to be alive, especially if you're a kid. That's precisely why adults love the show too. It transports us back to a pretty fantastic time when every day was an adventure of imagination, creativity and play. Like *Jack's Big Music Show*, *Yo Gabba Gabba* took me out of my seat. The music, stories and characters were alive and fun. It's like hearing a rocking sermon from the Rev. Charlie Jackson who, after watching *Gabba*, said: "Well if you need it, *Gabba's* got it. It's got everything thing you need. It's got everything a poor man needs."

The crappy state of most kids' TV animation makes you wonder if the creators were ever children. Maybe they had miserable childhoods and decided to have revenge on humanity by creating a steady stream of puerile, droning and agonizing screams and visions that feel more like a sampler from a life in hell than life here and now.

Yo Gabba Gabba has a soul. It makes you want to get off your ass and live.

Isn't that everything?

CHAPTER 30

Jonas Odell

Revolver Bang! Bang! (2008)

by Tom McSorley

Y<small>OU ALREADY KNOW</small> A lot about Sweden. You really do. Sweden is inescapable. Just look around.

Elements of the remarkable Swedish sensibility can be discovered in a number of places. Surprisingly, perhaps, given Sweden's relatively modest size, these elements are very easy to find because many of them are world famous. One element is discovered in the philosophically searching and internationally renowned cinema of Ingmar Bergman; more tangibly, perhaps, another resides in the ubiquitous, efficient and pragmatic Swedish products manufactured by IKEA, Volvo and Saab; in other international arenas, another is literally embodied in the cool athletic fires of tennis icons Bjorn Borg and Stefan Edberg, hockey legends Borje Salming, Nicklas Lidstrom and Daniel Alfredsson; and, in arguably the most spectacular example, in the enormous popularity of the music of ABBA (although I'd take The Soundtrack of Our Lives over that acronym band any day). While slightly more modest in terms of world domination, the multi-faceted animation work of Jonas Odell incorporates all of these same aspects of Swedish cultural output: pragmatism, craftsmanship and passion. The specifically "Swedish" elements, combined with a vital and vibrant internationalism that, in a sense, has always informed

DOI: 10.1201/9781003288022-31

the world of animation, make the multi award-winning Odell one of the most important figures in contemporary world animation.

Born in 1962, Odell is one of the founding members of Filmtecknarna, a prolific and renowned animation company based in Stockholm, founded in 1981 by Odell, Lars Ohlson and Stig Bergqvist. All students at the time, they shared a common interest in drawing and animating and decided to band together and combine their energies. All their time was spent at the animation desk and many films were produced, mostly independent short films, but when commercial television arrived in Sweden some two decades ago, Filmtecknarna's intelligent, unusual and entertaining animation found a place in this rapidly expanding television market. That combination of independent and commercial work has been the company's, and particularly Jonas Odell's, trademark ever since.

It is in his independent works that we can, at one level, locate Odell's auteurist animator persona, but it must be admitted that his persona is also present in the commercial work, too. Winner of the Golden Bear for Best Short Film at the 2006 Berlin International Film Festival, *Never Like the First Time!* is based on actual interviews with four people about their first sexual experiences. Each interview is animated in a different style, emphasizing the humorous, wistful, disturbing or, indeed, beautiful nature of the experience described. In a similar collective vein, the five stories in *Family and Friends* explore the strangeness of adult worlds from a child's perspective. As funny as it is sad, this perceptive work articulates, as Bergman did in his way, the often perplexing intensities and absurdities of family life and opens those obscure volumes of repressed family history to read a few chapters. *Atom Ant* is a critique of animation's complicity with Cold War ideology and not so tacit approval of the arms race. Odell's kinetic short incorporates Hanna-Barbera animation stylings with snatches of the original soundtrack with its toddler war cry, "Up and at 'em, Atom Ant!" It detonates any notion that animation, in general, is innocent or neutral and raises relevant, incisive questions about the politics of commercial animation.

Even earlier collaborative pieces that Odell made with fellow Filmtecknarnans, Stig Bergqvist and Martti Ekstrand, have a political dimension and explore dark, absurdist themes. *Exit* (1990) offers a mordant satire on how the entertainment industry exploits and deforms us, while 1993's *Revolver* (also with Lars Ohlson), is a Fleischer-meets-Beckett black and white meditation on repetition in modern society. The independent, noncommercial dimension of Jonas Odell's animation reveals him to be an astute and acute observer of his own art form, the idiosyncrasies and absurdities of our existential predicament and the idiocies of humankind.

As a member of an animation studio that does much commercial work to pay its bills, Odell is, of necessity, a chameleon – a pragmatic chameleon. Even a brief sampling of Odell's varied work in advertising reveals how talented a chameleon he is, for the intelligence and low-key humour evident throughout his independent work is also present. Moreover, his versatility is considerable, as his range of animation styles is impressively broad, always shifting to suit the product being sold. In *Moms Online*, for example, his simple (yes, almost childlike), line-drawn mothers and children against bold block-colour backgrounds fit the subject matter (advice about child-rearing) perfectly. In the cell-style animation for a Swedish candy, here rendered as a speedy small car, Odell evokes those anarchic Warner Bros. chase sequences. In one, he even has the candy car miss a turn, go off the road, and slide past the sprocket holes – are you watching, Mr. Tezuka? – before resuming the breakneck pursuit. In a Swedish ad for the aptly named Joker grocery store chain, he subtly satirizes the Swedish middle class with colourful mixed media. The range of styles employed in station identification spots for Cartoon Network runs the gamut from line drawings to cell to computer animation. His ads for IKEA, BMW, Virgin Atlantic, and other high-profile clients yield similar stylistic variances and equal amounts of invention and wit.

The other commercial side of his work, and again subject to the dictates of his clients (who, unlike the clientele for the ad spots, at least are fellow artists), are Jonas Odell's often sublime music videos. In a sumptuous visual array best described as

Lichtenstein-meets-Warhol-meets-Magritte Yellow Submarinesque dreamy pop-art psychedelic melancholia, is the video made for the band, Mad Action, *Smile*. The agit-prop Soviet Constructivist motifs, as well as architectural drawings and 1920s-style man-machine visuals, propel further the already propulsive Franz Ferdinand song, *Take Me Out*. The natural and the technological also collide and collapse into each other in *Strict Machine*, a MacLarenesque split-screen wonder made for the band, Goldfrapp. Another stunning example is the *Windows in the Sky* video for U2. Odell's stark and soaring monochromatic computer-manipulated technique of swirling still photographs and sending them through an ever-shifting myriad of spatial and temporal portals is mesmerizing in its ability to match and even enhance the experience of the song. These are but four examples of Odell's prodigious collection of videos, all commissioned, all subject to the input of others, and somehow, all Odell. Now *that's* a chameleon.

Art? Industry? Either-or? In between? In Odell's work, these hoary distinctions can be disregarded. His work both confounds and affirms the auteur theory. Even in his most commercial pieces, we can perceive his artistry, his signature; in the independent pieces, this signature is, of course, more pronounced. Auteur theories aside, Jonas Odell is an animation artist of the highest order who knows how to change, adjust, and cleverly balance his multi-media forms of animation to fit the task at hand. Perhaps he reflects the new Sweden – progressive and internationalist – or perhaps he's simply the latest to walk successfully along that art and commerce tightrope, imagining and drawing as he goes, honing his craft, doing his job. How Swedish. After all, even Ingmar Bergman admitted that he was ultimately a craftsman first, a filmmaker who hoped his films would be like a good table or chair, that would last and be useful to people. How Swedish. Under such an august metaphor, Jonas Odell can proudly sit on the furniture he's made so far, and it is our luck that he's invited us to join him.

CHAPTER 31

Michael Sporn (2008)

by Richard O' Connor

T URNING OFF SEVENTH AVENUE onto a tiny street, then another even
  tinier street, the New York of now – of the Real Housewives and the
Gossip Girls, of the luxury condos and high-rise hotels – recedes. The
crassness of reality draws back, pulling forward thoughts of New York as
we want it to exist. In our imagination, Audrey Hepburn is sipping coffee
at the corner café and Gene Kelly swings from every lamppost; Bob Dylan
is busking in the subway and Joey Ramone incites teenage riots down
the street. On this storyboard storybook street, an innocuous and easily
missed sign in a passageway next to a fortune teller – where a psychic fat
cat suns in the window, tail snuggling a crystal ball with a deck of tarot
cards as a pillow – marks the way: "Michael Sporn Animation."

A short tunnel leads to a garden – maybe Audrey Hepburn *will* drop
a serenade from the surrounding fire escapes. At the end of the garden
is (knock loudly) Michael Sporn's studio. Conspicuously absent its cat to
match stripes [with] the gatekeeper's (his previous space had an amiable
feline resident), the large semi-subterranean space has a comfort, a warmth
that fits with the films made there. The previous space on Broadway, now
most likely a bank or an American Apparel outlet, had the practical, efficient feel of a Henry Ford operation. As a producer, Michael is practical
and efficient, but here in this low-lit grotto, in this bustling part of the city
that real estate speculation and corporate claptrap seem to have forgotten,

DOI: 10.1201/9781003288022-32

he has found himself in a sort of Bauhaus in which the hand-hewn careful construction of his work is matched with an urban rusticity that has also disappeared from our landscape.

Michael walks through the studio filled with a mixture of moviolas, Macintosh computers and lightboxes. He's all bushy, unruly hair. He's still all eyes and lips that turn unexpectedly warm and smile with ease – looking every bit the part of an animator. Not surprisingly, a little like the Unabomber too, another solitary spirit out of place in the Walmart economy.

With such a ranging intellect, I would prefer to talk with Michael about anything instead of the mundane simplicity of animation. Our first ever conversation was at a dinner following a tribute to Tissa David at New York's Museum of Modern Art. He confessed that he read several books a week, usually devouring the work of a single author in the matter of a month. He modestly attributed this to insomnia. Other insomniacs are pros at Grand Theft Auto and channel changing. At that time, he was burning through John Updike. Updike, inspired by James Thurber, had wanted to be a cartoonist; writing novels, it turns out, was easier.

At that first conversation, just like now sitting across from the studio's picnic style lunch table, Michael's mind ranged the arts and sciences, always pulling back to animation – politics and animation, literary adaptations, Flash as a production tool (to be avoided, in his opinion), motion capture and its shortcomings. No matter how you try to avoid it, animation is inextricably tied up in his thought system.

Intelligence – book learning – is simple to relate to. Anybody can pick up a second-hand *Rabbit, Run* and a study guide and join the book club conversation. Experience is a sharper fanged monster. What librarian, even one who knows every decimal of Dewey's system, can claim to have stood side by side with Tolstoy as he plotted *War and Peace* or Dickens rhapsodizing on the French Revolution?

There's no way to phrase this, other than to just say it: I'm slightly (…just a little…) jealous of Michael's career. That dinnertime conversation took place a few years after we were first introduced. Something was daunting, slightly intimidating about his resumé, something so cool in his demeanour that made him seem unapproachable. In the early 70s, John Hubley hired him as an intern. In short order he graduated (or was demoted) to production manager, taking large responsibilities for the films from *Everybody Rides the Carousel* to the "Letter Man" series for Children's Television Workshop's *Electric Company.* "Letter Man," along with several shorts produced by Hubley and animated by Tissa David, rank with the most compelling and charming short films.

After Hubley's passing, he moved on to New York's next legendary production, Richard Williams' *Raggedy Ann and Andy.* Several years with John Hubley would teach anybody how to make films, and several months woodshedding with Williams and his assembled team of masters could teach anyone a few things about how to animate.

Michael often claims that he primarily does "work for hire" – making films for other people on other people's dime. While that may be true in an economic sense – in much the same way that Richard Williams' best work, it could be argued, is his commercial work, or that without CBS, Hubley never would have produced *Everybody Rides the Carousel* – Michael's works for hire all bear his personal touches and are as "independent" as animation gets concerning style and substance.

Amongst these notable commissions are two adaptations of William Steig books, the Academy Award-nominated *Doctor Desoto* and 1988's *Abel's Island.* Adapting a complex and ironic artist like William Steig can be particularly difficult. The story and the illustration all have to make sense on different levels of intellectual engagement. These pieces demonstrate a rare ability to understand the inner tonalities of an illustrated story and translate that feeling to film. The credit list of *Abel's Island* is a snapshot of influential East Coast animators. Rob Marianetti, John Dilworth, Doug Compton, Lisa Crafts, Tissa David, Steve Dovas all contributed to this (and other) films, thus perpetuating the cycle of influence and education that has made animation in New York an easily identifiable yet qualitatively indescribable art form.

Two centrepieces of this program, *The Marzipan Pig* and *The Man Who Walked Between the Towers* share the same softness and stylistic integrity demonstrated in Michael's two William Steig films. Much of that can be attributed to the touch of Tissa David, who has worked closely with Michael since his time with Hubley. Levity, respect, inquisitiveness – a space opens in these films, as though the artists are in communion with the material, and we are all brought privy to their understanding of the world.

The Hunting of the Snark also anchors the Festival's program selections. This film was completed over several years and was animated entirely by Michael in between projects. A Lewis Carroll poem recited by James Earl Jones, the film leaves off with a looming question, its characters teetering on the verge of new age. It's almost certain they'll all be devoured, a fate the film's director has managed to avoid as the brighter-than-neon signs of "progress" encroach.

CHAPTER 32

Jim Blashfield

"And Things Were Looking Like a Movie" (2009)

by Richard O'Connor

MAKE ART HOW YOU want to make it, and soon people will be knocking on your door asking for a portrait. Jim Blashfield began making films in the early 1970s, experimenting at Portland State University's Center for the Moving Image. These pieces ranged from optical experiments in camera to documentary – even some drawn animation – but always ranging back to photo collage. Self-taught, each piece a lesson in technique and technology, in an era long before every kid on the block could try their hand at filmmaking.

By 1985's *Suspicious Circumstances*, Jim, working out of Portland, had settled on a distinct photo cut-out technique. Roughly a decade after Xerox introduced the first colour copier, full-spectrum reproductions became relatively affordable. Prior to this, the development photo-rotos printed from negative could run several dollars per image. This economy allowed Jim to create a visual universe closely akin to reality, but substantially different.

This style turned out to ideally suit the nascent form of the music video.

Suspicious Circumstances' producer, Melissa Marsland, copied the address off the back of a Talking Heads album and mailed a tape, unsolicited, to the band's management. David Byrne called immediately giving creative carte blanche – and a month – to animate a video for "And She Was."

DOI: 10.1201/9781003288022-33

On its own, in an independent narrative like *Suspicious Circumstances*, Jim's imagery has a Dadaist feel: close to reality, but completely out of whack. Images are real, sort of, and the viewer has to work to reconstruct a mental universe which relates to the common world, but allows for the fantasy of Jim's animation. If you compare this to a drawn animation – or any other technique that uses representations of objects and not the real resemblances of photo-collage – then the drawn animation immediately signifies an alternate universe. There is no cognitive dissonance if a cartoon duck gets his beak shot off in scene two and then sings "The Marriage of Figaro" in scene three. It's all fake to begin with.

Now, begin with a man – a photograph of a man that looks like a "real" person – and a "realistic" set of rules is expected. Immediately, the imagery is unbalancing. Things are "real," yes, but they are different; they are like the things and people we know in some ways, but they are not the people we know (at least not how we think we know them). The viewer must reach a communion with the film, an understanding of the world's physics. In the music video, the soundtrack is that bridge.

Kids these days, they don't know what it was like: the scarcity of colour printers; "the push it a little, snap another picture" toil of under camera film animation; the visceral tingle of MTV and those images being thrown at you in exciting, previously forbidden ways. "And She Was" struck as one of the most energizing, awesome music film broadcasts. It wasn't just guys playing guitars; it wasn't a poorly lit performance of the lyrics, the video was as if the song was made out of pictures. Not only did the music bring communion between the audience and the notched visuals, but the song and picture also seemed to be the same. If the technique became more polished with The Talking Heads video, then the look reached its apex with Michael Jackson's "Leave Me Alone," which now stands as a monument to both the innovative era of 1980s music video and an accounting of two decades' mass sneering at the unmistakable former prodigy.

Most of Jim's music videos were created in a somewhat stream-of-consciousness manner, the images pulling along the story. "Leave Me Alone" was so complicated that it was completely storyboarded beforehand. Around 50 people worked on the project for roughly nine months. Still, the process was basically the same: First, a conversation with the musician, primarily to get ideas about their relationship to the song and to build a personal connection; from there, sketches and tests, followed by photography, editing, photo printing and a lot of cutting; then, a lot more testing of each item. This all culminated with around-the-clock under-camera animation sessions. Despite the moniker, these "videos" were shot on film, mostly on homemade animation stands.

After a long stretch of commissions from chart-toppers in search of innovative filmmakers to promote their singles – Peter Gabriel, Paul Simon, Joni Mitchell, Tears For Fears, Marc Cohn (which in turn prompted Madison Avenue to come calling with commercials for Nike, Kelloggs, Pepsi and others) – the 1990s ushered a return to personal work. The music video industry changed as MTV altered its programming. Multi-platinum acts produced ever more outlandish special-effects heavy videos, while everyone else greatly reduced the scope of their promotions. Furthermore, the painstaking under-camera techniques that had been honed to perfection soon became commonplace with the advent of the desktop computer.

Bunnyheads was seeded in 1996, after a show by the sculptor Christine Bourdette. Over the next decade, numerous ideas were tried; they were efforts to understand exactly how the figures would act, what sort of protagonists they would become. In his catalogue of works, Jim Blashfield has live-action, mixed media, effects films and multi-screen projections. *Bunnyheads*, through its technique, stands out. The mood and storytelling of the film are in line with the bulk of his work; but, there's a crispness here that hasn't been previously evident. This distinction in technique illuminates the earlier films and draws connections beyond differences.

Bunnyheads reminds us that collage requires a mental space to be constructed, allowing for the reality of the film to play. Collage creates a new world, based on reality in communion with the viewer. When a bunny sculpture crashes or gets sliced up, it's a visceral pain that we don't experience with cut-out collage. The story in *Bunnyheads* is the same sort of meta-realism of Jim's other animated and mixed media work; the "realism" of the characters creates a whole new effect.

Just as technique has not been a barrier, neither has media. Of late, Jim has created several environmental and public art projects. The forthcoming Riverwalk installation for Astoria, Oregon's waterfront revitalization, brings kinetic images to recognized sites. It projects to encompass video projection, animation, architecture, compositing, and audio design to create dreamlike spaces within the streetscape, making the ultimate leap. No longer are films morsels of heightened reality, but reality will become altered by the exotic visual and auditory experience of film.

CHAPTER 33

Stan Vanderbeek (2009)

by Amid Amidi

The whole commercial cinema of neo-reality is fundamentally porno-graphic and does not contribute to one's soul. It is not sensitive. The cinema needs people of private vision. We are living in an avalanche of entertainment fallout, and how does one survive when bombarded by clumsy ideas? The film should be in the hands of poets rather than just slick, literate stylists.

–STAN VANDERBEEK, 1964

Chuck Jones and Norman McLaren are fine filmmakers, but frankly, I wouldn't mind if I never hear their names again. As an animation historian, it's the thrill of discovery that keeps my motor running. There's nothing more exhilarating than unearthing the work of a filmmaker who did incredible things with the animation medium. It's especially exciting when it's the guy whose work inspired Terry Gilliam's cutout animation style, when it's the guy who started doing computer animation back in 19(friggin)65! and when it's the guy who so believed in the communicative power of cinema that he constructed a multi-screen, multi-projector theater in his backyard to carry out mad film experiments. The guy is Stan VanDerBeek.

I first discovered one of Stan's films, *Science Friction*, during a late-night jaunt around YouTube. My expectation was that the film I found would be only the beginning. Surely, there would be all kinds of information about

DOI: 10.1201/9781003288022-34

him scattered online and in print. After all, he appeared to be some kind of genius.

That's not how animation works, unfortunately.

We don't make Criterion special editions for our prized filmmakers. We don't write biographies of pioneering figures. We don't even bother to learn their names. VanDerBeek made eighty films (yes, eighty!) and was ignored by the animation community throughout his lifetime. Let me just put this out there for the record: he never won a single award at an animation festival. Animation art might receive respect from outsiders when – and if – we ever decide to respect it ourselves.

I compiled whatever I could find about poor, undocumented Stan and did a post expressing my enthusiasm on my blog, Cartoon Brew. It'd be nice if a few readers picked up on it, but the post was mostly for me, so I could remember his name for future reference. I figured that would be the end of it, except that Chris Robinson emailed me almost instantaneously, and all but commanded me to do this program for his festival. Nobody turns down Mr. Ottawa, and now I was in for the ride – deep in it. I started Googling VanDerBeek with a renewed sense of urgency, clicking on even the most minor of references. What I stumbled upon was almost too good to be true: a show of VanDerBeek's artwork at a Manhattan gallery was taking place just four days after my initial blog post. What luck! It was meant to be.

It gets better: the gallery putting on the show, Guild & Greyshkul, was run by VanDerBeek's two youngest children (artists themselves), Sara and Johannes VanDerBeek. As it turned out, they, too, were just discovering their father's work. "When he passed away in 1984, only a few months after an initial diagnosis of cancer, there were no instructions regarding how his artworks should be cared for or organized," Sara VanDerBeek said. "Everything was piled up in his office, and it was eventually split up among various family members."

The show shed light on their father's innovative spirit. He was a filmmaker, no doubt, but he was also a visionary who strived to marry art with technology and communications. Every technological breakthrough was grist for VanDerBeek's artistic mill. One of the pieces on display at the gallery was a recreation of his "Telephone Mural." At first glance, it was a bunch of pieces of 8x10 paper, with crude black-and-white images printed onto them, taped together across an entire wall. But there was more bubbling beneath the surface. VanDerBeek had conceived the mural as an experiment to create art via fax machine. The original piece had been pieced together over two weeks by faxing individual pieces of paper from VanDerBeek's station at M.I.T. to the Walker Art Center in Minneapolis. He dreamed that the fax machine could become a tool to promote dialogue between students from different parts of the world. As was often the case, his ideas were sound, but a few steps ahead of the technology: today, in our Internet-enabled society, we instantly share graphic files with thousands around the world without a second thought.

VanDerBeek was largely self-taught. A Cooper Union dropout, he began making films in the mid-1950s while painting backgrounds on the interactive children's TV series *Winky Dink and You*. VanDerBeek would return to the studio after-hours and inform the night watchman that he had work to do. He would then use the animation stand and camera for his experimental collage films and time paintings. He continued coming to the studio months after he was fired from the TV series for being non-union.

His enthusiasm for the magic of cinema carries the early films more than the actual content of the work. In *Dance of the Looney Spoons* (1959), he makes odd combinations of spoons, forks and kitchen utensils dance around the screen via stop-motion. He was so excited by the possibilities that he would sometimes shoot as much footage as he could around a particular theme and "slice a film off like a sausage," which explains why some of his films have titles like *Wheels #1*, *Wheels #2* and *Wheels #3*.

His films were beaten to the core – open-ended, spontaneous, non-conformist, pure. VanDerBeek tried just about every technique under-camera. He would film paintings created frame-by-frame, animate surreal pasteups of magazine photos, slice up existing newsreel footage and draw bits on top, create live-action segments, add the occasional bit of drawn animation, and combine his personal paintings with photographs through sophisticated cross-dissolves. It's a wonder he didn't have sex under the camera. There is nothing slick or polished about any of this work. Most of it appears to be done in one-take. There was no time for perfection; he had a million concepts to explore and admitted to having "impatience with mechanical execution."

Breathdeath is a fifteen-minute absurdist graphic hailstorm, an anti-war screed set, in part, to Screamin' Jay Hawkins' "I Put a Spell on You." In a 1964 article, a writer at *Time* magazine attempted in vain to describe the action he was witnessing onscreen –

A Merlin-like figure suddenly gets stuck in the back of the neck with a flying table fork. A nude appears, with two small skulls where her breasts should be. Another girl lies in bed caressing a TV set on the pillow beside her.

TIME (1964) 'CINEMA: IN THE YEAR OF OUR FORD', 3 APRIL. HTTPS://CONTENT.TIME.COM/TIME/ SUBSCRIBER/ARTICLE/0,33009,939493,00.HTML

In the hands of a lesser experimental filmmaker, this stream-of-conscious imagery would turn into a dreary, unwatchable ego trip. In Stan's universe, it's compelling, can't-take-your-eyes-away-from-the-screen filmmaking. His choice of raw filmmaking materials – newspaper photos, magazine advertisements – adds a light touch to the proceedings, as does his grab-bag use of techniques.

VanDerBeek shrewdly anticipated the remix styles of Paper Rad, Run Wrake and YouTube culture in general, in which everybody mashes up existing media into slick new digital forms. But he didn't make his career solely by reinterpreting the works of others. Films like *Mankinda* (1957) and *Oh* (1968) display his painting and drawing prowess, betraying a finely tuned aesthetic sensibility. One of his most impressive films (at least amongst those I've seen) is *See, Saw, Seams* (1965). In it, he uncovers new visual worlds by painting over found photos. In his words: "Juxtaposed to what we see, is what we think we see...that is, the memory of the dream is as real as the dream itself, but it is completely different from the dream."

In 1967, VanDerBeek made the *Panels for the Walls of the World* (1967), a film that was commissioned by WCBS-TV for a special called "Notes from the Underground." He dubbed it an "electric assemblage"; today, we'd call Stan a VJ. It is a dense video collage that mimics the barrage of sights and sounds that the average person experiences on a daily basis. To achieve the effect, he mixed eight separate video images through electronic mattes, superimpositions, pulsation effects, and various electronic means. The film had originally been planned for his Movie-Drome, a functional prototype movie theatre that he constructed in his backyard in which audiences laid down around the outer edges of the dome and saw dozens of images projected around the theatre's multiple screens.

Even though technological limitations of the time prevented VanDerBeek from performing his video compositions live, that's what he was thinking. He wrote,

> I envision in the future simplified image storage and retrieval systems, not to mention new image and graphic generating techniques – (via computer and videotape)... at which an artist will "perform" an image concept by instant selection plus image interplay...this could also be an "information concert"...(with literal and factual information in a very compact and intense form) we have turned a corner with film and TV when images can now be treated in much the same way that music is...endlessly and variable and dynamic...stored, and in motion...for instant recall.
>
> TAKE ONE, SEPT . 28, 1969, VOL 2, NO .3, PP . 16-17.

VanDerBeek was the subject of an early-seventies documentary called *The Computer Generation.* He appears onscreen with his hair bound in a ponytail and sporting a trucker's mustache and a neckerchief. He speaks in mellow and measured sentences. He recognizes his role as a teacher who is trying to inform the masses of the mysterious tool known as a computer. Even though he'd been exploring the possibilities of computer animation for more than half a decade at the time of the documentary, he admitted that "I frankly don't understand it and I'm trying to understand it."

VanDerBeek never earned any money from his films and survived largely on invitations and grants. In later years, he was a junkie whose drug of choice was computer hardware. He was willing to travel anywhere for his fix of digital technology and, in his lifetime, he held dozens of artist-in-residencies and teaching positions at universities and organizations, including the progressive Boston public TV station, WGBH, the Center for Advanced Visual Studies at M.I.T., CalArts, Columbia University, and everywhere in-between from Hawaii to Wisconsin.

Some of his earliest experiments with the computer – the "Poem Field" series – occurred in 1966 in collaboration with Kenneth Knowlton of Bell Telephone Laboratories, who had invented the BeFlix computer animation language. The films they created were in a resolution of 252x184 and were achieved by essentially turning small points of light on and off at high speeds. The films were created in eight shades of grey, with colour added afterwards through an optical process. The resulting digital mosaics, with their complex geometrical patterns, looked more like a Persian carpet of the future than the glossy CG animation we're used to seeing nowadays. He continued experimenting with the computer for the rest of his life, including *Symmetricks* (1972), which was made with an electronic stylus drawing tablet.

VanDerBeek's work was a catalogue of ideas for the future. He was a fearless optimist who believed in the potential of technology as much as he did in the poetry of art. He radically rewrote the role of filmmakers and animators in the second half of the 20th century and offered a roadmap for how artists can combine art, film, and technology towards the higher purpose of global visual communication. It was both his strength and weakness that he never paused long enough to achieve fluency in any particular field. Film critic Amos Vogel summed it best when he wrote VanDerBeek's obit in 1984: "His achievements lie less in individual works than in the staggering totality of his entire endeavour: a restless, passionate search for new techniques, new media, and new concatenations."

CHAPTER 34

Furniture of My Mind (2010)

by George Griffin

IN *WALDEN* (1854) THOREAU said, "A man is rich in proportion to the number of things which he can afford to let alone." And, with a bit more wit, "I had three pieces of limestone on my desk, but was terrified to find that they required to be dusted daily, when the furniture of my mind was all undusted still and threw them out the window in disgust." Our quintessential hippie philosopher here dusts off the Socratic maxim "the unexamined life is not worth living" and weaves in his own anti-materialist ethos of creative poverty.

Furniture is the stuff with which we fill up our living and working spaces. It's the functional, material culture, integral components for our "machine for living," yet often taken for granted, neglected, inert, invisible. The furnished room can display complex indications of status and taste, or it can be generic, sterile, institutional. In that peculiar zone of animation where reality is always synthetic and provisional, these things can come to life as ironic, comic, ornery, adversarial, even malign actors. The films in this program interpret furniture both literally (chairs, IKEA shelving) and symbolically, like Alexander Pope's "loads of learned lumber in his head" (language, advertising). There is often a tension between our expectations and what is actually happening in the frame and on the soundtrack.

DOI: 10.1201/9781003288022-35

Starting with Walerian Borowczyk's metaphorical parlour game, *Renaissance*, is no accident. My generation of animators may have come out of a cartoon childhood, but as adults in the '60s, the grim psychological realities of Eastern European animation, particularly from Poland, made a huge impression. Borowczyk's background in poster design strongly influenced his cut-out animation in *Les Jeux des Anges* and the *Kabal* films, but here he inverts the tidy accumulation of Victorian materialism with real objects captured by stop-motion. *Hommage à Hy Hirsch* refers to the legendary experimental animator from San Francisco living in Paris who helped Borowczyk escape Poland and gave him a place to stay and work. *Renaissance* perhaps refers to his newfound creative life in the West but drenched with a mordant Middle European skepticism.

In addition to being every American animator's Oedipal parent, Walt Disney was also an incurable optimist, glossing the nastiest realities with seductive diversion. In *Moving Day*, a classic Depression-era "Mickey" cartoon that still reverberates in our melt-down economy, an eviction is about to take place, and the ever-menacing Sheriff Pete threatens to seize "yer foinitcher." Donald does his inimitable dance with a plunger attached to his butt, then Goofy, in his first starring role, performs a rubbery-limbed set-piece with upright piano on a loading ramp. The brilliant comic choreography of Fred Spencer, Al Eugster and Art Babbitt propel this cast of innocent, inventive survivors to their well-deserved deliverance. We witness the evolution of animated characters from the generic pacing in a circle panic of silent-era Fleischer to the Goof's reflective personality of pragmatic nuttiness, a trait developed in countless "How To" cartoons, updated as recently as *How to Hookup your Home Theater* (2007).

Continuing the dubious yet inevitable national character scheme, we now turn to the delightful world of PES, the nickname of Adam Pesapane. Instead of ominous surrealism, we have a joyous playpen. PES brilliantly re-invents the relationships between everyday objects. They retain their autonomy while converging into an organically delirious alternative reality. Using cumbersome, overstuffed easy chairs (one of which he has suggested may have been the site of his conception) PES shows the carnal side of an "Up on the Roof" romance: in broad daylight, a breathless, awkward, moaning "quickie." Another chapter in the same book, one of his original "Plymptoons" made for MTV, before Bill became an introspective art-house auteur, involves a *folie à quatre* who at least seem to be aware that their naughty pursuit of illicit pleasure has a limit.

Real people interacting with real furniture in real space and in unreal time is the chief concern of three films that seem to be from different planets:

> Chomon's pioneering entertainments were called "trickfilms" rather than animation because they were essentially live-action interlarded with playful stop/motion effects and sequences. Yet even today the hand-cranked live scenes of stagey spectacles, jammed with over-acting, funny-dressed folks, retain an artificial flavour no less exotic than the skittering wardrobes and stuffy sofas that shuffle around them.

Before moving into authoring children's books and producing for Sesame Street, Jane Aaron created a suite of fresh, simple yet sophisticated stop-motion films that bypassed narrative and heavy symbolism for something close to pure-play. *Set in Motion*, like *Drawn to Light*, has no urgent agenda beyond the request that we re-consider our quotidian environment in a new light – as objects possessing a life of their own. An ironing board, a baby's crib, a young couple's waltzing embrace form a kind of democratic tableau vivant accompanied by Donald Fagen's infectiously unobtrusive music.

Jan Svankmajer rewrites the book on stop-motion so radically that his name has become an adjective. *Picknick mit Weissmann*, an early experiment shrouded in Teutonic mystery, produced by the perhaps nonexistent A.J. Puluj, presents an autumnal backyard furnished incongruously with domestic furniture. Ominous occurrences with phonographs and drawers, interspersed with rapid accumulations of leafy piles (or pyres) suggest that this will not be a pleasant outing.

Paul Bush approaches film from the realm of philosophy and literature, to create a diverse body of work, yet he is best known as a direct animator who manually scratches the surface (e.g., *The Albatross*, 1998). *Furniture Poetry* represents another side of Bush, like an alchemist of subjective consciousness. His domestic objects (the opening table reminiscent of Borowczyk's) may be pixilated, but they are stripped of all their narrative potential and reduced to a binary existence of either on or off. He tickles a proposition by Wittgenstein, similar to the question of the sound of a tree falling in a forest, and reimagines the existence of his furniture between their visual frames – a tart antidote to continuity.

Joseph Cornell's boxes of precious reconstructions evoking a lost European culture he never experienced, a niche of American surrealism, are reimagined in Joanna Priestley's *Utopia Parkway*. The title refers both to Cornell's home in Queens and to the impossibility of his nowhere world. The high priestess of personal animation, Priestley combines her signature card sequences of bio-morphism, sexual anxiety and exotic porcelain fauna with real environments, photographed through glass bottles and nestled in specimen boxes. Far from imitating Cornell, she pays homage as well to Morandi and Arp in this witty send-up of the Victorian fascination for collecting bibelots.

Alan D. Joseph's *"Construction Manual"* is so exactly what it is that it becomes a kind of hymn to our pathetically sexed-up world of brand identity and disposability, yet rendered without a whiff of condescension. Contrast this manual to *The Chair* for a delightful blast of ironically Anglophone mumbo-jumbo. The eponymous chair makes a late appearance acting as a kind of McGuffin, while all hell breaks loose around it. First, a load of verbiage piles itself into shaky, drunken architecture. Then loosely painted, flickery figures slide about in limbo. George Dunning is just warming up, experimenting with the pleasures of language and rotoscoping, which would re-emerge later in *The Yellow Submarine's* "Lucy in the Sky with Diamonds" sequence.

When MoMA honoured Pixar with a full-fledged 20th anniversary show of films and art in 2005, the most memorable attractions were the hand-drawn character designs which revealed that behind all the splines and vectors lurked the DNA of the comic pencil, scratching to find the perfect arc of comic hyperbole. Side by side were wire-frame models, perhaps by Alvy Ray Smith, and rough pastel sketches by John Lasseter. *Luxo, Jr.* wasn't just a cute short film, it was a hunch that the computer could be used to create empathic characters designed to look exactly, hyperphotographically, like real things: toys or furniture. The quotidian lamp has since become part of the Pixar logo, as recognizable as a silhouette of mouse ears.

Frank Film is the most unlikely and, for me, the best animated film to win an Oscar. Does it matter? Yes. Because it demonstrated, in 1973, that the animation world, so often burdened by an easy backslide toward professional craft, could still recognize genius. Here was a young artist, Alexander Pope, who had hoarded a trove of advertising images, precisely cut, cataloged into an eccentric taxonomy of form and stored as lumber in his hyperactive mind, to be issued as art when the opportunity arose. Animation, as he explains on the track, became the trigger that allowed him to jettison conventional graphic rules. These cascading, multilayered images are our stuff, our irresistible culture of narcissistic materialism, offered as a perfect storm of aspiration and memory. The uninflected first-person, autobiographical voice, threaded with Godardian self-reflexivity, is further layered with incantatory accumulations of witty puns. Twenty-five years later, Frank and Caroline Mouris released a sequel, *Frankly Caroline*, and more are promised, but the original remains a steamroller.

No ideas but in things.
                            —WILLIAM CARLOS WILLIAMS

CHAPTER 35

The Genius of Osamu Tezuka (2010)

by Tom McSorley

O NE OF THE MOST influential figures in postwar Japanese pop culture, Osamu Tezuka (1928–1989), occupies a unique place in Japan's
physical and philosophical reconstruction after its military defeat and
the unprecedented, direct and traumatic experience of the atomic bomb.
Singlehandedly creating manga, the enormously popular Japanese comic
book tradition, Tezuka expanded his creative vision to the world of animation after WWII and is widely considered to be the godfather of the wildly
successful contemporary phenomenon of anime. From a virtual infinity
of manga production (scholars estimate that he created over 150,000 pages
of manga alone) to his numerous films and television animation, Tezuka's
vast body of work constitutes one of the most impressive uses of the imagination to explore and express the uncertainties and anxieties arising from
a new atomic age, the waning of Japanese power and the veritable tsunami
of cultural influences thundering upon Japanese shores from the United
States of America after 1945.

Tezuka was a few months short of his 17th birthday when the cities of
Hiroshima and Nagasaki became the world's first scars of the atom bomb.
An inveterate doodler and drawer as a young man, and encouraged by his
parents to make images every day about things he loved and the things
that bothered him (perhaps this idea of image-making as a kind of therapy

DOI: 10.1201/9781003288022-36

appealed to his young sensibility), Tezuka had been producing his own comics even as a pre-teen. In his teenage years, the times were extremely dangerous. Indeed, the crucible of this wartime period fuelled Tezuka's life-long pacifism and his deep suspicion of technology. As a teenager, he witnessed the fire-bombing of his home city, Osaka. He also absorbed the ominous reality of the atom bomb and the Emperor of Japan's famous radio address which stated that in defeat Japan must "endure the unendurable" and surrender. Although after the war he trained to be a medical doctor, Tezuka never went into practice, instead, channelling his creativity and compassion into the production of images and drawings, both moving and still. His work reflected his profound recognition that postwar WWII Japan was a very different place from the country of his childhood; in one sense, Tezuka's work, from all that manga to *Astro Boy* to *Broken Down Film* and beyond, can be seen as a multi-faceted confrontation with the contradictions, paradoxes, and difficulties of that difference: escapist and realist, romantic and gritty, despairing and hopeful.

Like another towering figure of postwar Japanese image-making, Akira Kurosawa, Tezuka was attracted to the American pop culture that flooded Japan after the war, perhaps as a way of burying the recent past, as so much of the postwar Japanese society and sensibility appeared determined to do. As Kurosawa admired John Ford, so Tezuka embraced and even emulated Walt Disney. Tezuka is also known for his imaginative stories and stylized Japanese adaptations of western literature. He loved reading novels and watching films that came from North America and Western Europe. Specific to his manga and anime work, however, his early artistic style was largely inspired by Disney, to such an extent that Tezuka's early manga works include comic book versions of Disney movies.

While deeply influenced by American studio animation, the indefatigable Tezuka also developed his techniques, such as using more 'cinematic' camera angles and perspectives (dramatically and brilliantly depicted in 1984's *Jumping*), as well as panning, creating the illusion of watching a live-action film. This theme is humorously depicted in the masterful modernist miniature from 1985, *Broken Down Film*, in which the film elements themselves threaten to disintegrate as a romantic animated Western, literally and figuratively, unspools. Another element that distinguishes him from his American influences is that his work, like that of other manga creators of his generation, is sometimes gritty and violent, although Tezuka, *un*like many creators who followed, eschewed graphic violence in some of his later and popular creations, such as *Astro Boy*. Violence was present but never depicted as the answer to problematic situations. Indeed, the stupidity of violence and the catastrophic use of technology for violent ends emerge as insistent themes in almost all of Tezuka's animated films.

These themes are woven into the overlapping stories of *Tales from a Street Corner* (1962), a sprawling, symphonic film that alternates effortlessly between a sentimental love story and dark political allegory, using various animation techniques and styles, from figurative Disneyfied mice to abstract poster art reminiscent of Soviet Constructivism, tinged with hints of McLaren. As the little girl loses her Teddy Bear, as the mice struggle to survive, as seeds dropped by trees get destroyed or take root, as a cartoony moth ingratiates and irritates, and as the militarist totalitarians ultimately wreak havoc, Tezuka's film affirms the tenacity of hope and its stubborn possibilities. This sense of hope against considerable odds also informs *The Mermaid* (1964), a parable of how one young man's fantasy of discovering a mermaid cannot be defeated either by skeptical parents or the brutal, technological forces of a repressive government. Despite the fearsome obstacles, the determination and energy of the protagonist prevails.

Shadows persist, however. Tezuka is no blind utopian. His work often contains warnings, both wildly satirical and unabashedly sincere, of how easily worlds can be destroyed, how tenuous human life can be. In both *The Drop* (1965) and *Push* (1984), Tezuka explores the extremes of deprivation and consumerism, respectively. A desperate character adrift on a raft goes mad attempting to get the last drops of water off his tattered sails in *The Drop*, seemingly oblivious to the fact that there is water all around him. Slyly satirical of the Japanese predilection for vending machines and automation, *Push* depicts a man driving through a post-apocalyptic landscape still believing that humans can get anything they want at the push of a button: a new car, a new suit, a new Earth. Tezuka imbues this cogent satire with the sinister resonances, in a now very dangerous atomic age, of the phrase "pushing the button" and illustrates the real consequences for the planet of having done just that.

As the six films in this programme demonstrate, Tezuka's animated art stands as an engaged and prolific creative act of resistance to the tyranny of the masses over the individual imagination and a denunciation of those who would presume to dominate others by force. Paradoxically, he achieved this resistance through the popular and even populist art forms of comics and commercial animation. His work also constitutes an impassioned plea for the humane use of technology and an expression of the sanctity of life itself. This is not surprising for a man who had witnessed so much destruction in his young life and who subsequently, with hard-won pacificism driving his drawings, so nimbly navigated his way through the ruins and reconstruction of post-WWII Japan. Ultimately, perhaps Osamu Tezuka, the medical doctor who never practiced, understood that his manga and his anime could become modest instruments of healing and hope not only for his native Japan but also for an increasingly imperilled world.

CHAPTER 36

Decoding Narrative

The Animated World of
Gil Alkabetz (2011)

by Madi Piller and Patrick Jenkins

B ORN IN THE KIBBUTZ *Mashabei Sade* in Israel in 1957, Gil Alkabetz drew as a child and was fascinated by animation. At fifteen, he and his brother made a simple Zoetrope with some animated walk cycles. He went on to study Graphic Design at the Bezalel academy in Jerusalem, where he was exposed to films from the National Film Board of Canada and Zagreb Animation Studios, which encouraged him to try a more personal approach in his own animation. Upon graduating, he made his living mostly from illustration and teaching, as there was very little animation being done in Israel at the time. His student film *Bitzbutz* (1984) was shown at the Stuttgart Animation Festival and attracted the attention of Professor Albrecht Ade, an Animation Instructor at the Art Academy, who offered Gil a grant to come and make another film in his class. Gil has alternated between Stuttgart and Israel during his entire career, working as an animator, illustrator and teacher.

Gil Alkabetz is a fine art 2D animator with a very poetic approach to animation. A master of metaphor, his narratives are often told in an elliptical way, where the viewer is confronted with a series of narrative fragments or memories that gradually reveal the story. Each of his films has a distinct look, reflecting his graphic design background and illustration

DOI: 10.1201/9781003288022-37

work. Often he plays with the flatness of the screen image, in some cases abstracting characters to such an extreme that they are barely recognizable as an image.

Thoroughly storyboarded, his films come from many sources: ideas stored in his mind, stories he has read or ideas from past art school exercises. His work balances illustration, colour and sound with a touch of experimentation that makes each of his films a unique work of art and emotionally moving.

In his first film, *Bitzbutz* (1984), a plasticine stop-motion animated film, we see many of the themes that he will explore throughout his career. A high contrast white box appears on the screen, inside a black frame. A white bird squeezes out of the white box and starts to peck a series of white dots in the black frame. Appearing in the center, a huge black monster eats away the black frame and consumes the bird. Then in a reversal of the predator/prey relationship, the bird eats away the monster from inside, leaving a blank white screen. The high contrast, graphic look of this film explores the flatness of the screen, emphasizing the two-dimensionality of the image.

In *Swamp* (1992), Alkabetz explores this quality even further, "giving up any camera angles other than the frontal one"[1] and eliminating even the image of the swamp to create a poignant meditation on the futility of war. Here, armed with huge scissors instead of lances, two armies of armoured knights on horseback face each other. As an added twist, each mounted knight is attached by strings to balloons (blue for one side, red for another) that keep them from sinking into the swamp below them. They attack and defeat each other by snipping the strings with their oversized scissors, severing the balloons, losing their buoyancy and drowning in the swamp. In a variation of the hunter and hunted theme previously explored in *Bitzbutz*, after much slaughter, the two remaining knights kill each other, leaving no more combatants; completely draining all heroism from war.

In his next film, *Yankale* (1995), Alkabetz pushes simplifying, flattening and abstracting his characters and imagery until they become symbols or signs. Based on the short story *Where Do We Go from Here?* by Israeli writer Aharon Almog, this film tells the story of Yankale, a man who is uncharacteristically late for work one morning. Alkabetz tells Yankale's story three times, each time adding more detail. He lives with his domineering mother who excessively dotes on him, telling him not to take cold showers, eat his breakfast and not to forget his scarf. Yankale's world is made up of variations of the cross, plus and minus symbols that make his world look like a prison. As the story is retold in more detail, we see the reason that Yankale is late for work that morning is that he has stopped by a river made of plus and minuses and cuts off the image of a duck his mother has sewn on his shirt, symbolically cutting his umbilical cord to her. At the end of the film, the narration states that Yankale was never late for work again after this, but ironically, without his duck, Yankale now looks exactly the same as all his fellow workers. In a reflection on our search for personal freedom, the film suggests that Yankale, in making this symbolic act of liberation from his mother, hasn't really achieved emancipation. Instead, he now conforms to everyone else in his world.

In his next film *Rubicon* (1997), Alkabetz leaves aside plot and concentrates on the formal possibilities of using a repetitive structure. *Rubicon* is based on the classic logic riddle that asks: How do you transport a cabbage, a sheep and a wolf in a boat across a river when you can only take one at a time? Left alone the wolf will eat the sheep, or alternatively, the sheep will eat the cabbage. How will you safely transport all three across the river? Again, the theme of prey and predator is seen in this film. The central problem was first posed to Alkabetz fifteen years earlier at art school in a workshop given by the American designer Seymour Chwast.

Alkabetz has stated:

> I also connected it in my mind to the ongoing peace process that was going on at the time between Israel and the Palestinians in Oslo. The attempts to find a rational solution to the conflict reminded me of that classical riddle, and I wanted to show how rational solutions usually don't function in reality. But this context still gave me structural ideas, going from logical solutions to absurd ones, then to a conflict, which is suddenly solved without any apparent reason, till the next round…

FROM A 2011 INTERVIEW WITH GIL ALKABETZ
CONDUCTED BY MADI PILLER

The film follows this structure, at first attempting to solve the problem, before drifting into evermore humorous and surreal juxtapositions of the central characters until we are returned, full circle, to the beginning of the story again.

Morir de Amor (2004) finds Alkabetz returning to traditional narrative. Taking the song *Morir de Amor* (Dying of Love) by Charles Aznavour and Compay Segundo, Alkabetz started from, "a vague idea about music's power to awaken memories." The resulting film is a story of romantic betrayal told in a series of flashbacks. In an apartment, two caged parrots wait for a snoring old man to wake up and feed them. The parrots imitate the sound of everything in their environment, including the ticking of the clock and the snoring of the old man. Looking at the family photos on the walls and the picture of the parrots on the box of parrot feed, the parrots start to reminisce about when they first met and were captured by their owner many years before, when he was on a picnic trip with his wife and chauffeur in the jungle. The parrots sing the title song, which was playing on the portable record player during the picnic.

Reliving the scene, the parrots even mimic the sounds of the lovemaking between the chauffeur and the man's wife, while he is off hunting with a net that eventually will capture them. The parrots loudly repeat the ecstatic cries of the wife calling out "Pedro," the chauffeur's name, awakening the old man who realises that he had been betrayed many years earlier while looking at a family portrait, where he sees that his son has the same red hair as the chauffeur. The beauty of *Morir de Amor* is the complex way it tells the story through a series of flashbacks. It's a wonderful meditation on memory.

The theme of desire reappears in *Travel to China* (2002). Here, Alkabetz uses only one picture to tell the story of a man who dreams all his life of leaving his home and travelling far away. Movement is created through circular repetitions of different details of the image, but ultimately the man remains trapped in his room. Alkabetz then reprises the idea of animating a single image in *The Da Vinci Time Code* (2009). This time, secret movements in Leonardo Da Vinci's painting, *The Last Supper*, are revealed. Here, linear repetitions of fragments of the painting cause Christ and his Disciples to come to life: eating, dancing, discussing and arguing, until finally, all are silenced.

Over the past 27 years, Gil Alkabetz has juggled his work in illustration, teaching, and commercial animation to create an impressive body of independent animation.

NOTE

1. From a 2011 interview with Gil Alkabetz conducted by Madi Piller.

CHAPTER 37

Don't Stop

Animating Hip Hop (2011)

by Marley Rosen

Dirt McGirt comes from Dirt McGirt Island. It's a place that's right off the block from the next island off of Batman Island. I can't let you know exactly where it is–it's a secret, you know? Wonder Woman told me not to say nothing.

-ODB (AKA DIRT MCGIRT)

. . .

It's not easy having an alter ego. Besides wearing an extra layer of spandex under your tweed suit, that is. We spend enough psychological energy living one life; only a special kind of person would sign up for two. Rock stars, super heroes, professional wrestlers. You probably have to be a little unbalanced to voluntarily construct multiple personalities for yourself, to embrace that condition of scattered over-stimulation. But for any of us born in a post-modern urban soup – any of us who grew up in a flurry of media stimulation, a lifelong (cross)cultural electrical storm – for us, that kind of psychological fracturing and reconstruction might be the only kind of identity-making we know. Grab your parents' old records, your big brother's comic books, your cousin's 16-bit game console, your uncle's VHS collection of 70s sci-fi – slice it all up, layer it, rearrange it, and you've got one version of who you might be. Take those same bits, adjust the

DOI: 10.1201/9781003288022-38

pitch and the timing, change the context...and you become another you altogether.

The late 20th century came up with a word for this kind of slicing and repurposing – sampling. And no cultural or aesthetic form has been more explicitly and honestly founded on sampling than hip-hop. As a hip-hop producer, I might do all this quite literally. I might take my parents' old Coltrane records, layer them with SNES sound effects, and insert dialogue from my uncle's worn-out copy of *Tron* that he taped when it aired on CJOH-TV in 1986. While my selections and sampling style might be idiosyncratic or unique to me, the process itself is fundamental to the way that hip-hop culture is (and has always been) made. When we work this way, we build the past into the present.

In a very literal and visible way, hip-hop artists weave their influences right into the fabric of their creative process. It's no wonder, then, that artists who grew up in the 1970s and 1980s will always call back to the icons of their childhood in those eras. If you were a kid reading Marvel Comics and watching Saturday morning cartoons, you might grow up to become Kool Keith, who sometimes raps about space-travel under the alias Doctor Octagon. Or you might grow up to wear an ominous metal mask onstage and call yourself MF DOOM. Then again, you might call yourself Ghostface Killah (aka Iron Man, aka Tony Stark) and release a music video made up entirely of appropriated footage from the TV show *Speed Racer*. It's all fair game.

Not only do the animated and illustrated icons of childhood allow hip-hop to create and re-create itself, but the crate-digging style of hip-hop production also gives visual artists new material from which to draw. Montreal DJ Kid Koala, known not just for his eccentric scratch records but also for his albums' comic strip liner notes, has often collaborated with animator Monkmus to bring his sounds to life on-screen. When Kid Koala throws animal noises on his turntables and moulds them into a conversational exchange of warbling jibberish in the track 'Fender Bender,' Monkmus envisions a street corner lined with thirty-foot tall daisies and an argument between two well-dressed gentlemen, one wearing an oil lamp for a hat while the other carries a large, wind-up telephone. Only the imagination of an animator could do justice to the wordless eloquence of a scratch DJ.

Of course, the spoken word might be the most recognizable element of hip-hop culture, and there is no denying the power of moving images to bring the spoken word to life. Not only can lyrical content be played out visually, but even the very building blocks of verbal speed, complexity and delivery can be emphasized. It might be something as simple as a single verse flashing across the screen to show off Ludacris' double-time delivery in the video "Roll Out." Or it might be the elaborate, technical lyrical flow of Mos Def's 'Casa Bey' being transformed into syllabic dots and dashes that leap from his mouth, gradually accumulating and growing into individual phonemes, until eventually full words and verses fill the screen. It is these elements that make up an emcee's flow – and the living, moving word shows clearly that the term "flow" is not just arbitrary slang.

. . .

It's hard to explain what it's like to be rich, famous and from the hood. One way is to think of a superhero. Someone who has special powers, a double identity, maybe a secret weakness or two.

-THE RZA, *THE TAO OF WU*

. . .

When you build yourself an alter ego, it might be liberating to speak with a new voice, but things can change once that voice is heard. Once people are listening and doing so within a culture that (like any) has its own baggage and prejudices, suddenly you have expectations to live up to. For some, this means certain topics become off-limits. Issues of race, class, gender and sexuality often become virtually taboo in mainstream hip-hop. If you want to talk about these things, you're going to need another persona, and cartoons and comic books can give you just that. There is no better example of this phenomenon than *The Boondocks*. Created by American cartoonist Aaron McGruder, this television series based on his syndicated comic strip has explored every conceivable topic of controversy surrounding race in America. When it comes to hip-hop, McGruder and his team don't hesitate to challenge the status quo – from criticizing programming on BET to challenging the stigma of white folks using a certain N-word.

Perhaps one of the stickiest issues that the show has broached is that of homophobia and the Don't-Ask-Don't-Tell policy that remains in effect in much of mainstream hip-hop. It's an issue that the show explores over the first two seasons through the story of a fictional closeted rapper named Gangstalicious, as he wrestles with his fear of being outed and ostracized. What is most stunning about this multi-episode arc isn't so much the storyline itself (though it is brilliant and biting), but the roster of high-profile rappers who McGruber is able to enlist to play out the drama. It might come as no surprise that Mos Def would take part in a conscious social commentary like this, but to find Busta Rhymes, Snoop Dogg, Nate Dogg, and Xzibit starring in a revealing critique of sexuality in the hip hop industry is something worth noting. These guys aren't what most would call conscious rappers – on their own records, they've all been known to throw a certain F-word around. But the cartoon world of *The Boondocks* allows these icons to participate in a discussion they might not otherwise touch.

If you're reading this, chances are you already have some idea of the power of the animated image. Something about an image coming to life allows us to transport and re-imagine ourselves in ways that other aesthetic forms just can't equal. What is most remarkable about the way this phenomenon has played out in the hip-hop world is just how much this re-imagining has influenced the very fabric of the culture. When a turntablist cuts slide whistle sound effects into an off-kilter beat, he is using the language of Looney Tunes inside the language of scratch. When a graff artist paints a mural on the side of a train, she is using the language of typography inside the language of tagging. When an emcee dons an aluminum mask during a night-club performance, he's using the language of Marvel Comics inside the language of rap.

Everything is a sample. Sample everything.

CHAPTER 38

Remembering Karen Aqua (2012)

by Keltie Duncan with Ken Field

A T ONCE PERSONAL AND universal, the animated short films of Karen Aqua offer a tactile glimpse into the philosophies and experiences of a dynamic and creative woman. Aqua's films document the artist's playful self-exploration, undertaken to find her own unique place within the universal spectrum of human existence. Though Aqua lost her ten-year battle with cancer on May 30th, 2011, her films reveal and maintain a strong connection to the vibrant voice of the filmmaker who made them and, as such, become a patchwork portrait of Aqua herself. The films in this retrospective exude the pure essence that was Karen Aqua, and allow her very bright spirit to leap off the screen.

ABOUT KAREN AQUA

Karen Aqua began making animated films after her graduation from Rhode Island School of Design in 1976. Her award-winning films have been screened nationally and internationally, including at the New York Film Festival, and at international animation festivals in Zagreb, Hiroshima, Ottawa and Annecy, as well as museums and universities. She received film production grants from the American Film Institute, Massachusetts Council on the Arts and Humanities, New England Film/ Video Fellowship Program, New Forms Regional Initiative, Massachusetts

DOI: 10.1201/9781003288022-39

Cultural Council and the Puffin Foundation. She has been an artist-in-residence at The MacDowell Colony, Djerassi Foundation, Millay Colony, Roswell Artist-in-Residence Program, Atlantic Center for the Arts, and Fundacion Valparaiso (Spain).

Aqua was a Lecturer in Animation at Boston College from 1984–1991, and Animation Instructor at Emerson College in 1987. She served as a juror for major animation and film festivals in the US and Canada and presented one-person screenings of her work at museums and universities around the US, including the Boston Museum of Fine Arts, Institute of Contemporary Art (Boston), California Institute of the Arts, Dartmouth College, and the University of Oregon. Beginning in 1990, Aqua also produced, directed, and animated twenty-two segments for the acclaimed *Sesame Street* television program.

ARTISTIC IMPRESSIONS

Karen Aqua's earlier films document a time of self-discovery and lay bare the process of defining oneself through artistic exploration. These films are more explicitly subjective, providing glimpses into specific questions Aqua had about herself and her artistic process and how the two inform each other. Her very graphic style is reminiscent of ancient runes and symbols, even in films that do not directly deal with older civilizations. As a graduate of design education, Aqua's films reflect the evolving visual styles of the many years that span her career and serve to document her own lived time in much the same way she does for past generations.

In *Ground Zero / Sacred Ground*, Aqua looks at contemporary impacts of nuclear testing on nearby remnants of a past civilization. This film looks back to early ancestors to answer larger questions about the human condition hundreds of years afterward and raises more questions about humanity at large and how each new cycle of existence is influenced by those gone by. Similar questions are asked in films like *Vis-à-Vis*, where an animator is shown attempting to create a film through moments of daydreaming and self-reflection.

Many of Aqua's films contain visual metaphors for the journey and accumulation of human experience. Each one holds a sense of magic and whimsy, and often reveals love and longing for the allure of the exotic. Through the portrayal of distant creatures and locales, Aqua imparts an admiration for adventure that extends into an appreciation of those little everyday moments that compose our lives. Aqua's films inspire common bravery and encourage daily adventures so as not to miss one opportunity.

Vis-à-Vis is also directly referenced in *Experimental Animation: Origins of a New Art* by Robert Russett and Cecile Starr. This book was first published in 1976 to formally catalogue a budding and under-acknowledged art form one technique at a time, and the second edition includes mention of Aqua, framed as being amongst a group of strong, "liberated" female animators practising in the late 1970s and early 1980s. Cecile Starr says in this seminal text that Aqua's films are amongst those "concerned with serious feelings and true experiences" but, as has been my experience with her body of work, Aqua finds the truth of her existence more through a bright, light-hearted approach than through one with more serious tones (ibid).

Her films are filled with colour and rhythmic energy, fueled by exotic sounds that were often composed and performed by her husband, musician Ken Field. At a time when so much animation is made possible using computers, Karen Aqua's films stand out; they are created entirely from drawings done by hand. Her innovative films occupy a unique place in the world of independent and experimental animation. Created from exceptionally refined and colourful drawings, Aqua's style is characterized by extraordinary hand-drawn visual transformations and compelling subject matter, exploring themes of culture, ritual, and the human condition. Aqua stated, "I strive to create films which are more poetry than prose, making visible the invisible."

Aqua's films are alive with wild, exotic imagery from nature that lends a very rich visual and emotional tone to her work. Seashells, palm trees, and wild animals pervade and ground her work. Her films are so vividly personal that watching them feels like learning about her life philosophy from Aqua herself. Each one carries whispers from the woman who made them; they raise, in my mind's eye, glimpses of a nurturing, open, loving, perceptive, intelligent, warm and endlessly inquisitive person. Her later films maintain self-reflexivity, again paralleling the creative process to the process of living and dealing with life's inevitable questions. In *Afterlife,* a film in which Aqua reacts to her diagnosis, cancer becomes just another part of daily living to be examined and prodded with her unique vision and perspective. The body features quite prominently throughout all of Aqua's filmography, from the very beginning, through her changing relationship to her own body, so she was well-equipped to deal with the subject of cancer in her films. True to form, Aqua did so in a way that is sensitive and highly subjective; just like cancer itself.

Through chronicling the life of one of animation's most skilled practitioners and prolific champions, the films of Karen Aqua document an era and tradition of the artform seen less and less frequently. Self-exploration through animated film means that these films are both self-portrait and auto-biography, painting the picture of a woman keenly missed by those who knew her and, in a way, introducing her to those who wish they could have.

CHAPTER 39

Unseen Forces

A Spotlight on Emily Pelstring (2020)

by Keltie Duncan

L ET'S START WITH "SCIENCE."
Science, I'm sure you would agree, has conquered many of the simpler mysteries of our world: mysteries like gravity and light waves and how sound works. Using instruments – many of them analog, no less – to locate and quantify the invisible waves and frequencies that float around and through everything, humans have given form to these unseen forces and harnessed their power to create things like the projected image (yay!), a specific frequency that scares away teenagers (yay? yay.), and the Philips Hue lighting system which can turn a chores day into a smooth night at the jazz club (hallelujah!).

What, though, about the invisible mysteries that remain unsolved and unquantified; those in the realm of the paranormal, for example? Those of ghosts and magic and the effect centuries of existing in a heteronormative patriarchy has on social evolution?

What if a fresh mind came in and began using analog instrumentation to quantify *those* sorts of mysteries? What if said fresh mind didn't stop there, but tackled even those mysteries that are generally thought to be solved, like light waves and how sound works and... well probably not gravity, because I'm pretty sure that one's been done to death?

DOI: 10.1201/9781003288022-40

Who better to examine these paranormal mysteries than someone who's a little bit imagineer, a little bit tinkerer, a little bit artist, a little bit academic and a lot bit magician; and by 'magician' I mean both the fairy tale kind who have powers and tall hats and the real kind, who are masters of illusion, distraction and suspendable glass boxes á la David Blaine's 44 magical days above London. #neverforget

Emily Pelstring, if you haven't already guessed, is all of these things, yes, even a master of glass boxes! By day, Emily is a BFA graduate in Animation from the Rhode Island School of Design (RISD), holds her MFA care of Concordia University in Montreal and is currently a faculty member in the Department of Film and Media at Queens University (Kingston, Ontario, Canada). By night, she is a subversive punk whose mystical, fun and powerful work has enjoyed international success showing in both gallery and festival settings of all shapes and sizes.

Pelstring, as much a sound artist and performer as a visual artist and filmmaker, uses her superpowers for good, critiquing the world in which she lives indirectly by way of celebrating what makes it strong, rather than by explicitly exposing what makes it weak. Her interests and creative output make her as true a multi-disciplinary artist as ever I've seen, so like the analog experiments that have come before – wait for it – let's take a prism to this beam of light so we may examine all of her brilliant colours on their own.

BOOM.

– –

EMILY PELSTRING, MASTER OF GLOW (I.E., THE FILMS)

Animation is already something of an unquantifiable force. If you can separate the visual art in animation from its performance elements, its cinematic principles, or even its visual effects, then you'll have placed animation studies on the endangered departments list. Recognizing and capitalizing on these many facets of animation, Emily has incorporated the animated image in her practise for many years, ranging from recent fully-animated, good ol' fashioned short films, to components in her installation work and animated elements in live-action shorts and music videos.

Naturally, the best person to describe her work is the artist herself, but if I may:

I asked Emily to name a few common threads she sees running through her work. She describes one such thread as "a kind of cataloguing of images that appear out of dreams, arising from the subconscious." To me, the dream-like quality Emily describes is reminiscent of the colour palettes and general spookiness of *Susperia* (1977). Her images feel like they hold a physical space, that if I walked up to the image, I could touch it and feel a static charge, like when touching an old CRT TV. Her aesthetic is ephemeral, as if she, our intrepid magician-scientist, has harnessed actual light waves and forced them into as physical a form as they can take, giving her films and animated imagery an inner glow. They have a dark, cool colour palette, alive with an analog tactility, full of visual tracers that betray the wavelengths of colour which make up the image itself and provide an intriguing peek behind the curtain, so to speak.

Besides current thoughts, I also asked Pelstring to cite a few animated childhood memories that might still influence her work. She listed Maleficent's transformation scene from *Sleeping Beauty*, the bioluminescence of the plant life in *FernGully: The Last Rainforest*, and being just generally haunted by *The Last Unicorn*. I dare say I couldn't imagine a more fitting trio of references if I *tried* (I tried). Pelstring goes on to sum up her aesthetic in five words – "molten, nostalgic, figurative, hieroglyphic, prismatic" – which perfectly accounts for that unmistakable Emily Pelstring *Je ne sais quoi.*

Pelstring's visual language has one foot in the realm of the familiar, and one foot gleefully in a world of levitation, alternate histories and spells, which gives Pelstring's cinematic space an almost infinite and inexplicable depth. I can imagine her animated shorts being broadcast over the airwaves in Frankenstone, the fictional land home to the exiled characters of *The Hilarious House of Frightenstein* (and if you do not know of which I speak, do thyself a favour and Google it).

Experimental in nature, but with more than enough substance to grip, Pelstring's short films are spin art masterpieces combining old technology and techniques with contemporary iconography and themes. *Head Cleaner* (2015), for example, celebrates the technological tools of yore, imagining the filthy innards of a VCR, treating it like a wondrous hidden universe begging to be explored.

Though not all of Pelstring's short films reference technology so explicitly, they all share a familiar stylistic nod, bringing us to another self-declared creative thread: "experimentation with optical filtering and textural effects." Her films have a wonderfully contradictory crisp-yet-lo-fi quality that betrays her history of working with old video equipment. The images are compressed in a way that is reminiscent of a guitar signal making its way through a series of pedals to come out the other side, full of grit and texture. Pelstring's work relies on a principle that says frequencies are "real" even if you can't see them, including those frequencies and wavelengths that have yet to be proven, like ghostly dimensions and mystical powers.

Pelstring's sound work, often the soundtrack to her animation but not always, shares the same analog chewiness that her imagery does. In the most appealing way possible, her music has a tangible warp and weft to it, almost like it has an electromagnetic charge. It holds the quality of optical sound with a heap more dimension to it. Again, like her visual aesthetic, Emily's sound work takes the best of old, analog technology and puts it on a pedestal.

EMILY PELSTRING, SPACIAL MAGICIAN (I.E., THE INSTALLATIONS)

Animation as an art form shines in Pelstring's installation work. Animated elements become the link between a constructed physical environment and the imaginary veil being draped around it. In many of her installations, which can all be seen on her website, and are extremely well-documented, Emily combines glass structures, projections and reflections to create the illusion of floating objects, like a hologram. Pelstring cracks the barriers between our living existence and imaginary, or perhaps just unproven, hidden dimensions, not only blurring the line between physical reality and other realms but posing the question of whether or not the line exists at all.

Even when the image isn't animated, she applies a kind of graphic veneer to live people and objects, such as a life-sized line drawing of a car attached to a real car, or face paint on an actor to resemble a comic or a sketch, like in 'I Babysat for Those Fools', an installation created with Inflatable Deities, a collective established with her creative partner, Jessica Mensch. (It should be noted here that Pelstring is also in a musical collaboration with Mensch and their bandmate, Katherine Kline, called The Powers. Shout out to The Powers.)

For "The Haunted Blob," an installation staged at Montreal's historic Rialto Theatre, Pelstring created the illusion of huge gashes in the walls, revealing a secret dimension teeming with swimming, floating, life-sized ghosts. Like the Wizard of Oz, Pelstring augments reality the old-fashioned way, using tricks of the eye or "in-camera effects" like projection and masks to bend the experience of her surroundings. These elements create a sense of childlike wonder, like some of the best animated films do, and speak to Emily's third self-proclaimed creative thread: her sense of humour.

Looking ahead to her next project, Pelstring is planning to free herself from the shackles of storyboarding in favour of a more liberated workflow. She says she's done both highly planned projects and more stream-of-consciousness shoots and wants to focus on the latter, while experimenting with some multi-plane effects and techniques, expanding on her exploration of reflection and surface.

Now to sum up, if I may heavy-handedly return to "science" – *ahem* – my conclusions find Emily's work consistently combines sombre whimsy and powerful mysticism with an eerie semi-translucence to create a phenomenon I would like to call Saturated Haunting Bioluminescence (SHB), or, The Pelstring Effect. Prepare to be tickled, intrigued, entranced, provoked, impressed and, of course, improved. Maximum exposure encouraged.

All of the above hypotheses can be considered at emilypelstring.com.

CHAPTER 40

Flannel Fever Dream

The Films of Mike Maryniuk (2021)

by Devin Hartley

Y OU NEVER QUITE KNOW what you're going to get when you watch a
Mike Maryniuk film, but it's always guaranteed to be an experience.
Born in Winnipeg and raised in rural Manitoba, Maryniuk has
described himself as a "self-taught film virtuoso" inspired by a love of
Norm MacLaren, Jim Henson, Looney Tunes, Stan Brakhage and the
often-over-the-top physical acting in silent films. Over the years he has
cited two formative moments in his development as an artist and filmmaker. The first involved the accidental discovery of a bunch of old 1920s
film posters while working on a demolition crew in a soon-to-be demolished shoe store that used to be a movie theatre. The second was taking
one of Sol Nagler's 16mm workshops at the Winnipeg Film Group, which
introduced him to a passion for hand-processing.

The Winnipeg Film Group would also play a key role in facilitating
many of his productions in the years following that fateful workshop,
seven of which he also worked for them as their Production Director.
Working in 16mm – frequently paired with scratch animation – his initial films highlight the almost absurd and surreal sense of humour that
would become a mainstay of his work, featuring characters that include
a crime-fighting chicken boy and a possessed water bed. As he continued
developing his skills as a filmmaker, he began to add new techniques to his

DOI: 10.1201/9781003288022-41

repertoire, experimenting with everything from different ways to hand-alter found footage, to claymation, collage film, cut-outs and more. From there he would also go on to make three films with the National Film Board of Canada, and in 2018 he directed his first feature film, *The Goose*.

His work with the Winnipeg Film Group also put him in the orbit of frequent collaborator Matthew Rankin. In 2006 he teamed up with Rankin and Walter Forsberg, under their collective L'atelier national du Manitoba, to make *Death by Popcorn: The Tragedy of the Winnipeg Jets*, a fictionalized pseudo-documentary about the not-so-fictional demise of the Winnipeg NHL franchise (which has since been resurrected). *Death by Popcorn* was assembled using found footage rescued from the dumpster of local CTV affiliate CKY-TV and donated to the collective. While the film was a success, selling out the Winnipeg Film Group's Cinematheque on multiple nights, CTV ended up suing over their use of the footage, complicating further screenings of the film. Two years later, Matt Rankin and Maryniuk teamed up again for the fast-paced, hallucinogenic documentary *Cattle Call*, which made the rounds on the film festival circuit and quickly gathered a bit of a cult following (fortunately without any more lawsuits).

While all of Maryniuk's films blend his knack for inventive DIY methods with an irreverent sense of humour and a flair for the surreal, it's almost impossible to give a specific label in terms of technique, genre, or medium to his overall body of work. While he started with 16mm and scratch animation, he quickly expanded his horizons to, well, pretty much every technique you could possibly imagine, and several you probably couldn't. Whether it's surreal documentaries like *Cattle Call* and *The Yodelling Farmer*, adapting his signature home brew style to a commissioned music video, the experimental abstract animation of *Blotto 649* and *Tattoo Step*, or a "3DIY" short about the horrors of combining a satellite, a microwave and the live broadcast of a horseshoe match (do they actually even broadcast those?), Mike Maryniuk doesn't seem interested in restricting the types of films he makes or the methods he uses to make them. His work is consistent in its inconsistency, careening from one technique to the next, scratch animation, cut-outs, time lapse, stop motion and everything in between, all while maintaining a distinctive handmade style that's as resourceful as it is imaginative.

There's a hard-working, prairie sensibility to his art, something that is immediately familiar to anyone from there – "there" encompassing the provinces of Alberta, Saskatchewan and Manitoba – but still gives anyone who isn't a means of seeing into the heart of the place, a glimpse behind the curtain to reveal the dusty, oft-forgotten corners in all their glory. While the techniques he uses may constantly change, Maryniuk's approach to animation rarely differs, gravitating towards practical, hands-on methods that are frequently labour-intensive, (like *June Night*'s 14,000+ Buster Keaton cut-outs, which were individually cut by hand), literally experimental (like the repurposed thrift store spin art machine used for *Blotto 649*), or both. The films that result are unpretentious, balancing the craft involved in their execution with a willingness to lean into moments of goofball or absurdist humour. Lorne Collie, the subject of *Home Cooked Music*, unintentionally describes Maryniuk's work best when he laments in the film that "We get too used to everything being made in a factory someplace, and you buy it in a store somewhere. There isn't enough make it yourself anymore."

Despite his varied and prolific oeuvre, one thing that is ever-present in his films is his love for his home province and its people. Beyond his frequent collaborations with mainstays of Winnipeg's arts scene like Matthew Rankin, the Winnipeg Film Group, and the band D. Rangers, Maryniuk's films often centre on subjects or figures that speak to the spirit or character of Manitoba and the lives of the people who live there, while also, in equal measure, confronting and embracing the stereotypes and assumptions made about prairie life from those on the outside. Even his films that aren't explicitly Manitoba-centric often have some kind of small nod, like *Blotto 649*'s spin art animation being set to a cover version of "These Eyes" by The Guess Who, arguably the one band most associated with the province (for better or worse).

His preoccupation with Manitoba and with prairie life shouldn't, however, be interpreted as simply nostalgia or some kind of blind worship for the place where he grew up. The visions of prairie life Maryniuk captures are much more dreamy surrealism than documentary "reality." He has a knack for presenting the familiar in unfamiliar ways, taking the imagery of urban and rural Manitoba life and transforming it into something from a half-remembered fever dream. While that transformation can be found to varying degrees in all his films, it's most obvious in his feature film, *The Goose*, a hypnotic and kaleidoscopic love letter to Manitoba as Mike Maryniuk knows and loves it, disguised as a young man's existential journey to escape his small town and find his voice. In *The Goose*, as with many of his films, he uses surrealism and absurdity as a means to lovingly poke fun at the realities and shared experiences of living in Manitoba. Much like how it's totally ok to make fun of your own sibling for their flaws and foibles, but if someone else tries there'll be hell to pay, Maryniuk is only able to pull it off *because* of his love for the place.

Beyond capturing his clear affection for his home province, in a way, many of his films (and not just those related to his homeland) are an act of preservation, of the fragments of other lives, other memories, that would otherwise be lost to time. It's fitting that his artistic "origin story" begins with discovering those long-forgotten and abandoned movie posters, as so much of his work is directly concerned with preventing things from being discarded or forgotten, which also comes across in his penchant for hands-on, home brew techniques. Whether it's stories, archival footage, or whatever recent treasure he found at a thrift store, Maryniuk is sure to not only salvage it, but to also transform it into something new and imaginative, without losing the spirit of the original.

Take, for example, the real-life people whose stories he captures. His documentaries often centre on very prairie-specific figures who are frequently overlooked or unknown by the rest of Canada (let alone outside of Canada), like Indigenous hockey legend Reggie Leach in *The Riverton Rifle* or folk artist Armand Lemiez, whose attempts to will his artworks to the province of Manitoba are the focus of *No Cultural Value*. Maryniuk also tends to focus on those who are involved in what could be called "dying arts," like Tim Dowler, the auctioneer at the heart of *Cattle Call*, *The Yodeling Farmer*'s eleven-time World Champion yodeller Stew Clayton, or retired machinist Lorne Collie's truly one-of-a-kind string instruments profiled in *Home Cooked Music*. While all documentaries are arguably trying to preserve through documenting something, it's hard to overlook how specific Maryniuk is about selecting his subjects.

Despite being an artist who frequently works with techniques that are both time-consuming and laborious, Maryniuk definitely doesn't have a problem with just winging it when he needs to. In early 2021, Maryniuk participated in a virtual artist talk for the Regina Public Library, "Sculpting in Pandemic Times," to discuss *June Night*. While describing printing and cutting by hand the roughly 14,000 cut-outs of Buster Keaton used in the film, he noted that "as you mature as an artist you start to realize that really all that you keep is the mistakes." While mistakes seem like they might be an inherent risk when using the more DIY methods Maryniuk favours, whether it's repurposing misprinted cut-outs for *June Night* or the sudden and very pandemic-relatable surprise cat appearance in his music video for Paul Leary's "Gary Floyd Revisited," that risk seems to fuel his creativity rather than wear him down, "it's the mistakes that set you apart, so embracing your mistakes is probably the most important advice I could give to someone."

Index

ABBA, 191
Abel's Island (Steig), 197
Absolute realism and unrealism, 12
Advertising film, 7, 26, 54–56
Akira Kurosawa, 129, 216
Alkabetz, Gil
  Bitzbutz (1984), 219–220
  The Da Vinci Time Code (2009), 222
  fine art 2D animator, 219–220
  Graphic Design at the Bezalel
    academy, 222
  illustration, and commercial
    animation, 222
  Morir de Amor (2004), 222
  Rubicon (1997), 221
  Swamp (1992), 220
  Travel to China (2002), 222
  Yankale (1995), 220–221
American animation, 47–49, 80, 82, 131
American Bandstand, Clark's television
  program, 65
American classic cartoon esthetics, 56
American Film Institute, 65, 227
Animation
  absolute realism and unrealism, 12
  description, 12
  frame-by-frame animation technique,
    12
  second mode of expression, 12
  "stop-action" technique, 12
  trend of comic action, 12
  use of trick pictures, 12
Aqua, Karen
  Afterlife, 229
  artistic impressions, 228–230
  colour and rhythmic energy, 229

  early life, 227
  emotional tone, 229
  graphic style, 228
  Ground Zero/Sacred Ground, 228
  hand-drawn visual transformations, 229
  impacts of nuclear testing, 228
  lecturer in animation, 228
  self-exploration, 230
  Vis-a-Vis (1982), 228–229
  visual metaphors and human
    experience, 228–229
Art Association of Montreal, 15
Avery, Tex, 152
Baden-Baden International Festival of
  New Music, 42

Barré-Bowers Studio, 14
Barré, Raoul
  Animated Grouch Chaser (1915), 3, 9,
    10, 13
  Au bord de la mer (1911), 4
  Barré-Bowers Studio, 14
  birth and family, 4
  and Bowers, 15
  caricatures for "Le Soufflet," 5
  caricatures in *Cartoons on a Yacht*
    (1915), 12
  cartoons in "La Patrie," 6
  Cartoons in the Country (1915), 11, 13
  Cartoons in the Hotel (1915), 13
  Cartoons in the Laundry (1915), 11
  Cartoons in the Parlour (1915), 13
  Cartoons on the Beach (1915), 11, 13
  cell animation techniques, 9–10
  children of Dirk's "Katzenjammer
    Kids," 7

comedy–parody metaphor of human
life, 7
comic zoo in *Hunts the Hunter*, 15
Contes Vrais (1905), 5
in daily newspapers, 6
development of comic strips and film
animation, 3
Edison Studios, American animated
films, 11
Edison workshops, 7
"Educational Art and Film Company
of Montreal," 16
elegant and descriptive style, 11
"En roulant ma boule," satiric album, 5
exhibitions, 15
Felix in Germ-mania (1927), 15
first animation film and studios, 7–8
frame-by-frame shooting, 4
funny fat women in *Felix Trumps the
Ace* (1926), 15
interview for "Le Devoir," 16
invention and development of
animated film, 3
La Baigneuse (1913), 4
Les mines de l'ensoleillee (1929), 4
live-action sequence, 16
Mariette (1902), 5
newspaper comic strips in Quebec, 3
Outcaut's "Buster Brown," 7
Pamphile LeMay's books, 5
peg system, description, 8–9
Phables (1916), 13–14
portraits of actresses and women, 15
positioning and superimposition of
images, 8
predictions, 10–11
pseudonym as E. Paulette, 16
representation of habitants and
explorers, 5
sequences of live-action, 11
sequences of *Two Lip Time* (1926), 15
slash system, 9
"syndicated" comic strips, 13
technical procedures for picture-by-
picture drawing, 4
"Tourism in Quebec", 16

transparent material, use of, 9
trip to Europe, 4
use of impressionistic techniques, 4
visual arts in Quebec, 3
work in George Batten and Co, 6
work on stained glass windows, 15
Bartlett, Craig, 146
Bendazzi, Giannalberto, 105, 121
Berlin International Film Festival, 192
Blanchard, Gerard, 58
Blashfield, Jim
Bunnyheads (1996), 201
multi-platinum acts, 201
music videos, 200
Suspicious Circumstances (1985), 199
Boston public TV station, 207
Bray, John Randolph, 14
Breer, Robert
Blue Monday (1988), 139
early life, 137
experimental animator, 140
Fist Fight (1964), 139
Form Phases IV (1954), 138
influencing factors, 138
A Man and His Dog Out for Air (1957),
139
mimes in LMNO (1978), 138
Neo-Plasticism, 137
Recreation (1956), 138–140
sound, role of, 139
technique and personal associations,
139–140
Bride and the Bachelors (Tomkins), 25
Bringing Up Father (1946), 13
Buddha, 25, 30
"Business Office" Ads, 53

CalArts, 87, 207
Cell animation techniques, 9–10
Center for Advanced Visual Studies at
M.I.T, 207
The Chamber of Horrors (1916), 14
Chomon, Segundo de
colouring of films, 33
The Dandys of The Park, 35
Danse Cosmopolite, 34

early life, 33
El Hotel Electrico, 36, 37
fairy tale, 37
first technical discovery, 34
frame-by-frame technique, 38
La Legende Du antome, 36
La Maison antee, 38
Le Chevalier Mystere, 37
Le Roi Des Aulnes, 37
Les Ombres Chinoises, 37
Life and Death of Our Lord Jesus
        Christ, 38
Liquefaction Des Corps Ours, 36, 37
Los Cuapos De La Vaqueria Del
        Parque, 35
"natural scenes," 35–36
150-metre comedies, 36
one turn, one picture technique,
        34, 36
Samson et Daila, 34
shot of an eclipse of the, 36
spirit of imitation, 35–36
stop motion animation, 37
use of a transparent screen, 38
Voyage ans La Lune (1908), 37
Voyage Au Centre De La Terre, 37
Voyage Dans La Planete upiter, 37
Clampett, Bob at Warner Bros.
    Arsenic and Old Lace (1944), 154
    Baby Bottleneck (1946), 153
    Baby Bottleneck spoofs Dumbo
        (1940), 154
    "Beany and Cecil" episodes, 156
    "big five" Warner Bros animation
        directors, 152
    Book Revue (1946), 154
    character in a positive light, 153
    Clampett's Daffy, 153–154
    Coal Black and de Sebben Dwarfs
        (1943), 154
    Corny Concerto (1944), 155
    The Daffy Doc (1938), 153
    Disney techniques, 155–156
    employment at Los Angeles Examiner, 151
    Fantasia (1940), 154
    Flowers and Trees (1932), 154

The Great Piggy Bank Robbery (1946), 154
    Gruesome Twosome (1945), 153
    The Hare and the Tortoise (1940), 154
    influence on animators, 157
    An Itch in Time (1946), 155
    Kitty Kornered (1946), 154
    "Merrie Melodies" cartoon, 151
    moral and psychological approach of
        animators, 152–153
    Mutual Broadcasting Network, 154
    Porky's Duck Hunt (1937), 152
    Rabbit Seasoning (1952), 152
    Snow White and the Seven Dwarfs
        (1937), 154
    The Three Little Pigs (1934), 155
    Tortoise Wins by a Hare (1943), 153
    The Ugly Duckling (1938), 154
    with Walt Disney, 154–155
Cohl, Emile, 7, 54, 138
Comedy–parody metaphor of human
        life, 7
Comic action, 12
Comic strips and film animation, 3;
        see also Barré, Raoul
Crafton, Donald, animation historian, 64
Cramps (1916), 14
Cutout animation style, Terry Gilliam's, 203
Cut-outs, 238
Czechoslovakia, animation in
    advertising, 54
    IRE Films, 54
    Maar sound-film advertising
        studio, 54
    Pole Sergije Tagatz set up shop, 54

Daffy Duck, evolution of
    aggressive and urban, 49–50
    Blanc's original voice for Daffy
        Duck, 51
    block-booking system, 47
    Book Revue (1946), 50
    Colonel Heeza Liar (1913), 48
    The Daffy Doc (1938), 50
    Daffy soldiers, 50
    Disney's Mickey Mouse, 48
    Duck Amuck (1953), 51

Duck Dodgers in the 24 1/2th Century (1953), 49, 51
The Duxorcist (1987), 47
Fleischers' Betty Boop, 48
Frank Tashlin's Daffy, 49, 50
Goofy or Donald Duck, 49
The Great Piggy Bank Robbery (1946), 50
Hardaway – Woody Woodpecker, 49
interpreted by Chuck Jones, 51
large-scale production, 48
Little Red Riding Hood (*Book Revue*), 50
live-action pictures, 47
Looney Tunes series (1930), 48
Merrie Melodies series (1934), 48
Nasty Quacks and *Plane Daffy* (1944), 50
parameters of Daffy's character, 50
Porky Pig's Feat (1943), 49
Porky, reactive character, 48–49
Porky's Duck Hunt (1937), 49
Porky's Hare Hunt (1938), 49
Rabbit Seasoning (1952), 51
Robin Hood Daffy (1958), 50
Silly Symphonies, 48
Song Car-Tunes, 48
Stupor Duck (1956), 50
Tashlin's cartoons, 50
Warner Bros., 47
You Ought to Be in Pictures (1940), 49, 50
Daniels, Dave, 146
Disney, 13, 17, 22, 48, 49, 60, 64, 69, 77, 80–82, 98, 151–152, 154–156, 161, 167, 168, 176, 210, 216
Doctor Desoto (Steig), 197
The Dog Pound (1916), 14
Don't-Ask-Don't-Tell policy, 225
Dumala, Piotr
    "alchemy" of animation, 103
    artist-driven animation, 104–105
    Crime and Punishment (2000), 105, 107
    Czarny Kapturek (The Little Black Riding Hood, 1983), 105
    Dostoevsky, Fyodor, 105, 107

Dostoevsky's Underground Man, 104
    early life, 104
    "free market" economy, 105
    Kafka, Franz, 105, 107
    Lagodna (Gentle, 1985), 106
    Latajace Vlosy (Flying Hair, 1984), 105
    literary influences, 104
    Lykantrophia (Lycanthropy, 1981), 105
    Nerwowe Zycie Kosmosu (The Nervous Life of The Universe, 1986), 105
    "poetry of pessimism," 105
    Sciany (Walls, 1987), 106
    unmistakable style, 106
    Wolnosc nogi (Freedom of the Leg, 1988), 106

Eclecticism, 56, 124
Edison Studios, American animated films, 11
Edison workshops, 7
"Educational Art and Film Company of Montreal," 17
Eggeling, Viking, 41–42
    Diagonal Symphony (1924), 41
    Horizontal–Vertical Orchestra (1921), 41
"En roulant ma boule" satiric album, 5
Exercises, Whitney brothers', 24
Experimental Animation: Origins of a New Art (Russett and Starr), 229

Fantasia (1940), 81, 115, 154, 155
Farmer Alfalfa, Paul Terry's, 10
Fart of art, *see* Grillo, Oscar
Felix the Cat, Sullivan and Messmer's, 9
Film Culture, 26, 27
Fischer, Hans, 45
    Blue Wonder, 45
    The Ravaged Melody, 45
    The Snowman, 45
    studio in Mehlem-on-the-Rhine, 45
Fischinger, Hans, *Dance of the Colours*, 45
Fischinger, Oskar, 43–44
    Art in Cinema catalogue, 26
    astrological principles, 23
    Blavatsky's theosophy, 24

Cage's work with Fischinger, 25–26
commercial work for money, 26–27
Composition in Blue, 29
continuity and polytechnical
    diversity, 44
Ding le Mei's Institute, 28
Disney, 22
early films, 27
electric Tibetan prayer wheel, 24
formal writings, 23
individualism, 24
internal facts of Fischinger's life, 21–22
Kandinsky, memoirs, 30
MGM, 22
Motion Painting I (1947), 22, 29
opposed in theory to representational
    imagery, 26
Paramount, 22, 44
Pasadena Museum notes, 27
private writings, 23
Radio Dynamics (1942), 28
representational cartoons, 22
Spiral film (1926), 29
Spiritual Constructions (1927), 43
Steiner's anthroposophy, 24
Study 11A, 28
suspicion of other artists, 24
Swiss Rivers and Landscapes (1934), 29
three-colour subtractive tripack
    film, 22
wax-slicing machine, 21
Woman on The Moon (1929), 44
"working process," 28
Yogananda's Vedanta, 24
Frame by frame, animated commercials
    1920–1990
advertising film, 55
animation in Hungary, 54
Czechoslovakia, 54
eclecticism and evolution of
    techniques, 55
era of hypersignalisation, 55
France in 1919, 54
Germany, in 1911, 54
graphic creation for TV, 55
graphic symbolism, 55

Italian animation, 55
Mondschen-Maar brothers, 55
slice-of-life approach, 57
style and sensitivity of thye era, 57
2001: A Space Odyssey (1968), 57
ultra-synthetic imagery, 55, 56
Yellow Submarine (1968), 57
Frame-by-frame animation technique,
    4, 12
France in 1919, animation in, 54
Freleng, Friz, 152
Furniture in animation!
    Construction Manual (Joseph), 212
    description, 209
    Frank Film (1973), 212
    Frankly Caroline, sequel, 213
    How to Hookup your Home Theater
        (2007), 210
    Kabal films, 210
    Moving Day (2012), 210
    Picknick mit Weissmann (1968), 211
    "Plymptoons" for MTV, 210
    Renaissance, Borowczyk's
        metaphorical parlour game, 210
    Set in Motion, like *Drawn to Light*, 211
    Utopia Parkway (Priestley), 212
    The Yellow Submarine (1968), 212
Furukawa, Taku
    anime TV series, 100
    Bird (1985), 100
    Coffee Break (1977), 100
    contribution, 102
    digital tools, 100–101
    Disney's *Snow White*, 98
    early life, 97
    "family tree," presented by Furukawa, 98
    1st Tokyo Animation Festival, 99
    Hayao Miyazaki, 99
    Head Spoon (1972), 100
    heroes and villains, images, 97
    Kuri's studio, 99
    megalomaniacal culture in late 60s, 100
    "Memorial Day," 98
    New Trends in Japanese Popular
        Culture, 100
    New York Trip (1970), 100

"Ombro cinema," 98
Osamu Tezuka, 99
Phenakistoscope (1975), 100
Portrait (1977), 100
post-war western-style studios, 98
Rin Tarou, 99
The Room (1967), 99
Ryuichi Yokoyama, 98
short films for children, 101
Sleepy (1980), 100
Taku Furukawa, 99
Takun Jikken Manga Box, 99
TarZAN (1990), 101
techniques and imagery, 100
Tetsuo Kagawa, 100–101
Toei Animation Studios, 98
Tyo Story (1999), 101
Yoji Kuri, 99
Zuraw (1964), 99

German animation pioneers (1988)
    Eggeling, Viking, 41–42
    Fischer, Hans, 45
    Fischinger, Hans, 45
    Fischinger, Oskar, 43–44
    German avant-garde artists, 41
    Horizontal–Vertical Orchestra
        (1921), 41
    "non-figurative" animators, 41
    Pinschewer, Julius, 44–45
    provocative avant-garde art, 45
    Reiniger, Lotte, 45–46
    Richter, Hans, 42
    Ruttmann, Walter, 43
    Seeber, Guido, 44
German avant-garde artists, 41
Germany in 1911, animation in, 54
    Pinschewer, Julius, 54
Goeslowski, Richard, 146
Graphic creation for TV, 56
Graphic symbolism, 56
The Great American Cartoon, 98
Grillo, Oscar
    "appropriating" images, icons,
        geometries and techniques, 123
    Grillo CARTOON, 125

Help! and *Hard Day's Night?*, 126
The Man Who Couldn't Help It', 126
McCartney, Linda Eastman, 124–125
Monsieur Pett, 126, 127
"Parker's Mood," 126
Grimault, Paul, 119

Harps and Halos (1917), 14
The Haunted Hotel (1907), 12
Hip hop, animating
    crate-digging style, 224, 225
    hip-hop artists, 224, 225
    issues of race, class, gender, 225
    McGruber, Aaron, 225–226
    sexuality, 226
    spoken word, 224–225
Hoedeman, Co
    Charles and Francois (1988), 143–144
    children's films, 141
    fairy tales, 144
    Four Seasons in the Life of Ludovic
        (2002), 144
    Garden of Ecos (1996), 144
    Ludovic: Magic in the Air (2002), 144
    Masquerade (1984), 144
    Matrioska (1970), 144
    National Film Board animator, 141
    Odd Ball (1969), 144
    The Sand Castle (1977), 141–143
    The Sniffing Bear (1992), 144
    Tchou-Tchou (1972), 142
    transformative magic, 141
Homophobia, 225
Hopi shaman, 30
Horizontal–Vertical Orchestra
    (1921), 41
The Hospital (1918), 14
Hungary, animation in, 54, 55
Hurd, Earl, 9, 15
Hypersignalisation, era of, 55

"Illustrative" artists
    Hart Benton, Thomas, 60
    Riggs, John, 60
    Wood, Grant, 60
Impressionistic techniques, use of, 4

The Interpreters, 14
The Inventors and Wall Street (1918), 14
Italian animation, 55
   Carosellian star system, 55
   "commercial extravaganzas," 55
   Italian star system, 55
   production of ads, 55

Janie Geiser
   career background, 109
   complexities of psychic knowledge, 109
   The Fourth Watch, 112
   Gothicism, 111
   gothic tendency, 109
   language and emphasizing
      impressions, 109
   The Red Book, 110–111
   silence, accuracy of, 112
   silent film actors, 112
Jerry on The Job (1913–1930), 13
Jones, Chuck, 49, 50, 51, 82, 83, 152, 157,
   178, 203

Kenneth Knowlton of Bell Telephone
   Laboratories, 207
Krazy Kat (1913–1944), 13
Kricfalusi, John
   coloration as concept, 115
   Mighty Mouse blockbuster, 116
   plethora in pink, 114–115
   same-gender interspecies cohabitation, 114
   self-referential, 116
   themes, 114
   Yogi's pal Boo Boo, 115

La Baigneuse (1913), 4
Laguionie, Jean-Francois, 119, 121
   Centre d'art dramatique, 119
   French animation, 119
   La Traversee de l'Atlantique a la Rame,
      (1978), 120
   Le Masque du Diable (1976), 120
   paradoxical work, 120
   Potr' et la Fille des Eaux (1974), 120
   presence of the ominous, 120
   style, naïf painting and Magritte, 121

Une Bombe Par Hasard (1969), 120
Lamb, Derek, *see* Pindal and Lamb,
   art and careers
Lasseter, John, 129, 212
"Leave Me Alone" (Michael Jackson), 200
Les mines de l'ensoleillee (1929), 4
L'Hotel Electrique (1908), 12
Live-action sequence, 17
London Film Society, 43
Lortac (Robert Collard), collaboration of
   Emile Cohl, 54
Lumiere brothers, 53

McCartney, Linda Eastman, 124
McGruder, Aaron, 225
McLaren, Norman, 68, 71, 203, 217
Mariette (1902), 5
Maryniuk, Mike
   artistic "origin story," 240
   Blotto 649', 237–239
   Cattle Call, documentary, 238, 240
   cut-outs, 238
   *Death by Popcorn: The Tragedy of
      the Winnipeg Jets*, pseudo-
      documentary, 238
   "dying arts," 240
   experimental abstract animation, 238
   "Gary Floyd Revisited," music video,
      238, 241
   The Goose (2018), 238–240
   Home Cooked Music, 239–240
   June Night, 240–241
   preoccupation with Manitoba, 239
   scratch animation, 238
   "self-taught film virtuoso," 237
   stop motion, 238
   Tattoo Step, 238
   time-consuming and laborious
      techniques, 239–240
   time lapse, 238
   3DIY methods, 238, 241
   virtual artist talk for the Regina Public
      Library, 240
   Winnipeg Film Group, 237, 239
   The Yodelling Farmer, documentary,
      238, 240

Massachusetts Council on the Arts and Humanities, 227
Massachusetts Cultural Council, 227–228
Melbourne-Cooper, Arthur, 53
Messmer, Otto, 4, 9, 10, 15
  comic strip adventures of *Felix the Cat*, 4
MGM, 22, 152
Mills, Christopher, 181, 183, 184
  After Effects, 182
  animated documentary *Macroscopic*, 183
  early life, 182
  live action video and film, 182–183
  "mixed media" technique, 183
  music videos, 182
  101 Uses for a Sparkler, 183
  3D animation, use of, 183–184
  Vaccination Scar, 184
Miyazaki, Hayao
  Academy Award, the Golden Bear, 129
  animator and co-founder of Studio Ghibli, 129
  "apocalyptic pantheism" of *Nausicaa*, 132
  economic miracle period, 133
  firearms technology period, 133
  Future Boy Conan (1978), 130
  gender-biased attitude, 134
  Horus: Prince of the Sun (1968), 130
  Howl's Moving Castle (2004), 129
  Imperial and post-war, industrialized democratic Japan, 133
  Japanese animation or *anime*, 130
  Japanese style, 131
  Kiki's Delivery Service (1989), 131
  Laputa: City in the Sky (1986), 131
  Laputa: The Castle in the Sky (1986), 132
  "Les Temps des cerises" in *Porco Rosso* (1992), 130
  Lupin III: The Castle of Cagliostro (1979), 130
  mecha-anime, 132
  "Miyazakiness," 132
  Nausicaa of the Valley of the Wind (1984), 130
  Princess Mononoke (1997), 132–133
  Sailor Moon or *Hello Kitty*, 130
  science-fiction *Nausicaa of the Valley of the Wind* (1984), 129
  Spirited Away (2001), 129
  "3H" approach, 130
Mondschen-Maar brothers, 55
MTV, animation of
  Aeon Flux (1995), 86
  Beavis and Butthead (1993), 86
  The Brothers Grunt (1994), 86
  Celebrity Deathmatch (1999), 86–87
  The Children's Television Workshop, 85–86
  creative programmers, 85
  Daria (1998), 86–87
  Dougherty, creative director, 86
  expansion into Europe, 85–86
  The Head (1994 & 1997), 86
  influence of alternative comics, 86–87
  The Maxx (1995), 86
  MTV Downtown (1999), 86–87
  Saturday Night Live (1986), 86
  Seibert, Fred, 85
  Slow Bob in the Lower Dimensions (1990), 86
  social issue series, 87–88
Mulloy, Phil
  compared to Wood, Edward D., 91
  line drawings, 90
  primitive, 89
  timing and sequence, 90
Muratti cigarette ads, 57
Mysterious Box (Black), 11, 13

Nazi Germany, 27
New England Film/Video Fellowship Program, 227
New Forms Regional Initiative, 227
Newspaper comic strips, 3
New York's Museum of Modern Art, 196
"Non-figurative" animators, 41

Odell, Jonas
  ads, films, 193
  auteurist animator persona, 192, 194
  contemporary world animation, 191–192

Exit (1990), 192
    member of Filmtecknarna, 92, 192
Moms Online, 193
monochromatic computer-
    manipulated technique, 193
multi-media forms of animation, 194
music videos, 193–194
Never Like the First Time! (2006), 192
    range of styles, 193
Revolver (1993), 192
"Swedish" elements, 191
Windows in the Sky, 193–194
    winner of the Golden Bear, 192
Outcaut's "Buster Brown," 7
Out of the Inkwell (Fleischer), 9, 10

Pamphile LeMay's books, 5
Paramount, 22, 44
Park, Nick, 146
Pee-wee's Playhouse (2005)
    Panter, Gary, work of, 148
    Reubens, Paul, interview, 145–149
Peg system, description, 8–9; *see also*
    Barré, Raoul
The Pelstring Effect, 235
Pelstring, Emily
    artist and filmmaker, 232
    early life, 231
    "The Haunted Blob," an installation, 235
    Head Cleaner (2015), 233
    The Hilarious House of Frightenstein
        (1971), 233
    "in-camera effects," 235
    The Last Unicorn (1982), 233
    life-sized line drawing, 234
    plant life in *FernGully: The Last*
        Rainforest, 233
    Saturated Haunting Bioluminescence
        (SHB), 235
    short films reference technology, 234
    Susperia (1977), 233
    transformation scene from *Sleeping*
        Beauty (1959), 233
    visual aesthetics, 234
    visual language, 233
The Phable of a Busted Romance (1916), 14

Picture-by-picture drawing, 4
Pindal and Lamb, art and careers
    Academy Award for *Special Delivery*, 73
    "animation is movement," 68
    "cartoony" animation technique, 75
    CD-ROMs, 67
    The City (Osaka '70), 71
    early life, 68
    Every Child (1979), 74
    Goldtooth (1994), 76–77
    The Great Toy Robbery (1964), 67, 69–70
    Hors d'oeuvre, 68
    The Hottest Show on Earth (1977), 72
    I Know an Old Lady Who Swallowed
        a Fly, 67
    International Exposition at Osaka,
        animated lightboard piece, 71
    Karate Kids (1990), 67, 76–77
    The Last Cartoon Man (1973), 72
    "laughing dog" sequence, 72
    Laugh Lines: A Profile of Kaj Pindal
        (*1979*), 73–74
    Living Books programme, 77
    McLaren's role as a mentor, 68
    My Financial Career (1962), 69
    Nesbitt Spoon, 67
    1980 Referendum crisis, 73
    the Old Lady, 67
    Peep and the Big Wide World (1988),
        75–76
    The Peep Show (1962), 67, 69, 75
    Pot-pourri, 68
    principles of animated art during, 67
    The Shepherd, Oscar-nominated, 72
    social situations, 68
    Sports Cartoons, 75
    Street Kids International, 76
    Third World Animation, 67
    2001: A Space Odyssey, 68
    Very Nice, Very Nice (1961), 69
    Why Me? (1978), 73
Pindal, Kaj, *see* Pindal and Lamb, art and
    careers
Pinschewer, Julius
    film animators, work on, 44–45
    producer and filmmaker, 53

Pintoff, Ernest
  advertisements, 62
  American Film Institute, 65
  animated shorts, 61
  BFA in Painting and Design, 60
  Blade (1973), 64
  Bolt from The Blue (1992), 66
  Bullitt (1968), 64
  CinemaScope, 61
  *The Complete Guide to American Film
    Schools* (1994), 66
  The Critic (1962), 62–63
  Dynamite Chicken (1971), 64
  Edgar Award for Best Young Adult
    Mystery, 65
  Flebus (1957), 61–62
  The Gerald McBoing Boing Show
    (2005), 61
  Harvey Middleman, Fireman
    (1965), 64
  illustrations, 60
  improvisational jazz, 60
  The Interview (1959), 62–63
  The Old Man and the Flower
    (1960), 62
  Pintoff-Lawrence Productions, 61
  positions at positions at Michigan
    State University, 65
  Q-Tips, 63
  *The Select Guide to Studies in
    Animation and Computer
    Graphics* (1994), 66
  The Shoes (1962), 62–63
  teenage and early life, 59–60
  television, direction, 64
  University of California, 65
  The Violinist (1958), 62–63
  wife and children, 66
  Zachar (1991), first book, 65
Plato, 30
Porter, Edwin S., 53
Portland State University's Center for the
    Moving Image, 199
The Promoters, 14
Provocative avant-garde art, 45
Puffin Foundation, 228

Quinn, Joanna
  advertisements, 164
  Beryl Productions International Ltd, 165
  Body Beautiful (1990), 165
  "body consciousness," 164
  The Canterbury Tales, 165
  career as an animator, 164
  Dreams and Desires: Family Ties
    (2000), 165
  feminism, 165
  figure of Beryl, 165
  Girls Night Out (1986), 164

Regnier, Jean, 18
Reiner, Carl, 62
Reiniger, Lotte, 45
  The Adventures of Prince Achmed
    (1923–26), 45
  Aucassin and Nicolette (1975), 46
  Cinderella (1922), 45
  La Marseillaise, sequence of Chinese
    shadows, 46
  1979 *The Rose and Ring*, 46
  Ornament of The Loving Heart
    (1919), 45
Reubens, Paul, interview, 145–149
  Panter, Gary, work of, 148
  Pee-wee Herman's Playhouse (1986 to
    1991), 145–146, 149
  The Pee-wee Herman Story, 149
  problems with the network, 147
  transition to doing a kid's show, 146
  use of animation, 148
Rex, Epicurus
  Adventures in Telly, 94
  being *vs* becoming, 94
  Epicurean notion of pleasure, 95–96
  Fruits of The Earth (Spalding), 95
  moving pleasure, 94
  pleasure, feeling of, 95
  Rex the Runt, 94
  surrealist tendencies, 93
  things, 95
  The Trials of Wendy, 95
Rhode Island School of Design (RISD),
    227, 232

Richter, Hans, 42
   *Film Enemies Today – Film Friends
      Tomorrow (1929)*, 42
   Filmstudie (1926), 42
   frame-by-frame breakdown, 42
   Ghost Before Breakfast (1927–28), 42
   Rhythmus 21, 42
Royal Canadian Academy, 15
Ruttmann, Walter, 43
   'Absolute films,' 43
   Berlin, Symphony of a Great City
      (1927), 43
   Lichspiel, 43
   Olympia, 43
   Opus I, II, III and IV, 43

Saturday Evening Post or *Colliers*, 60
Scher, Jeff
   Area Striata (1985), 161
   artwork in an animated cartoon, 161
   Cunning Stunts, collage film, 160–161
   Goodnight Moon, 160
   Lost and Found (2016), 160–161
   Rorschach of the Kuleshov Effect, 160
   "showing," 161–162
   Sid, 161
   singular technique, 161
Scratch animation, 237, 238
Seeber, Guido
   cinematography, 44
   co-publisher of *Filmtechnik*, 44
   predilection for tricks, 44
Slash system, 9
Slice-of-life approach, 57
Soviet Constructivism, 217
Sporn, Michael
   adaptations of William Steig books, 197
   conversation, 195–197
   Electric Company, 197
   Everybody Rides the Carousel (1976), 197
   The Hunting of the Snark, 198
   *The Man Who Walked Between the
      Towers*, 197
   The Marzipan Pig, 197
   Michael Sporn's studio, 195
   "work for hire," 197

Stained glass windows, work on, 15
Steinberg, Saul
   animation and design, 175–176
   Another Bad Day for Philip Jenkins
      collage, 179
   awareness of self-conscious
      psychology, 178
   background, 174
   The Characters (1986), 180
   collection of drawings (1945), 174
   Communism or racial integration, 175
   Curriculum Vitae (1986), 180
   Diary (1974), 179
   drawings and sculptures, 173
   Everything is a Number (1967), 179
   Feeling My Way (1997), 179
   illustrations for films, 177
   literal educational illustrations, 176
   "modernistic" design and limited
      animation, 175
   Steinbergian animation, 178
   Steinberg-inspired character designs,
      175–176
   sui generis, 174
   UPA paradigm, 176
   "virus" of psychoanalysis, 179
"Stop-action" technique, 12
Stop motion, 38, 205, 210, 211, 220, 238
Style and sensitivity of thye era, 57
"Syndicated" comic strips, 13

Tad's Indoor Sports, 15
Tashlin, Frank, 49, 50, 79, 152
   appreciation of Tashlin, 79
   Army–Navy Screen Magazine, 82
   career, 79–80
   Daffy soldiers, 82
   Dawn Patrol (1938), 81
   entry into the workforce, 83
   and faster sense of timing to
      animation, 83
   The Fox and the Grapes (1941), 81–82
   The Fuller Brush Girl (1950), 83
   The Fuller Brush Man (1947), 83
   Fun and Fancy Free (1947), 81
   The Girl Can't Help It (1956), 81

Got Plenty of Mutton (1944), 81
The Home Front (1943), 82
Lady and the Tramp (1956), 81
The Lemon Drop Kid (1950), 83
Love Happy (1948), 83
Make Mine Music (1946), 81
Miss Grant Takes Richmond (1949), 83
Monsieur Beaucaire (1945), 83
Nasty Quacks (1944), 82
A Night in Casablanca (1945), 83
Plane Daffy (1944), 80, 81, 82
Porky as model, 82
Porky of the North Woods (1936), 81
Porky's Poultry Plant (1936), 81
Porky's Romance (1937), 81
puppet animated films, 83
quick cutting and extreme angles, 83
self-reflexive quality, live-action films, 81
strike of 1941, 81
Stupid Cupid (1945), 82
Ub lwerks' Celebrity Productions, 81
Walt Disney Studio, 81
Warner Bros., 82
Will Success Spoil Rock Hunter?
    (1957), 81
Terry, Paul, 8–10, 13, 14, 79
Tezuka, Osamu
    Broken Down Film (1985), 216
    The Drop (1965), 217
    early life, 215–216
    imaginative stories, 216
    Japanese adaptations of western
        literature, 216
    manga creator, 215
    manga works, 216
    The Mermaid (1964), 217
    Push (1984), 217
    Tales from a Street Corner (1962), 217
    use of technology for violence, 217
Thurber, James, 60, 196
Time lapse, 21, 29, 238
"Tourism in Quebec", 16
Transparent material, use of, 9
Trick pictures, use of, 12
2001: A Space Odyssey (1968), 57, 68

Ultra-synthetic imagery, 56
United Productions of America (UPA),
    56, 60, 82
Updike, John, 196

Vanderbeek, Stan
    artwork at a Manhattan gallery, 204
    BeFlix computer animation
        language, 205
    Breathdeath, 205
    The Computer Generation,
        documentary, 207
    Dance of the Looney Spoons (1959), 205
    Mankinda (1957), 206
    Panels for the Walls of the World
        (1967), 206
    "Poem Field" series, 205
    raw filmmaking materials, 206
    recreation of "Telephone Mural," 204
    Science Friction, 203
    See, Saw, Seams (1965), 206
    style, 205
    Symmetricks (1972), 205
    TV series *Winky Dink and You*, 205
Vukotić, Dušan
    "abstract humanism" (and abstract
        graphism), 171
    The Avenger (1958), 169
    The Big Scare (1958), 169
    commercials, 168
    A Concert for a Machine Gun
        (1958), 169
    Cowboy Jimmy (1957), 169
    The Enchanted Castle in Dudinci
        (1952), 167
    fairy tales, 168
    horror movies, 168
    How Kico was Born (1951), 167
    modernist cartoon-film style, 168
    modernist style, 170
    parody, 168–169
    Piccolo (1959), 169
    science fiction, 168
    "second wave" authors of Zagreb's
        animated films, 170

Surrogate (1962), 171
thematic turn and the focus on
    graphics, 170
Zagreb film animation production, 168
Zagreb school of animation, 171
Warner Bros. cartoons, 47, 48, 51, 79–83,
    151–153, 155–157, 193
Warner Studios, 17

WGBH, 207
Winnipeg Film Group, 237–239

Yellow Submarine (1968), 57, 193, 212
Yo Gabba Gabba Revolution (*2008*)
    description, 187–188
    Jack's Big Music Show, 187
    music, stories and characters, 188

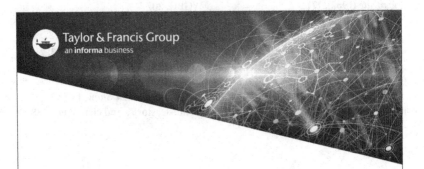

Printed in the United States
by Baker & Taylor Publisher Services

Printed in the United States
by Baker & Taylor Publisher Services